THE
EVERYTHING
Quick Meals Cookbook
2nd Edition

Dear Reader,

As a professional writer working from home, I never had a problem finding time to cook dinner. A flexible schedule meant I was free to whip up meals on the spur of the moment, making a quick trip to the neighborhood supermarket for supplies if needed.

That all changed when I took a part-time afternoon position. Faced with the challenge of driving home in rush hour traffic (picking up my son from child care on the way) and then quickly assembling dinner before we all headed out the door to sports, Scouts, or other activities, it became more and more tempting to rely on the corner fast-food restaurant for evening meals.

Clearly, my unstructured approach to meal preparation wasn't working. Over time, I developed several strategies to make this everyday task less stressful. Along with becoming better acquainted with my supermarket's offering of healthy convenience foods, I found that a little advance preparation on the weekend makes an enormous difference.

In this book, I hope to show you that it's easy to prepare quick and easy meals for your family every night of the week. I hope you enjoy the recipes as much as I've enjoyed making them up for you.

Rhonda Lauret Parkinson

Welcome to the EVERYTHING Series!

These handy, accessible books give you all you need to tackle a difficult project, gain a new hobby, comprehend a fascinating topic, prepare for an exam, or even brush up on something you learned back in school but have since forgotten.

You can read an *Everything*® book from cover to cover or just pick out the information you want from our four useful boxes: e-questions, e-facts, e-alerts, e-ssentials. We give you everything you need to know on the subject, but throw in a lot of fun stuff along the way, too.

We now have more than 400 *Everything*® books in print, spanning such wide ranging categories as weddings, pregnancy, cooking, music instruction, foreign language, crafts, pets, New Age, and so much more. When you're done reading them all, you can finally say you know *Everything*®!

QUESTION?

Answers to
common questions

FACT

Important snippets
of information

ALERT!

Urgent
warning

Quick
handy tips

PUBLISHER Karen Cooper

DIRECTOR OF ACQUISITIONS AND INNOVATION Paula Munier

MANAGING EDITOR, EVERYTHING SERIES Lisa Laing

COPY CHIEF Casey Ebert

ACQUISITIONS EDITOR Kerry Smith

DEVELOPMENT EDITOR Brett Palana-Shanahan

EDITORIAL ASSISTANT Hillary Thompson

Visit the entire *Everything*® series at *www.everything.com*

THE
EVERYTHING
QUICK MEALS
COOKBOOK

2nd Edition

Whip up easy and delicious meals
for you and your family

Rhonda Lauret Parkinson

Aadamsmedia
Avon, Massachusetts

An Everything® Series Book.
Everything® and everything.com® are registered trademarks of F+W Publications, Inc.

Published by Adams Media, an F+W Publications Company
57 Littlefield Street, Avon, MA 02322. U.S.A.
www.adamsmedia.com

ISBN 10: 1-59869-605-X
ISBN 13: 978-1-59869-605-9
Printed in the United States of America.

J I H G F E D C B A

Library of Congress Cataloging-in-Publication Data
available from the publisher.

This publication is designed to provide accurate and authoritative information with regard to the subject matter covered. It is sold with the understanding that the publisher is not engaged in rendering legal, accounting, or other professional advice. If legal advice or other expert assistance is required, the services of a competent professional person should be sought.

     —From a *Declaration of Principles* jointly adopted by a Committee of the
American Bar Association and a Committee of Publishers and Associations

Many of the designations used by manufacturers and sellers to distinguish their products are claimed as trademarks. Where those designations appear in this book and Adams Media was aware of a trademark claim, the designations have been printed with initial capital letters.

This book is available at quantity discounts for bulk purchases.
For information, please call 1-800-289-0963.

Dedication

This book is dedicated to my two favorite taste testers: my husband, Anthony, and son, Robert.

Acknowledgments

I would like to thank everyone at Adams Media for their help and support throughout this project. In particular, I would like to thank my Project Editor, Kerry Smith, and Executive Editor, Brielle Matson. Special thanks to my agent Barb Doyen, for her guidance and encouragement. Finally, I would like to thank About.com, a part of the New York Times Company, for providing me with a forum for sharing my passion for all things food-related with an entire online community.

Contents

Introduction

In today's busy world, it seems that no one has time to cook anymore. At the end of a busy workday, few people have the inclination to pour over recipe books trying to decide what to make for dinner, let alone to prepare and cook it. It's all too easy to join the growing trend of "fast-food families" who rely on the corner drive-through restaurant for their meals.

Why should you prepare home-cooked meals? For one thing, they're healthier. A steady diet of burgers, French fries, and other fast-food standbys has a high nutritional cost. Despite the best efforts of fast-food and family restaurant chains, the average takeout meal is loaded with excess fat, sodium, and calories. Enjoying the occasional Sunday breakfast or celebration dinner at a restaurant is one thing, but eating out regularly can wreak havoc with your waistline, and lead to long-term health problems.

Studies show that children of families that frequently eat fast-food dinners also tend to make poor food choices at home, favoring chips and soda over fresh fruit and vegetables. This can signal the start of a lifelong struggle with obesity and the health problems associated with being overweight.

Cooking at home saves money. True, it's easy to splurge when you're inspired to create a special meal on the spur of the moment; a trip to the farmer's market for organic vegetables, to the butcher for a special cut of meat, and finally to the supermarket for ingredients to make that special sauce all add up. But the meal's high price tag comes from making numerous one-time purchases, with no plans for using up excess ingredients or leftovers. Instead of discarding that unused half cup of canned herbed tomatoes, why not incorporate it into another meal? Planning in advance enables you to get the most for your food dollar.

Believe it or not, cooking at home saves time. Once you develop a regular routine—writing up a grocery list, taking a spare hour to do advance prep work on the weekend, and planning for leftovers—you'll find it's easy to quickly pull together a meal. From start to finish, dinner can be on the table in under thirty minutes (frequently under twenty). That's less time than it takes for a pizza to arrive during the busy dinner hour.

Besides, having a plan and sticking to it—instead of struggling to throw something together—may help you to discover cooking's therapeutic side. Preparing a nutritious home-cooked meal for your family is a great way to unwind at the end of the day.

Finally, preparing home-cooked meals can help bring back family mealtime. Numerous studies demonstrate the benefits of regularly eating together, from stronger family bonds to improved socialization and communication skills for children. But we all lead such active lives that this can be hard to arrange. Some stressed-out parents see the fast-food restaurant as a convenient solution, allowing them to spend time with their children while avoiding the hassles of cooking and cleanup. Being able to whip up a meal in under thirty minutes will give back that extra time you need to sit down for a family meal before rushing off to other activities. And you'll feel better knowing that you are helping your children establish healthy eating habits that will last a lifetime.

Chapter 1
Quick-Cooking Essentials

One of the biggest challenges for today's cooks is figuring out how to prepare meals that are quick, easy, and healthy. The lure of the local takeout restaurant can be strong, especially on busy weeknights. However, you do have alternatives. There are many timesaving strategies and tips that can help turn cooking family meals from a seemingly impossible chore into a joy—without requiring too much time in the kitchen!

Shopping for the Week

In response to the needs of a fast-paced society, there are numerous culinary shows dedicated to showing you how to whip up a meal in minutes. While celebrity chefs such as Rachael Ray make it seem easy, it takes a bit of advance planning to put together fast and healthy meals every night of the week. It all begins with the weekly trip to the supermarket.

Smart Shopping with a List

Never go grocery shopping without a list. There's nothing worse than having to make repeated trips to an overcrowded supermarket for a few items. A list also helps eliminate impulse purchases, which inflate your shopping bill and, worse, may end up forgotten in the vegetable crisper or back of the pantry shelf.

Before you begin writing a list, plan your meals for the week. Don't forget to take previously frozen food and leftovers into account. For example, if you're making Quick Tuna with Marinara Sauce (page 136), you could prepare a double batch of the sauce to use for soup (see Turning Sauce into Soup, page 57). Those cooked chicken breasts you froze earlier can be thawed and used to make Leftover Coconut Chicken (page 200). For lettuce and other highly perishable vegetables, buy as much as you need to last a few days and then plan a return trip to stock up in the middle of the week.

Consider the supermarket layout when formulating your list. Most supermarkets (including ethnic groceries) tend to work from the outside in, placing the fresh produce and perishable items around the perimeter, and the dried goods in the aisles in the middle. Organize the list so that the items are placed in the order you would find them in the store. This will prevent wandering back and forth between aisles, and shorten your total shopping time.

Let Your Computer Do the Work

A computer can be an invaluable aid in preparing a grocery list. When working out a meal plan, it's easy to forget staples (both food and nonfood items) that need replacing on a regular basis, such as cereal or soap. Keeping a basic list of items on file, and adding or subtracting from it each week as needed, will make this task much easier and help prevent repeated trips to the supermarket. Besides, a printed list is often much easier to read!

Always read a recipe through completely before making up a shopping list. That way, you'll know what ingredients you have on hand and which ones you need to purchase. When you are ready to start cooking, read the recipe through one more time. This will help you get organized, since most recipes list the ingredients in the order in which they are used.

Quick-Cooking Tips

Organization is key when it comes to quick cooking. Professional chefs follow a philosophy called *mise en place*. Literally meaning "everything in its place," it refers to a system of advance preparation that is designed to help the cooking process unfold more smoothly. The quick cook's version of *mise en place* includes advance preparation, making use of convenience foods, and incorporating leftovers.

Thinking Ahead: Advance Preparation

At home, get a head start on meal preparation by chopping vegetables and cooking rice or noodles to use during the week. How much advance prep work you do will depend on how much time you have during the week, as well as whether or not you enjoy it. If the thought of peeling and chopping onions after a long workday is enough to send you out the door to the nearest restaurant, do the prep work on the weekend when you're not so stressed. Store the amount you need for each meal in a resealable plastic bag and refrigerate until needed.

Saving Time with Leftovers

Incorporating leftovers into your meal plan is a great way to speed up cooking time during the week. When preparing pasta or rice for dinner, it's just as easy to cook a double portion and store half to use later. (This is a particularly good idea if you're not a fan of instant rice.) Similarly, it's easy to broil or grill an extra chicken breast, piece of beef, or seafood steak. Besides saving time later, preparing a double portion of sauce may actually add extra flavor to your meals, since the sauce ingredients will have more opportunity to blend together. Just be sure to always follow basic food hygiene rules for storing and reheating food.

In order to avoid foodborne illnesses, always follow the four "Cs" of food hygiene. Make sure your hands and work area are Clean before you begin cooking. Cook food through to the required level of doneness. Make sure food is Chilled at the correct temperature. Finally, avoid Cross-contamination by keeping cooked and raw food separate, and by using different cooking equipment and work surfaces for raw and cooked foods.

Many leftovers can be frozen until needed. Wrap the food in individual portions in freezer bags, label with the date, and store until needed. When it comes time to cook, simply reheat the frozen food in the microwave, oven, or stovetop as required.

Always be sure to label leftovers with the name and date before storing them in the freezer. The length of freezing time will vary depending on the type of food. Besides, it can be difficult to differentiate one solid mass of frozen food from another!

A Matter of Convenience

Be sure to take advantage of your supermarket's selection of convenience items. Cooked deli chicken, precut vegetables from the salad bar, and prepared fruit (such as cored pineapple) are great timesavers. Just bag them into individual meal portions when you get home, store in the refrigerator, and you're all set! Thanks to growing demand from consumers, many supermar-

kets are expanding their offerings of prepared canned and bottled foods—
it's becoming easier to find everything from canned squid to bottled minced
garlic. Greater awareness of the need to eat healthy meals means that many
of these foods are low in fat and sodium.

The freezer section of your supermarket is a great resource for prepped
foods—such as precut vegetables—along with specialty items such as frozen
cooked meatballs. Regularly incorporating frozen foods into your meal plan
will reduce preparation and cooking times. And if you're concerned about the
nutritional value of frozen foods, relax: freezing is the healthiest form of food
preservation. Studies have shown that the nutritional value of frozen vegetables is equal to, and sometimes even surpasses, that of fresh vegetables.

Stocking the Kitchen

Just because your cooking time is limited doesn't mean you should skimp
when it comes to purchasing quality cooking equipment. It's easier to work
quickly and efficiently in a well-organized, properly equipped kitchen. For
the cook whose main goal is to prepare quality home-cooked meals in a hurry,
there are a few appliances that are essential.

Microwave Magic

Cooking food in a microwave oven (instead of in a conventional oven or
on the stovetop) has several advantages: it reduces cooking time, uses less
energy, and doesn't heat up the kitchen. Nonetheless, despite the fact that
the microwave oven celebrated its sixtieth birthday in 2007, in many homes it
is still used primarily to reheat leftovers, or cook fast food such as pizza. However, a microwave can dramatically shorten cooking times at every meal.

FACT

An invention based on radar-related technology developed in World
War II, the first commercial microwave oven was released in 1947
by the Raytheon Company. Called the "Radarange," it stood over
five feet tall, weighed more than 750 pounds, and cost thousands
of dollars.

A microwave oven cooks food when the microwaves hit the food, causing water molecules in the food to vibrate and produce heat. This makes it perfect for cooking food with a high liquid content, such as soups and casseroles, or for boiling rice and vegetables. And nothing beats a microwave for making chocolate-based desserts such as Microwave Fudge (page 270) or Fast Chocolate Fondue (page 266). It's so much easier to melt heat-sensitive chocolate in the microwave, stirring occasionally, than to stand over the stovetop constantly stirring and adjusting the temperature to prevent the chocolate from scorching.

A microwave will help with the preliminary stages of cooking a meal, such as thawing or defrosting frozen food, blanching vegetables, quickly boiling water, or reheating rice. Within certain limits, you can even prepare complete meals in a microwave. Just remember that, since the microwave cooks food from the outside inward, it's important to make sure that meat, poultry, and seafood are thoroughly cooked.

The precise cooking times needed to microwave food will depend on the model of microwave you are using—everything from the wattage level to the microwave stirrer can affect the amount of time it takes for food to cook. There can even be differences in cooking times between two microwaves of the same make and model, as "hot spots" develop over time. When a recipe calls for cooking food in the microwave, always start with the minimum cooking time given, and then continue cooking at shorter intervals as needed until the food is cooked.

Adjusting recipes can be a little tricky when you're cooking with a microwave, since exact cooking times depend on the quantity of food being cooked. When doubling a recipe, increase the cooking time by at least 50 percent, and check carefully to make sure the food is thoroughly done.

Mixing and Processing Food

A blender is the ultimate timesaving device, used for everything from chopping onions to crushing ice and puréeing vegetables for soup. As with the microwave, the culinary possibilities of the blender are sometimes overlooked. While the blender's main claim to fame is liquefying ingredients for smoothies and mixed drinks, it can also be used to make sauces (such as Italian pesto or cold tomato sauce) and cold soups.

Another useful tool is a mini food processor. Much less expensive than higher-end models designed to perform complex tasks such as making bread dough, a mini food processor is excellent for mincing garlic, chopping herbs, grating cheese, and crushing bread crumbs. The size and shape of its work bowl makes a mini food processor more efficient than a blender at performing these tasks when you're only using a small quantity of food.

Essential Cooking Utensils

Quality, not quantity, is what counts when it comes to buying cooking utensils. A basic supply of high-quality pots, pans, bakeware, and other assorted kitchen utensils—many nonstick and dishwasher safe—will making cooking easier and cleanup time shorter. Here is a basic list of tools that every busy cook should have:

- **Nonstick baking sheets:** Be sure to buy two or more.
- **Complete set of pots and pans:** Be sure to include a large pot for cooking noodles.
- **Complete set of plastic mixing bowls:** For sifting and mixing ingredients.
- **Pepper mill:** It takes only seconds to grind a few peppercorns in the mill, giving you fresh ground pepper with significantly more flavor than store-bought.
- **A metal whisk:** Sometimes called a balloon whisk, a small metal whisk is perfect for mixing sauces.
- **Plastic cutting boards for cutting and chopping food:** Plastic boards are easier to clean than traditional wood chopping boards.
- **Heatproof rubber spatula:** Use to stir and turn food during cooking.
- **Measuring cups and spoons:** Along with a complete set of regular measuring cups for liquid ingredients, be sure to buy a set of nested measuring cups that can be easily leveled off for measuring flour and other dry ingredients. Try to find liquid measuring cups that

are microwave-safe—these are very convenient for quickly heating specific amounts of water or sauces in the microwave.

- **A complete set of knives:** Buy the best that you can afford and have them sharpened regularly.
- **A metal steamer:** For steaming vegetables quickly.
- **Strainer and colander:** Look for metal or silicone colanders that are heat-resistant to high temperatures.
- **Containers for storing dry goods:** Plastic is fine; just make sure there is a tight seal between the container body and the lid.
- **Microwave accessories:** Microwave-safe plastic wrap and wax paper are frequently used in recipes that call for covering food while it is cooking.

FACT

It may sound contradictory, but a sharp knife is safer than a dull one. Trying to cut food with a dull knife forces you to use more pressure, increasing the chances of slippage. To avoid accidents, have your knives regularly sharpened by a professional, or consider buying a sharpening steel.

Staple Ingredients

Stocking the pantry is a key strategy in preparing home-cooked meals fast. Whether you're cooking for friends, family, or just yourself, having to repeatedly make emergency trips to the supermarket for that one essential ingredient you forgot to buy will lower your enthusiasm for cooking considerably. This isn't meant to be an exhaustive list of what every kitchen should have, but rather a rundown of staples that should always be on hand:

- **Flour:** All-purpose flour is a blended wheat flour that can be used for most types of baking.
- **Baking powder and baking soda:** Staples in any kitchen, these are essential for baking recipes such as quick breads.

- **Sugar:** Keep both granulated and brown sugar on hand for use as sweeteners in sauces and for baking.
- **Olive oil:** Use extra-virgin olive oil—the healthiest type of olive oil—for marinades and salad dressings. For sautés, use pure olive oil (also called simply olive oil).
- **Vegetable oil:** While pure olive oil is acceptable for most stir-fries, at times it may contrast with the flavors in a dish. To avoid potential problems, stick with a vegetable oil, such as canola oil, for stir-fries.
- **Bottled minced garlic and ginger:** These are great timesavers on nights when you just don't feel up to peeling and mincing.
- **Dried spices:** Spices are perfect for enhancing flavor without adding fat and calories. While literally hundreds of spices exist, there are certain ones you'll find yourself using regularly. These include dried basil, dried parsley, dried oregano, ground cinnamon, ground nutmeg, paprika, red pepper flakes, and chili powder.
- **Instant rice:** Instant rice is a great timesaver for nights when you don't have time to cook rice on the stovetop or in a rice cooker. While instant white rice can taste rather bland, a number of other varieties, such as quick-cooking brown and jasmine rice, can be found in many supermarkets or purchased online.
- **Regular rice:** Be sure to also keep regular long-grain white rice and scented jasmine rice on hand to cook ahead of time and reheat, or for nights when you have at least thirty minutes to cook dinner.
- **Pasta:** You'll want to keep a selection of small-shaped pasta, such as penne and macaroni, in the cupboard. Smaller pastas come in a variety of unusual shapes that enhance the appearance of a dish. Better still, they cook more quickly than longer pastas!
- **Asian rice noodles:** Available in a variety of different widths and sizes, rice noodles add a different texture and flavor to a dish. An added plus is that they are gluten-free. Round rice-paper wrappers (used to make Asian spring rolls) only require a quick dip in water before being ready to use.
- **Canned beans:** High in fiber and loaded with vitamins and minerals, beans are the healthiest type of plant food. Most stores carry a wide selection of beans, including red, black, white, navy, and chickpeas.

- **Canned tomatoes:** Canned chopped or diced
  tomatoes will save preparation time.

Safe Storage

Since a major part of your cooking strategy depends on advance preparation, you'll need to have necessary supplies for storing food. Be sure to have small and large resealable bags for storing leftovers at room temperature or in the refrigerator—these are also ideal for marinating food. For freezing, containers, bags, and paper specifically designed for the freezer will keep out excess moisture and vapor that can cause freezer burn. The ultimate all-purpose food storage wrapper, aluminum foil, molds easily to the shape of the food and can withstand extreme temperatures.

Shelf Life

Using dry ingredients that are past their prime can affect flavor, or even cause a recipe not to turn out properly. Cookies and other baked goods don't taste the same; older rice needs more water, which increases the cooking time. Be sure to store staples such as flour, rice, and sugar in tightly sealed canisters in a cool, dry place. Here is a chart showing the maximum shelf life for staples commonly used in cooking:

Ingredient	Maximum Storage
Flour	1 year
Baking powder	1 year
Baking soda	1 year
Granulated sugar	18 months
Brown sugar	6 months
Rice	2 years
Dried spices	2 years

While it's becoming increasingly rare, it is possible that a bag of flour or rice you bring home from the grocery store may be infected with weevils or other small pests. Once the bugs find their way out of the bag and into your kitchen cupboard, they can be extremely difficult to get rid of. To guard against an infestation, freeze all dry ingredients for forty-eight hours before storage. This will kill both the bugs themselves and any eggs that may be residing in the food.

Speedy Cooking Techniques: Sautéing, Steaming, and Stir-Frying

Quick-cooking techniques such as stir-frying and steaming are very easy to learn. An added plus is that they are healthier than longer cooking techniques: shorter cooking time means that the food retains more of its nutrients.

Stir-Frying

Invented by the Chinese to cope with a shortage of oil, stir-frying consists of cooking food by stirring it rapidly at high heat in a small amount of oil. Traditionally, Chinese stir-fries are prepared in a bowl-shaped utensil called a wok, but a deep-sided skillet makes an acceptable substitute. Stir-frying requires more advance preparation than other cooking methods. However, the short cooking time more than makes up for the extra prep work, as the average stir-fry dish takes less than ten minutes to make.

Here are the basic steps needed to prepare a stir-fry:

- **Prepare all the ingredients:** Cut the meat and vegetables into bite-size pieces and place on a dish near the stove.
- **Preheat the pan:** Heat the pan on medium-high heat before adding the oil.
- **Heat the oil for stir-frying:** Add vegetable or peanut oil, tilting the pan so that the oil coats the bottom and halfway up the sides of the pan.

- **Test the oil to see if it is hot:** The easiest way is to drop a piece of fresh gingerroot into the hot oil. If it starts sizzling immediately, the oil is ready.
- **Add the first set of ingredients:** Usually the meat, poultry, or seafood is added first. Lay the meat out flat and let it sear for about thirty seconds before you begin stirring.
- **Add the second set of ingredients:** Usually these are the vegetables. Unlike meat, vegetables need to be stir-fried continually to prevent burning.
- **Add a sauce:** The sauce is normally added near the end of stir-frying.

Before you begin stir-frying vegetables, try adding a few pieces of fresh gingerroot or crushed garlic cloves to the hot oil to season it. The advantage of seasoning oil is that it removes any raw taste from the oil.

Sautéing

Like stir-frying, sautéing consists of cooking food in a small amount of oil over high heat. However, sautéed food doesn't need the constant stirring required for stir-frying (although it will need to be turned over to ensure that each side is browned and cooked through). Furthermore, the food does not need to be cut into bite-size pieces, but can be cooked whole.

Both sautéing and stir-frying have their advantages. Stir-frying takes less time, as cutting food into bite-size pieces makes it cook more quickly. On the other hand, there is less preparatory work required to sauté food.

Steaming

Generally considered to be the healthiest cooking technique, steaming consists of using moist heat, commonly called steam, to cook food. Unlike stir-frying, grilling, and other quick-cooking methods, steaming does not destroy important nutrients in the food. Even a simple method such as cooking food in boiling water is less healthy, since you lose many nutrients when you drain the cooking water. Furthermore, steaming does a better job of coaxing out the subtle flavors of the food.

The only potential disadvantage of steaming is that it can sometimes (although not always) take longer than other cooking methods. Still, even cooks in a hurry will find it's a great way to cook many types of food, particularly fish and vegetables.

Whether you're using traditional Chinese bamboo steamer baskets placed in a wok or a simple metal steamer inserted into a saucepan, steaming is easy if you follow a few simple steps:

- When using a bamboo steamer, place a bamboo base into a Chinese wok, making sure it doesn't fit too snugly.
- When steaming larger items (such as fish) in a bamboo steamer, place the food on a heatproof dish. For smaller items, you can use a bamboo steaming basket placed on top of the base.
- Pour enough boiling water in the sides of the wok so that the water comes within an inch of the food.
- When using a metal steamer insert, add water to a medium-sized saucepan, and then add the insert. The water should come within an inch of the food.
- Whatever type of steamer you are using, it's important to make sure the water doesn't touch the food. Let the steam cook the food.
- Keep the water at a rolling boil while cooking the food. Add more boiling water as needed.

To steam vegetables, cook over the boiling water until they are tender but still crisp when pierced with a fork (about two to three minutes for most vegetables). To steam poultry, cook until the chicken is tender and the juices run clear when pierced with a fork. To steam fish, cook until the fish flakes easily with a fork.

Chapter 2
Breakfast

Bagel and Cream Cheese with Italian Seasonings

Serves 4

Preparation time:
5 minutes

4 plain bagels
½ cup plain cream
   cheese
½ teaspoon dried
   oregano leaves
½ teaspoon dried basil
   leaves
¼ teaspoon garlic salt
4 teaspoons lemon juice
1 teaspoon balsamic
   vinegar

Here's an easy way to spice up plain cream cheese, using ingredients on hand in the cupboard. If you like, feel free to replace the dried oregano and basil with an equal amount of Italian seasoning mix, which contains a blend of several herbs, including rosemary, thyme, marjoram, basil, and oregano.

1. Cut the bagels in half and place in an 8-slice toaster.

2. While the bagels are toasting, prepare the cream cheese: in a bowl, stir the oregano, basil, garlic salt, lemon juice, and balsamic vinegar into the cream cheese, blending thoroughly.

3. Use a knife to spread about 1 tablespoon of the cream cheese mixture on each bagel half.

Ten-Minute Yogurt and Rice Pudding

Serves 4

Preparation time:
2–3 minutes
Cooking time: 10 minutes

1 cup coconut milk
1 cup water
2 cups instant rice
¼ teaspoon salt
½ cup raisins
2 cups peach-flavored
   yogurt

Using instant rice means this simple pudding takes just over 10 minutes to make. Feel free to replace the peach yogurt with your favorite variety of yogurt, or to spice up the pudding by adding ½ teaspoon of ground cinnamon or nutmeg.

1. Bring the coconut milk and water to boil in a medium saucepan.

2. Stir in the rice, making sure it is thoroughly wet. Stir in the salt.

3. Cover the saucepan and let stand for 5 minutes, or until the water is absorbed. Fluff up with a fork.

4. In a large bowl, combine the cooked rice with the raisins and peach-flavored yogurt. Serve immediately, or chill until ready to serve.

Instant Granola

Be sure that the melted margarine covers the bottom of the cooking dish, and to spread out the granola mixture so that it doesn't burn. You can increase the brown sugar to 3 tablespoons if desired.

1. Place the margarine in a 1-quart microwave-safe casserole dish.

2. Heat the margarine in the microwave on high heat for 15 seconds, or until it is melted.

3. In a medium mixing bowl, stir together the quick-cooking oats, vegetable oil, and brown sugar. Spoon the oat mixture into the dish, spreading it out evenly.

4. Microwave on high heat for 1 minute. Add the apple juice and the dried fruit and nut mixture, stirring to mix thoroughly into the oats.

5. Give the dish a quarter turn and microwave on high heat for 1 more minute, then another 30 seconds if needed, until the granola is cooked, stirring the granola and making another quarter turn. Be sure not to overcook the fruit. (Do not worry about foaming at the top of the granola.)

Marvelous Muesli

The uncooked version of granola, muesli is a nutritious dish combining fruit and nuts with oats. While the exact origins of muesli are unknown, the modern version was invented by Dr. Maximilian Bircher-Benner, who wanted to provide a healthy meal for patients in his sanatorium. Using oats makes this dish high in fiber, while the fruit provides a healthy source of sucrose.

Serves 2

Preparation time:
5 minutes
Cooking time:
2–3 minutes

3 tablespoons margarine
1 cup quick-cooking oats
¼ cup vegetable oil
2 tablespoons brown sugar
2 tablespoons apple juice
½ cup dried fruit and nut mix

Easy Cheese Frittata

Serves 4

Preparation time:
5 minutes
Cooking time: 15 minutes

6 eggs
¼ teaspoon nutmeg
Salt and black pepper to
   taste
2 cups shredded cheese,
   divided
2 teaspoons olive oil

The Italian version of an omelet, a frittata is served open-faced instead of folded over. A blend of shredded Italian cheeses would be ideal for this recipe.

1. In a large bowl, whisk the eggs with the nutmeg, salt, and pepper. Stir in 1½ cups cheese.

2. Heat a medium-sized skillet over medium-high heat. Add the oil, tilting so that it covers the bottom of the pan. Pour the egg mixture into the pan. Cook the frittata on low-medium heat, using a heatproof turner to lift the edges occasionally so that the uncooked egg flows underneath.

3. When the frittata is firm on top, remove from the pan, turn it, and slide it back into the pan.

4. Sprinkle the remaining cheese on top and cook for a few more minutes, until the cheese is melted and the frittata cooked through.

Flipping a Frittata

Traditionally, a frittata is flipped over before adding the cheese topping. To flip over the frittata, cover the frying pan with a plate, and then turn the pan over so that the frittata falls on the plate. Set the skillet back on the stove element, and carefully slide the frittata off the plate and back into the pan. Sprinkle the cheese over the top. Cook for 1 to 2 more minutes, until the cheese has melted.

Fast Frittata with Beans

For an extra touch, serve the frittata with a flavorful red or green salsa.

Serves 4

Preparation time: 10 minutes
Cooking time: 10 minutes

4 large eggs
¼ teaspoon salt
⅛ teaspoon black pepper
2 tablespoons minced onion
1 cup frozen vegetables, thawed
½ cup fat-free evaporated milk
1 teaspoon bottled minced garlic
¾ cup drained canned black beans
¾ cup drained white beans
½ cup shredded Cheddar cheese

1. In a small bowl, beat the eggs with the salt and pepper.

2. Stir in the minced onion, vegetables, milk, and garlic. Stir in the beans.

3. Pour the egg mixture into the pan. Cook the frittata on low-medium heat, using a heatproof turner to lift the edges occasionally so that the uncooked egg flows underneath.

4. When the frittata is firm on top, remove it from the pan, turn it, and slide it back into the pan.

5. Sprinkle the cheese on top and cook for a few more minutes, until the cheese is melted and the frittata cooked through.

Simple Cinnamon Toast

The combination of ground cinnamon and granulated sugar is the secret behind this simple, fragrant breakfast treat.

Serves 4

Preparation time: 5–10 minutes

2 tablespoons granulated sugar
1 tablespoon ground cinnamon
4 slices bread
8 teaspoons margarine

1. In a small bowl, stir together the sugar and ground cinnamon.

2. Toast the bread. Spread 2 teaspoons margarine over one side of each slice of bread.

3. Sprinkle the cinnamon and sugar mixture on top of each slice of bread (2 to 2½ teaspoons for each slice).

Basic Banana Muffins

Yields 12 muffins

Preparation time:
10 minutes
Cooking time:
20–25 minutes

1 cup milk
1 large egg
⅓ cup vegetable oil
1 teaspoon vanilla extract
3 medium bananas,
   peeled and mashed
2 cups all-purpose flour
½ teaspoon baking soda
1¼ teaspoons baking
   powder
½ cup granulated sugar
½ teaspoon salt
½ teaspoon ground
   cinnamon

Fresh-baked banana muffins have a sweet flavor. For an extra touch of flavor, add 2 to 3 tablespoons of sweetened coconut flakes to the muffin batter.

1. Preheat the oven to 375°F. Grease one muffin tin.

2. In a medium mixing bowl, whisk together the milk, egg, vegetable oil, vanilla extract, and mashed banana.

3. In a large mixing bowl, stir together the flour, baking soda, baking powder, sugar, salt, and ground cinnamon, mixing well.

4. Pour the milk mixture into the dry ingredients. Stir until the mixture is just combined and still a bit lumpy (do not overbeat).

5. Fill each muffin cup about two-thirds full with muffin batter. (If you have leftover muffin batter, refrigerate and use within a few days.) Bake the muffins for 20 to 25 minutes, until they are a light golden brown and a toothpick inserted in the middle comes out clean.

Muffin Cooking Tips

Muffins are easy to make if you follow a few simple steps. Don't overbeat the batter—a good muffin batter has a few lumps. Once the batter is mixed, fill the cups and put the muffins in the oven immediately. Be sure not to fill the cups over two-thirds full, or the muffins will have an uneven shape. Remove the muffins from the oven when a toothpick inserted in the middle of a muffin comes out clean.

Chocolate Chip Muffins

*Easy-melting semisweet chocolate chips are perfect
for baked goods.*

1. Preheat the oven to 375°F. Grease one muffin tin.

2. In a medium mixing bowl, whisk together the milk, egg, and vegetable oil.

3. In a large mixing bowl, stir together the flour, sugar, salt, and baking powder, mixing well. Gently stir in the chocolate chips.

4. Pour the milk mixture into the dry ingredients. Stir until the mixture is just combined and still a bit lumpy (do not overbeat).

5. Fill each muffin cup about two-thirds full with muffin batter. (If you have leftover muffin batter, refrigerate and use within a few days). Bake the muffins for 20 to 25 minutes, until they turn a light golden brown and a toothpick inserted in the middle comes out clean.

Yields 12 muffins

Preparation time:
10 minutes
Cooking time:
20–25 minutes

1 cup milk
1 large egg
⅓ cup vegetable oil
2 cups all-purpose flour
⅓ cup granulated sugar
½ teaspoon salt
2 teaspoons baking
  powder
1 cup semisweet
  chocolate chips

Tofu Breakfast Shake

Serves 2

Preparation time:
7–10 minutes

1 (12-ounce) package soft
    tofu
1 banana
1 cup raspberries, fresh
    or frozen
½ cup orange juice
1 cup soymilk
2 tablespoons liquid
    honey

*The soft texture of silken tofu makes it perfect for everything
from shakes or smoothies to custards and puddings. For
an interesting twist (and to increase the health benefits
of this nutritious breakfast even further), try adding
2 tablespoons of brewed green tea.*

1. Carefully remove the tofu from the package and cut into loose chunks.
    Cut the banana into chunks.

2. Combine all the ingredients in a blender. Process until smooth.

Tofu By Any Other Name

*Originating in Japan, silken tofu is made by a process similar to yogurt
making. This gives it a creamier, more custardy texture than regular
tofu—perfect for puddings, smoothies, dressings, and other blended
dishes.*

Make-Ahead Muffin Batter

Nothing beats enjoying fresh muffins in the morning without having to do any stirring or mixing! When preparing make-ahead muffin batter, it's even more important than usual to not overbeat the batter. Refrigerate the batter and use within one week.

Yields 12 muffins

Preparation time:
10 minutes
Cooking time:
20–25 minutes

1 cup buttermilk
1 large egg
⅓ cup vegetable oil
1 teaspoon vanilla extract
2 cups all-purpose flour
½ cup granulated sugar
½ teaspoon salt
½ teaspoon baking soda
1½ teaspoons baking powder
¾ cup semi-sweet chocolate chips

1. In a medium mixing bowl, whisk together the buttermilk, egg, vegetable oil, and vanilla extract.

2. In a large mixing bowl, stir together the flour, sugar, salt, baking soda, and baking powder, mixing well.

3. Pour the buttermilk mixture into the dry ingredients. Stir until the mixture is just combined and still a bit lumpy (do not overbeat).

4. Fold in the chocolate chips. Cover the bowl and store in the refrigerator until ready to use.

5. When ready to bake the muffins, fill greased muffin cups about two-thirds full with the muffin batter. Bake the muffins in a 375°F oven for 20 to 25 minutes, until they turn a light golden brown and a toothpick inserted in the middle comes out clean.

Basic Blender Pancakes

Serves 12

Preparation time:
10 minutes
Cooking time:
5–6 minutes per pancake

2 cups plain yogurt
2 large eggs
3 tablespoons vegetable
    oil
2 tablespoons granulated
    sugar
2 tablespoons brown
    sugar
2 cups all-purpose flour
½ teaspoon salt
4 teaspoons baking
    powder
Water, as needed

If desired, you can replace the yogurt with 2½ cups of either small curd cottage cheese or ricotta cheese.

1. Preheat a griddle or skillet over medium-high heat.

2. In a blender or food processor with knife blade attached, blend the yogurt, eggs, and vegetable oil. Add the sugars, flour, salt, and baking powder. Blend until smooth, adding as much water as needed until you have a pancake batter that is neither too thick nor too runny.

3. Grease the griddle or skillet as needed.

4. Pour the batter in ¼ cup portions into the pan. Cook the pancakes until they are browned on the bottom and bubbles start forming on top. Turn the pancakes over and cook the other side.

5. Continue cooking the remainder of the pancakes, adding more oil or margarine to grease the pan as needed.

How to Freeze Pancakes

Got leftover pancakes? To freeze, place a sheet of wax paper between each pancake to keep them separate, and wrap in a resealable plastic bag. To reheat the pancakes, unwrap, remove the wax paper, and cook the pancakes in stacks of two in a microwave on high heat for 1 to 1½ minutes, or in a 375°F oven for 10 to 15 minutes.

High Protein Peanut Butter Pancakes

The total cooking time for pancakes will depend on the size of the skillet and how many pancakes you can cook at a time.

Serves 6

Preparation time:
10 minutes
Cooking time:
5–6 minutes per pancake

1 cup all-purpose flour
2 tablespoons brown
    sugar
¼ teaspoon salt
2 teaspoons baking
    powder
1 large egg
1 cup coconut milk
2 tablespoons melted
    butter
⅓ cup peanut butter
4 tablespoons water, or
    as needed

1. In a medium mixing bowl, stir together the flour, brown sugar, salt, and baking powder.

2. In a large mixing bowl, beat together the egg, coconut milk, melted butter, and peanut butter.

3. Grease a griddle or skillet and heat over medium-high heat. Combine the dry and wet ingredients, stirring until they are just combined. Add as much water as needed until you have a batter that is neither too thick nor too runny. Don't overbeat the batter, and don't worry if there are a few lumps.

4. Pour the batter in ¼ cup portions into the pan. Cook the pancakes until they are browned on the bottom and bubbles start forming on top. Turn the pancakes over and cook the other side.

5. Continue cooking the remainder of the pancakes, adding more oil or margarine to grease the pan as needed.

Perfect Pancake Toppings

Maple syrup is the traditional pancake topping, but if you're not a fan there are other options. For a more nutritious dish, top the pancakes with fresh fruit that is mixed with either plain yogurt or cottage cheese. When you want something a little more decadent, melted butter mixed with sugar, warmed fruit preserves, or even icing sugar are all good choices.

Microwave Scrambled Eggs

This recipe makes a very light, fluffy scrambled egg. The paprika adds extra flavor, but doesn't overpower the other ingredients.

Serves 2

Preparation time:
5 minutes
Cooking time:
1–2 minutes

3 large eggs
3 tablespoons milk
¼ teaspoon salt
⅛ teaspoon black pepper
⅛ teaspoon paprika
1 tablespoon margarine

1. In a small bowl, lightly beat the eggs with the milk, salt, pepper, and paprika.

2. Place the margarine in a microwave-safe bowl. Microwave on high heat for 30 seconds, and then for 5 seconds at a time until the margarine melts (total cooking time should be 30 to 45 seconds).

3. Pour the egg mixture into the bowl, stirring.

4. Microwave the egg on high heat for 45 seconds. Stir to break up the egg a bit, then continue microwaving for 30 seconds, and then for 15 seconds at a time, stirring each time, until the egg is just cooked through. Serve immediately.

Scrambled Egg Variations

A few additions can transform basic scrambled eggs into a hearty meal that will easily serve as a lunch or light dinner. For cheesy eggs, add ½ cup shredded American or other processed cheese to the eggs after they have begun to thicken. For a heartier dish, add ½ pound of cooked and drained bulk sausage to the thickening egg mixture. And to create Denver-style scrambled eggs, cook ⅓ cup chopped onion, ⅓ cup diced green pepper, and ⅓ cup diced ham in the melted butter before adding the eggs to the bowl.

Vegetarian "Egg" Scramble

Most of the preparation time for this vegetarian version of scrambled eggs comes from draining the tofu. If you drain the tofu ahead of time (storing it in the refrigerator), this easy dish can be ready in under 10 minutes.

Serves 4

Preparation time:
20 minutes
Cooking time:
5–7 minutes

12 ounces extra-firm tofu
1 teaspoon turmeric
1 teaspoon dried dill
¼ teaspoon garlic powder
1 teaspoon salt
½ teaspoon black pepper
2 tablespoons nutritional
    yeast
1 teaspoon bottled
    minced ginger
2 tablespoons minced
    onion
1 tablespoon vegetable oil
2 tablespoons soymilk

1. Drain the tofu and cut into ½-inch cubes. Place the cubes in a bowl and use your fingers to crumble and break them up until the tofu has the texture of scrambled egg.

2. Stir in the turmeric, dried dill, garlic powder, salt, pepper, nutritional yeast, minced ginger, and minced onion.

3. Heat the oil in a skillet over medium-high heat. Add the crumbled tofu. Cook, stirring the tofu continually, for about 2 minutes, then stir in the milk.

4. Continue stirring until the tofu has a light, fluffy texture, adding more oil as needed.

The Vegetarian Version of Scrambled Eggs

The two key ingredients in vegetarian scrambled eggs are nutritional yeast and turmeric. An inactive yeast fortified with vitamins, nutritional yeast adds a savory cheese and nutty flavor to the dish. Turmeric, a spice frequently used in Southeast Asian cooking, gives the scrambled tofu a golden yellow color similar to regular scrambled eggs.

French Toast

Crusty French or sourdough bread, sliced 1-inch thick, is ideal for making French toast.

Serves 4

Preparation time:
5–10 minutes
Cooking time: 15 minutes

4 eggs
1 cup milk
¼ teaspoon salt
⅛ teaspoon ground
    nutmeg
2 tablespoons margarine
8 slices bread
¼ cup brown sugar,
    optional
½ cup maple syrup, or as
    needed

1. In a medium-sized bowl, whisk the eggs with the milk, salt, and ground nutmeg.

2. Heat the margarine in a skillet on medium to low-medium heat.

3. Dip one of the pieces of bread in the egg mixture, coating well. Continue with the remaining pieces of bread, but only dip as many pieces of bread in the mixture as you are cooking at one time.

4. Lay the soaked bread in the skillet. Cook on one side for about 2 minutes until browned, then turn over and cook the other side.

5. Serve the French toast with the brown sugar and maple syrup.

The Best French Toast

French toast should be firm enough to cut into, and not too soggy. For best results, use a good crusty bread such as French bread, or white bread that is several days old.

Fun French Toast Sticks with Cinnamon

Kids love making this fun twist on traditional French toast. While maple syrup is the traditional French toast topping, these also taste delicious topped with jam or powdered sugar.

Serves 4

Preparation time:
5–10 minutes
Cooking time: 15 minutes

8 slices raisin bread
4 eggs
1 cup milk
¼ teaspoon salt
¼ teaspoon ground
*   cinnamon*
½ teaspoon vanilla extract
2 tablespoons margarine
½ cup maple syrup, or as
*   needed*

1. Cut each piece of bread lengthwise into four equal pieces.

2. In a small bowl, whisk the eggs with the milk, salt, cinnamon, and vanilla.

3. Heat the margarine in a skillet on medium to low-medium heat.

4. One at a time, dip the bread slices in the egg mixture, coating well. Only dip as many pieces of bread in the mixture as you are cooking at one time.

5. Lay the soaked bread pieces in the skillet. Cook on one side for about 2 minutes until browned, then turn over and cook the other side.

6. Serve the French toast sticks with the maple syrup.

Marshmallow Breakfast Bars

Breakfast bars make a fun change from regular breakfast cereal. Be sure to keep an eye on the marshmallow mixture so that it doesn't burn.

Serves 6

Preparation: 5–8 minutes
Cooking time:
10–15 minutes

4 tablespoons margarine
½ cup peanut butter
2 cups mini marshmallows
½ cup sugar
½ cup milk
2 cups quick-cooking
   oats
½ cup raisins
¼ cup dried cranberries

1. In a heavy medium-size saucepan, melt the margarine on low-medium heat. Add the peanut butter, stirring. Turn the heat down to low and add the marshmallows. Continue cooking over low heat, stirring occasionally, until the peanut butter and marshmallows are almost melted.

2. While melting the marshmallow and peanut butter, heat the sugar and milk to boiling in a separate small saucepan, stirring to dissolve the sugar.

3. Stir the oats into the melted marshmallow and peanut butter mixture. Stir in the heated milk and sugar, raisins, and cranberries.

4. Spread the mixture in a greased 9" x 9" pan, using a spatula or your hands to press it down evenly.

5. Chill for at least 15 minutes. Cut into bars.

Replacing Marshmallows with Mini Marshmallows

Replacing regular-size marshmallows with mini marshmallows gives you a greater assortment of colors. Use 10 mini marshmallows for every regular-size marshmallow called for in a recipe.

Chapter 3
Midday Meals

Leftover Meat Loaf Sandwich

This recipe would also work well with leftover Sweet-and-Sour Meat Loaf (page 104)—instead of honey mustard, use fiery hot mustard.

Serves 1

Preparation time:
3–5 minutes
Cooking time: 7–8 minutes

2 tablespoons margarine, divided
2 slices crusty Italian or French bread
2 teaspoons honey mustard
1 slice provolone or mozzarella cheese
1 leaf romaine lettuce, washed
1 slice leftover Five-Ingredient Meat Loaf (page 103), about ½-inch thick

1. Spread 1 tablespoon margarine over the inside of one slice of bread and the mustard over the inside of the other slice.

2. Lay a slice of cheese and the lettuce leaf on the inside of one bread slice. Add the meat loaf on the inside of the other bread slice. Close up the sandwich.

3. Heat a frying pan on medium heat. Melt the remaining tablespoon of margarine in the frying pan, tilting the pan so that the margarine coats the bottom.

4. Place the sandwich in the frying pan. Cook until the bottom is golden brown, then turn and coat the other side. Add more margarine to the pan if needed. Serve hot.

Swiss Cheese and Ham Sandwich

Adding a spice or combination of spices is a great way to create your own gourmet mayonnaise. In addition to cayenne pepper, good choices include curry powder, prepared Italian pesto sauce, or even sweet Thai chili sauce.

Serves 1

Preparation time:
5 minutes

1½ tablespoons mayonnaise
¼ teaspoon cayenne pepper, or to taste
2 slices rye bread
2 slices processed Swiss cheese
2 teaspoons mustard
1 slice cooked ham
½ medium tomato, thinly sliced

1. In a small bowl, combine the mayonnaise and cayenne pepper.

2. Spread the mayonnaise on the inside of one slice of bread and place the Swiss cheese on top.

3. Spread the mustard on the inside of the other slice of bread and add the sliced ham. Add the sliced tomato. Close up the sandwich.

Fast Chicken Fajitas

Deli chicken and packaged coleslaw mix take a lot of prep work out of this recipe. Instead of deli chicken, you can also use stir-fry chicken strips—stir-fry the chicken strips with the lime juice and paprika until they turn white and are nearly cooked through. If you like, top each fajita with 2 tablespoons of shredded cheese before rolling it up.

Serves 6

Preparation time:
5 minutes
Cooking time: 5 minutes

1 tablespoon vegetable oil
½ teaspoon chili powder
1 cup cooked deli
    chicken, shredded
1 tablespoon lime juice
1 cup packaged coleslaw
    mix
½ teaspoon salt
1 tablespoon apple juice
½ cup canned black
    beans, drained
6 tortilla wraps

1. Heat the vegetable oil in a skillet over medium-high heat. Stir in the chili powder. Add the deli chicken and cook for a minute, stirring to heat through. Stir in the lime juice while cooking the chicken.

2. Add the packaged coleslaw mix. Stir in the salt. Cook, stirring frequently, until the packaged coleslaw mix is heated through (1 to 2 minutes). Splash with the apple juice while cooking.

3. Stir in the black beans. Cook briefly, stirring to mix everything together.

4. Lay a tortilla wrap in front of you. Spoon ⅙th of the chicken and bean mixture in the center of the tortilla wrap, taking care not to come too close to the edges. Fold in the left and right sides and roll up the wrap. Repeat with the remainder of the tortillas.

Fantastic Fajitas

Originally conceived of as a creative way to add extra flavor to a tough cut of beef, fajitas are now one of the most popular items on Mexican restaurant menus. Traditionally, fajitas are made with skirt steak. In this recipe the beef is replaced with chicken from the delicatessen.

Herbed Cottage Cheese Wrap

Serves 2

Preparation time:
10 minutes

1 cup cottage cheese
1 tablespoon low-fat
    French dressing
¼ cup chopped chives
¼ teaspoon salt, or to
    taste
Black pepper, to taste
4 tortilla wraps

*Chives are a great way to add extra flavor to cottage cheese—
besides adding onion flavor, they are low in fat and calories.
Feel free to use a flavored tortilla wrap, such as spinach or
red pepper.*

1. In a medium bowl, combine the cottage cheese, French dressing, chopped chives, salt, and pepper, stirring to mix well.

2. Lay out a tortilla wrap in front of you. Spread one-quarter of the cottage cheese mixture on the bottom half of the wrap, taking care not to come too close to the edges. Roll up the wrap.

3. Fill the rest of the wraps. Serve immediately or store in a resealable plastic bag in the refrigerator until ready to serve.

Spicy Cottage Cheese

The mild flavor of cottage cheese pairs nicely with many types of herbs and spices. Instead of French dressing and chives, try adding a pinch of ground cinnamon and ½ teaspoon of vanilla extract. For more heat, blend the cottage cheese with a pinch of cayenne pepper and 1 tablespoon of lemon juice.

Hot and Spicy Cucumber Sandwich

Paprika adds extra heat to the traditional cucumber sandwich, while cream cheese turns it from an afternoon snack into a nutritious midday meal.

1. In a small bowl, stir the lemon juice into the cream cheese. Stir in the paprika and chopped red onion.

2. Lay two slices of bread out in front of you. Spread 2 teaspoons of margarine on the inside of one slice of bread. Lay out half of the cucumber slices on top.

3. Spread half the cream cheese mixture on the inside of the other slice of bread.

4. Close up the sandwich. Cut in half or quarters as desired.

5. Repeat with the remaining two slices of bread.

Serves 2

Preparation time:
10 minutes

1½ teaspoons lemon juice
4 tablespoons cream
    cheese, softened
¼ teaspoon paprika, or to
    taste
1½ teaspoons chopped
    red onion
4 slices bread
4 teaspoons margarine, or
    as needed
½ medium cucumber,
    thinly sliced

Deviled Egg Sandwich

Serves 2

Preparation time:
10 minutes

3 hard-boiled eggs
1½ tablespoons cream cheese
¼ teaspoon paprika, or to taste
1½ teaspoons lemon juice, or as needed
1 tablespoon chopped red onion
4 slices bread
4 teaspoons honey mustard
2 lettuce leaves
1 medium tomato, sliced

Using cream cheese instead of mayonnaise makes a healthier version of classic deviled eggs. If you like, use a small amount of juice from the tomato instead of lemon juice to moisten the mashed egg mixture.

1. Carefully peel the hard-boiled eggs and chop. Place the eggs in a medium bowl and mash with the cream cheese. Stir in the paprika, lemon juice, and red onion, until everything is mixed together.

2 Toast the bread.

3. Lay two slices of toast in front of you. Spread 2 teaspoons honey mustard over one side of a slice of bread. Add a lettuce leaf and half the sliced tomato. Spread half the deviled egg mixture over the inside of another slice of bread. Place on top of the other slice and close. Cut diagonally in half.

4. Repeat with the remaining two slices of bread.

Make-Ahead Hard-Boiled Eggs

Eggs can be hard-boiled ahead of time and used as needed during the week. Store the eggs in their original container in the refrigerator. The eggs will last for about seven days.

Grilled Cheese Sandwich

You can add extra protein to this simple sandwich by adding a thin slice of ham or leftover cooked chicken.

Serves 1

Preparation time:
2 minutes
Cooking time:
7–8 minutes

2 tablespoons margarine,
    divided
2 slices sourdough bread
2 teaspoons prepared
    mustard, or as needed
⅛ teaspoon paprika, or to
    taste
2 slices Swiss cheese

1. Spread 1 tablespoon margarine over the inside of one slice of bread. Spread the mustard on the inside of the other slice and sprinkle the paprika over it. Add the Swiss cheese and close up the sandwich.

2. Heat a frying pan on medium heat. Melt 1 tablespoon of margarine in the frying pan, tilting the pan so that the margarine coats the bottom.

3. Place the sandwich in the frying pan. Cook until the bottom is golden brown, then turn and coat the other side. Add more margarine to the pan if needed. Serve hot.

Leftover Chicken with Bruschetta

You can use leftover Teriyaki Chicken (page 209) or Thai-Style Lime Chicken (page 210) in this recipe. If you don't have a microwave, heat the sandwich in a 250°F oven for 5 minutes, or until it is browned.

Serves 1

Preparation time:
5–7 minutes
Cooking time: 1 minute

2 ounces goat cheese,
    softened
2 slices crusty French or
    Italian bread
2 Marinated Artichoke
    Hearts (page 229),
    sliced
2 tablespoons leftover
    Italian-Inspired
    Bruschetta (page 235)
½ cup leftover grilled
    chicken breast,
    shredded

1. Spread the softened goat cheese over the inside of both slices of bread.

2. Lay the marinated artichoke hearts on top of the cheese on one slice of bread. Spread the Italian-Inspired Bruschetta over the inside of the other slice.

3. Add the shredded chicken and close up the sandwich.

4. To heat the sandwich, place on a microwave-safe plate and microwave on high heat for 20 seconds, then for 5 seconds at a time until it is heated.

Thai Chicken and Rice Wraps

Serves 4

Preparation time:
5 minutes

4 tortilla wraps
¼ cup peanut sauce
½ cup Steamed Coconut
Rice (page 153)
1 cup cooked chicken,
chopped

Peanut sauce is available in Asian markets, or in the international section of many supermarkets. Feel free to load up the wrap by adding shredding carrots and sliced cucumber.

1. Lay a tortilla wrap out flat. Spread 1 tablespoon of the peanut sauce over the inside of the wrap.

2. Spread 2 tablespoons of the coconut rice onto the tortilla, taking care not to go too close to the edges. Add ¼ cup of the chopped chicken on top. Roll up the wrap.

3. Continue with the remainder of the tortilla wraps.

Make Your Own Peanut Sauce

It's easy! In a small bowl, whisk together ½ cup peanut butter and ¼ cup coconut milk. Add 2 teaspoons lime juice, 1 teaspoon fish sauce or soy sauce, 1 teaspoon brown sugar, and red curry paste to taste.

Easy Enchiladas

Preparing enchiladas in the microwave instead of baking them in the oven substantially reduces the cooking time. To speed things up even further, use leftover cooked ground beef and reheat in the microwave.

Serves 4

Preparation time:
5 minutes
Cooking time:
10–15 minutes

1 cup ground beef
¼ teaspoon ground cumin
¼ teaspoon salt, or to
   taste
⅛ teaspoon black pepper,
   or to taste
8 corn tortillas
2 cups store-bought
   enchilada sauce
1 cup shredded Cheddar
   cheese

1. In a bowl, season the ground beef with the cumin, salt, and pepper, using your fingers to mix it in. Let the ground beef stand while you are preparing the tortillas and sauce.

2. Place the corn tortillas on a microwave-safe plate. Microwave at high heat for 30 seconds, and then for 10 seconds at a time until the tortillas look slightly dried out and are cooked. Dip each of the tortillas into the enchilada sauce, letting the excess sauce drip off.

3. Place the ground beef into a 1-quart microwave-safe casserole dish, using your fingers to crumble it in. Microwave on high heat for 2 minutes. Stir and cook for another 2 to 3 minutes, until the ground beef is cooked through. Remove from the heat and drain off the fat. Stir in ½ cup leftover enchilada sauce and cook for another minute.

4. Lay a tortilla flat and spoon a portion of the meat and sauce mixture in the lower half of the tortilla. Roll up the tortilla and place in a shallow, microwave-safe 9" x 13" baking dish. Continue with the remainder of the tortillas. Spoon any leftover enchilada sauce on top. Sprinkle with the cheese.

5. Microwave on high heat for 5 minutes, or until the cheese is melted and everything is cooked through. Let stand for 5 minutes before serving.

Basic Tuna Salad Sandwiches

Serves 4

Preparation time:
10 minutes

1 (7-ounce) can tuna,
    drained
3 tablespoons low-fat
    mayonnaise
1 teaspoon red wine
    vinegar
4 strips red bell pepper,
    finely chopped
1 tablespoon chopped
    fresh parsley
⅛ to ¼ teaspoon cayenne
    pepper, optional
8 slices whole-wheat
    bread
4 lettuce leaves
5 tablespoons margarine

Red wine vinegar adds a bit of bite to this easy-to-make sandwich filling. If you want, you can replace the red bell pepper with finely chopped celery, or use a combination of both.

1. In a medium bowl, stir together the canned tuna, mayonnaise, red wine vinegar, red pepper, parsley, and cayenne pepper, if using, until they are well mixed.

2. To prepare the sandwich, butter two bread slices and add 1 lettuce leaf to one slice. Spread about 2 tablespoons filling on the other slice and close up the sandwich. Repeat with the remainder of bread and sandwich filling.

Make-Ahead Sandwiches

Sandwiches can be prepared up to a day ahead of time—just wrap and refrigerate until you're ready to eat. You can also make sandwich spreads up to three days in advance; keep covered and stored in the refrigerator.

Shrimp-Filled Avocados

For a more attractive presentation, sprinkle a bit of extra lime juice on the avocados to prevent discoloration, and serve the shrimp-stuffed avocados on a bed of lettuce leaves.

1. In a large bowl, combine the shrimp, pineapple, reserved pineapple juice, lime juice, yogurt, green onions, crushed red pepper, and salt. Stir to mix well.

2. Cut the avocados in half lengthwise, removing the pit in the middle.

3. Fill the avocados with the shrimp mixture and serve.

Amazing Avocados

Its buttery flesh leads many people to mistake the avocado for a vegetable, but it is actually a type of fruit. Avocado leads all other fruits in protein content, and is a good source of vitamin E. An avocado filled with shellfish, or cottage or ricotta cheese, makes a quick and healthy midday meal. Just don't get carried away—a single avocado has more than 300 calories.

Serves 4

Preparation time:
10 minutes

2 cups cooked shrimp
1 cup drained pineapple
    tidbits
2 tablespoons reserved
    pineapple juice
1 tablespoon lime juice
2 tablespoons natural
    yogurt
2 green onions, finely
    chopped
½ teaspoon crushed red
    pepper, or to taste
Salt, to taste
4 avocados, peeled

Grilled Chicken Sandwich

Serves 1

Preparation time:
5 minutes
Cooking time:
15 minutes

*1 boneless, skinless
     chicken breast half*
¼ teaspoon salt
*¼ teaspoon black or white
     pepper*
*2 slices crusty French or
     Italian bread*
2 teaspoons margarine
*1 tablespoon low-fat
     mayonnaise*
*½ medium tomato, thinly
     sliced*

For a fancier sandwich, try replacing the margarine and mayonnaise with Italian pesto. Instead of broiling, the chicken breast can also be cooked on the grill.

1. Preheat the broiler.

2. Rinse the chicken breast under running water and pat dry. Rub the salt and pepper over the chicken to season.

3. To broil the chicken, place it on a broiling rack sprayed with nonstick cooking spray. Broil the chicken on high heat, 9 inches from the heat source, for about 7 to 8 minutes, or until cooked through.

4. Lay out the bread in front of you. Spread the margarine over the inside of one slice of bread and the mayonnaise over the inside of the other.

5. Add the sliced tomato on the slice with mayonnaise. Add the broiled chicken on the other side. Close up the sandwich.

Greek Pita Pockets with Tzatziki

A popular Greek dip, tzatziki also makes a satisfying sandwich filling. To turn this recipe into an appetizer, simply cut each pita round into eight equal wedges and bake at 250˚F until crisp. Spread the dip on the pita wedges.

Serves 8

Preparation time:
10 minutes

1 English cucumber
1½ teaspoons virgin olive
   oil
1½ teaspoons lemon juice
1 cup plain low-fat yogurt
2 tablespoons chopped
   red onion
½ teaspoon garlic salt
Freshly ground black
   pepper, to taste
8 pita wraps

1. Peel and grate the cucumber until you have ½ cup. Thinly slice the remainder of the cucumber and set aside.

2. In a small bowl, stir the olive oil and lemon juice into the yogurt. Stir in the chopped red onion and garlic salt. Taste and season with the pepper.

3. Lay out a pita wrap in front of you. Spread up to 2 tablespoons tzatziki over the inside of the wrap. Lay a few cucumber slices on top and roll up the wrap.

4. Continue with the remainder of the pita wraps.

Choosing Olive Oil

Virgin olive oils are the best choice in recipes where the dressing isn't being heated, such as Marinated Artichoke Hearts (page 229) or Greek Pita Pockets with Tzatziki (above). Either the virgin or extra-virgin variety of olive oil can be used, although extra-virgin olive oil has less acidity and a better flavor. Pure olive oil (also simply called olive oil) has a higher smoke point than virgin oils—use it in stir-fries or whenever the oil is going to be heated.

Easy Skillet Zucchini Quiche

Serves 4

Preparation time:
5 minutes
Cooking time: 15 minutes

4 eggs
½ teaspoon salt, or to
    taste
Black pepper, to taste
¼ teaspoon dried
    oregano, or to taste
1 teaspoon onion powder
2 ounces canned sliced
    mushrooms
1 tomato, diced
½ cup grated Swiss
    cheese
¼ cup grated mild
    Cheddar cheese
1 tablespoon margarine
1½ cups chopped
    zucchini, fresh or
    frozen

Removing the crust from a standard quiche recipe substantially reduces the time it takes to make. On days when you do have a bit more time, feel free to bake the quiche instead of broiling it— after combining the ingredients in the bowl, bake at 325°F for 30 minutes, or until the quiche has set.

1. Preheat the broiler.

2. In a medium bowl, lightly beat the eggs with the salt, pepper, dried oregano, and onion powder. Stir in the mushrooms, tomato, and cheeses.

3. Melt the margarine in a heavy skillet over medium heat. Add the chopped zucchini and sauté for a couple of minutes, until the zucchini turns dark green.

4. Pour the egg and cheese mixture into the skillet, stirring to mix it in with the zucchini. Cook for 7 to 8 minutes, until the cheese is melted and the quiche is cooked through but still moist on top.

5. Place the skillet in the broiler. Cook until the top has set but has not yet browned.

Easy Tomato Sandwich

A simple tomato sandwich is a great way to enjoy tomatoes in season. For a heartier version, add sliced cucumbers and top with a slice of Swiss cheese.

1. In a small bowl, combine the mayonnaise, lemon juice, garlic salt, and pepper.

2. Spread the mayonnaise mixture over one side of each slice of bread.

3. Lay the sliced tomato on top of the mayonnaise mixture. Close up the sandwich.

Tomato Lore

A New World fruit, the tomato is one of the many foods Christopher Columbus introduced to Europeans following his journeys to the Americas. The tomato was slow to catch on in Europe, as it was widely believed to be poisonous. It wasn't until the 1800s that tomato consumption took off in Britain and other parts of Europe. Today, tomatoes are one of the many antioxidant-rich foods that physicians believe may help prevent cancer.

Serves 1

Preparation time:
8 minutes

2 tablespoons
   mayonnaise
1 teaspoon lemon juice
⅛ teaspoon garlic salt, or
   to taste
⅛ teaspoon black or white
   pepper, to taste
2 slices bread, toasted
½ medium tomato, thinly
   sliced

Fish Stick Tacos

Serves 3

Preparation time:
5–8 minutes
Cooking time:
5–7 minutes

¼ cup plain yogurt
2 tablespoons tartar
    sauce
1 teaspoon chili powder,
    or to taste
2 teaspoons chopped red
    onion
6 leftover cooked fish
    sticks
3 corn tortillas
2 cabbage leaves,
    shredded

Want something a little more authentic? Try a chunky red or green salsa instead of tartar sauce, such as Simple Salsa Verde (page 248).

1. In a small bowl, stir together the yogurt, tartar sauce, chili powder, and red onion.

2. Place the fish sticks on a microwave-safe plate. Use your microwave's reheat setting, or 70 percent power for 1 to 2 minutes, until the fish sticks are heated through.

3. Place the corn tortillas on a microwave-safe plate. Microwave at high heat for 30 seconds, and then for 10 seconds at a time until the tortillas look slightly dried out and are cooked.

4. Lay a tortilla in front of you. Spread a third of the yogurt mixture over the tortilla. Add a third of the shredded cabbage. Place two fish sticks inside. Fold the tortilla in half.

5. Continue filling the remainder of the tortillas.

Chapter 4
Soups

Easy Frozen Split Pea Soup

Serves 4

Preparation time:
10 minutes
Cooking time:
15–20 minutes

3 cups frozen peas
1 tablespoon olive oil
1 teaspoon minced garlic
¼ cup chopped red onion
3½ cups canned or
    packaged chicken
    broth
1 cup light cream
½ teaspoon salt
Juice of 1 lemon
2 tablespoons fresh
    chopped mint leaves

This refreshing soup makes a nice alternative to a plain vegetable side dish. For an extra touch, garnish with a few mint sprigs before serving.

1. Place the frozen peas in a mesh strainer. Run warm running water over them until they are defrosted.

2. Heat the olive oil in a medium saucepan over medium-high heat. Add the garlic and onion. Sauté until the onion is shiny and softened (adjust the heat, turning it down to medium if the onion is cooking too quickly).

3. Add the peas, chicken broth, and cream. Stir in the salt and lemon juice. Bring to a boil. Reduce the heat to medium-low, cover, and simmer until the peas are tender (about 5 minutes).

4. Place the soup in the blender with the mint. Purée until smooth.

5. Pour the soup into four serving bowls. Cover and chill until ready to serve.

How Much Lemon Juice?

Don't feel like squeezing lemons? While freshly squeezed lemon juice is always nice, you can also use presqueezed lemon juice. When a recipe calls for the juice of one lemon, use 2 tablespoons of presqueezed lemon juice.

Easy Coconut Soup

Toasted coconut enhances the appearance and flavor of this simple soup. Serve with Curried Chicken and Rice (page 88).

1. Preheat oven to 325°F. Spread out the coconut flakes on a baking sheet.

2. In a medium saucepan, bring the milk, coconut milk, water, and light cream to a boil.

3. While waiting for the soup to boil, place the coconut flakes in the oven. Toast for 5 minutes, or until they turn a light brown and are fragrant.

4. When the soup comes to a boil, stir in the cinnamon, sugar, and salt. Turn the heat down to medium-low, cover, and simmer for 5 minutes.

5. To serve, garnish the soup with the toasted coconut.

Serves 4

Preparation time:
5 minutes
Cooking time:
10–15 minutes

¼ cup unsweetened
    coconut flakes
1 cup whole milk
1 cup coconut milk
1 cup water
⅓ cup light cream
⅛ teaspoon ground
    cinnamon
3 tablespoons granulated
    sugar
¼ teaspoon salt, or to
    taste

Blender Beet Borscht

You can garnish this filling Russian soup with hard-boiled eggs for a complete meal. Leftover cooked beets can be used in this recipe, and the sour cream can be replaced with low fat natural yogurt.

Process all the ingredients in a blender for 30 seconds, or until smooth. Serve immediately or cover and chill until ready to serve.

Serves 4

Preparation time:
5–10 minutes

2 (14-ounce) cans sliced
    beets
1 cup reserved beet juice
1 cup beef broth
2 tablespoons red wine
    vinegar
5 teaspoons chopped
    fresh dill leaves
4 teaspoons Dijon
    mustard
¾ teaspoon salt
4 tablespoons sour cream

Easy Microwave Onion Soup

Serves 4

Preparation time:
5 minutes
Cooking time:
7–10 minutes

2½ cups low-sodium beef
    broth
1 package (¼ cup) instant
    onion soup mix
2 slices bread
½ cup shredded
    Parmesan cheese

This quick and easy version of classic French onion soup takes only minutes to make. If possible, use a good crusty bread such as French or sourdough.

1. Place the beef broth and instant onion soup mix in a microwave-safe casserole dish or bowl, stirring the soup mix into the broth.

2. Microwave the soup on high heat for 2 minutes. Stir and heat for 1 minute more, and then for 30 seconds at a time if needed until the soup is heated through.

3. While the soup is cooking, toast the bread and cut into small cubes.

4. Pour the heated onion soup into four microwave-safe bowls. Sprinkle one-quarter of the cheese over each bowl and add one-quarter of the bread cubes.

5. Place the soup bowls in the microwave. Microwave on high heat for 2 minutes. Stir and continue cooking if needed until the cheese is melted.

Warming Herbed Tomato Soup

Using canned tomatoes that are already flavored with herbs such as basil and oregano adds extra flavor. You might also add two Roasted Red Peppers (page 221), chopped into bite-size pieces.

Serves 4

Preparation time:
5 minutes
Cooking time:
10–15 minutes

1 teaspoon olive oil
1 teaspoon bottled
    minced garlic
1 (19-ounce) can
    tomatoes with herbs
2 cups beef broth
¼ teaspoon ground cumin
½ teaspoon salt
¼ teaspoon black pepper
¾ cup croutons

1. Heat the olive oil in a saucepan over medium heat.

2. Add the minced garlic and cook for about 1 minute until it begins to brown.

3. Add the canned tomatoes and beef broth. Cover and turn the heat up to medium-high to bring to a boil.

4. Stir in the ground cumin, salt, and pepper. Turn the heat down to medium-low, cover, and simmer for 2 to 3 minutes.

5. Serve the soup hot, garnished with the croutons.

Tomato Soup Toppers

Shredded cheese is a traditional garnish for tomato soup—Italian and Swiss cheeses such as Parmesan, Romano, and Gruyère are all good choices. For something different, add a dollop of your favorite Italian pesto to the cooked soup, or keep it simple with a few handfuls of chopped fresh herbs such as basil or parsley.

Frozen Garden Vegetable Soup

Serves 4

Preparation time:
5 minutes
Cooking time:
15–18 minutes

2 teaspoons olive oil
1 teaspoon minced garlic
1 onion, peeled, chopped
1 teaspoon dried parsley
2 cups frozen vegetables
2 cups low-sodium beef
    broth
1 cup water
¼ teaspoon salt
Black pepper, to taste
½ teaspoon Tabasco
    sauce

Frozen vegetables take the work out of peeling and chopping fresh vegetables in this quick and easy recipe. While the soup doesn't take long to make, if you want to speed up the cooking time even more, cook the frozen vegetables in the microwave while sautéing the onion.

1. In a medium saucepan, heat the olive oil over medium-high heat. Add the garlic and onion. Sprinkle the dried parsley over the onion. Sauté for about 4 minutes, until the onion is softened.

2. Add the frozen vegetables. Cook for about 4 to 5 minutes, until they are thawed and heated through, using a rubber spatula to break them up while cooking.

3. Add the beef broth and water. Bring to a boil (this takes about 4 minutes).

4. Stir in the salt, pepper, and Tabasco sauce.

5. Turn down the heat and simmer for 3 to 4 minutes. Serve immediately.

New England Clam Chowder

Traditionally, New England's take on clam chowder is served with hexagon-shaped oyster crackers. For a special touch, sprinkle ¼ cup of bacon bits over the soup.

Serves 4

Preparation time:
5 minutes
Cooking time: 15 minutes

1 cup frozen corn
1 tablespoon margarine
¼ cup chopped onion
½ cup clam juice
1½ cups whole milk
1 cup cream
1 teaspoon dried parsley
¼ teaspoon paprika, or to
   taste
¾ teaspoon salt
½ teaspoon black pepper
1½ cups canned chopped
   clams

1. Place the frozen corn in a microwave-safe bowl. Cover with microwave-safe plastic wrap, leaving one corner open to vent steam. Microwave on high heat for 2 minutes and then for 30 seconds at a time until cooked, stirring each time (total cooking time should be about 3 minutes).

2. Heat the margarine over medium-high heat. Add the onion. Sauté for 4 to 5 minutes, until the onion is softened.

3. Add the clam juice, milk, cream, dried parsley, paprika, salt, and pepper. Bring to a boil.

4. Stir in the cooked corn. Return to a boil.

5. Turn down the heat, cover, and simmer for 3 minutes. Add the clams and cook for 2 more minutes. Serve hot.

Soup Facts

A bisque is a creamy soup made with shellfish, while chowder is a heartier soup with fish or shellfish and vegetables in a milk-based broth. A southern U.S. specialty, gumbo is a thick soup made with meat or seafood, served over rice.

Hearty Roasted Vegetable Soup

*Here is a great way to turn leftover vegetables
into a nutritious soup.*

Serves 4

Preparation time:
5 minutes
Cooking time:
10–15 minutes

1 teaspoon olive oil
1 teaspoon bottled
   minced garlic
1 cup tomato juice
2½ cups beef broth
2 cups leftover Roasted
   Fall Harvest
   Vegetables (page 222)
1 teaspoon dried thyme
½ teaspoon salt
¼ teaspoon black pepper,
   or to taste

1. Heat the olive oil in a saucepan over medium heat.

2. Add the minced garlic and cook for about 1 minute until it begins to brown.

3. Add the tomato juice and beef broth. Cover and turn the heat up to medium-high to bring to a boil.

4. Add the roasted vegetables. Stir in the dried thyme, salt, and pepper.

5. Turn the heat down to medium-low, cover, and simmer for 2 to 3 minutes. Serve hot.

Chicken and Corn Soup

*Cayenne pepper adds a bit of spice to this nourishing chicken
and vegetable soup. You can replace the frozen corn with your
favorite type of corn in this recipe, including canned cream corn.*

Serves 4

Preparation time:
5–10 minutes
Cooking time: 15 minutes

2 teaspoons olive oil
2 shallots, peeled,
   chopped
5 cups chicken broth
2 cups frozen corn
½ teaspoon salt
⅛ teaspoon cayenne
   pepper
1 teaspoon ground cumin
1 leftover chicken breast,
   shredded
¼ cup chopped fresh
   parsley

1. Heat the olive oil in a saucepan over medium heat. Add the shallots and sauté until softened.

2. Add the chicken broth. Bring to a boil.

3. Add the frozen corn. Return to a boil.

4. Stir in the salt, cayenne pepper, and cumin.

5. Add the shredded chicken pieces. Stir in the fresh parsley. Simmer for a minute and serve hot.

Minestrone

Minestrone—literally, big soup—is one of Italy's signature dishes. Every region has its own special way of preparing this popular vegetable soup.

Serves 6

Preparation time:
5 minutes
Cooking time: 15 minutes

5 cups water
2 packages instant onion
   soup mix
1 zucchini, cubed
12 baby carrots
1 cup drained canned
   white beans
1 cup drained canned
   green beans
1 cup elbow macaroni
1 (28-ounce) can plum
   tomatoes
1 teaspoon dried parsley
1 teaspoon dried oregano
½ teaspoon salt, or to
   taste
¼ teaspoon black pepper,
   or to taste
⅓ cup grated Parmesan
   cheese

1. In a large saucepan over medium-high heat, bring the water to a boil. Stir in the onion soup mix.

2. Add the zucchini, carrots, white and green beans, and macaroni. Return to a boil.

3. Add the tomatoes with their juice. Return to a boil.

4. Stir in parsley, oregano, salt, and pepper.

5. Turn the heat down to medium-low, cover, and simmer for 10 minutes or until the zucchini is tender and the elbow macaroni is cooked. Pour the soup into serving bowls and garnish with the Parmesan cheese.

Turning Sauce into Soup

Your favorite pasta sauce can easily be transformed into a flavorful soup. For example, when preparing Simple Linguine with Tomato Sauce (page 166) reduce the amount of pasta to ¾ pound and reserve 1 cup of the sauce. To make the soup, simply combine the reserved sauce with 2½ to 3 cups of canned or packaged beef broth. Bring to a boil and simmer for 5 minutes to allow the flavors to blend.

Easy Egg Drop Soup

Serves 4

Preparation time:
5 minutes
Cooking time:
5–8 minutes

5 cups canned or
    packaged low-sodium
    vegetable broth
1 cup frozen peas
10 baby carrots, cut in
    half
2 green onions, finely
    chopped
¼ teaspoon white pepper,
    or to taste
½ teaspoon granulated
    sugar
2 large eggs, lightly
    beaten

The secret to this popular Chinese soup is the beaten egg, which is slowly streamed into the soup to form thin shreds. You can season the soup with salt to taste, if desired.

1. In a medium saucepan, bring the vegetable broth to a boil.

2. Add the frozen peas, baby carrots, green onion, white pepper, and sugar.

3. Cover and return to a boil. Cook for a minute.

4. Slowly stream in the eggs, stirring rapidly with a fork until it forms thin shreds.

5. Remove the soup from the heat. Serve hot.

Green Onion Safety

Like bean sprouts and other foods that are eaten raw, green onions are a frequent source of foodborne illnesses such as hepatitis A. While it's tempting to sprinkle freshly chopped green onion over soups and salads, for safety's sake it should always be cooked before serving.

Speedy Chicken Noodle Soup

Don't have leftover chicken on hand? This recipe uses canned chicken, a quick and easy alternative that is very economical.

1. Bring the water to a boil on medium-high heat. Add the ramen noodles and the contents of the flavor packet. Return to a boil, stirring.

2. Add the frozen peas. Return to a boil, reduce the heat, and simmer for 2 to 3 minutes, until the peas are cooked.

3. Add the canned chicken. Stir in the soy sauce and red pepper flakes.

4. Return to a boil, then reduce the heat and simmer for 5 more minutes.

Serves 4

Preparation time:
5 minutes
Cooking time:
12–15 minutes

3 cups water
1 package chicken-flavored ramen noodles
1 cup frozen peas
1 cup canned chicken
1 tablespoon soy sauce
¼ teaspoon red pepper flakes

Chicken Noodle Soup

Feel free to adapt this recipe according to what ingredients you have on hand. To make a quick and easy seafood version, for instance, replace the leftover chicken and vegetables with crabmeat and canned asparagus.

1. Heat the margarine over medium-high heat. Add the onion and sauté until it begins to soften. Stir in the minced garlic and cook for another minute until it begins to brown and the onion is softened.

2. Stir in the celery and carrots. Cook for a minute.

3. Add the chicken broth. Cover and turn the heat up to medium-high to bring to a boil.

4. Stir in the salt, pepper, and parsley. Add the chicken and pasta.

5. Turn the heat down to medium-low, cover, and simmer for 2 to 3 minutes. Serve the soup hot.

Serves 4

Preparation time:
5–8 minutes
Cooking time: 15 minutes

2 teaspoons margarine
1 medium onion, peeled, chopped
2 teaspoons bottled minced garlic
1 rib celery, thinly chopped
12 baby carrots, cut in half
5 cups reduced-sodium chicken broth
½ teaspoon salt
¼ teaspoon black pepper
1 teaspoon dried parsley leaves
1 leftover cooked chicken breast, chopped
1 cup leftover cooked pasta

Chicken Soup with Two Types of Mushrooms

Mushrooms add a savory flavor to warming chicken soup. Instead of wine, you can use 5 cups of chicken broth or substitute 1 cup of milk or light cream.

Serves 4

Preparation time:
5 minutes
Cooking time:
12–15 minutes

1 tablespoon olive oil
2 shallots, peeled, chopped
1 tablespoon chopped
    garlic
1 cup sliced portobello
    mushroom caps
1 cup sliced oyster
    mushrooms
1 cup dry white wine
3 cups chicken broth
¼ teaspoon salt
¼ teaspoon freshly
    ground white pepper
1 tablespoon chopped
    fresh parsley

1. Heat the olive oil in a saucepan over medium-high heat. Add the shallots and garlic. Sauté for 3 to 4 minutes, until the shallots are softened.

2. Add the mushrooms. Cook until softened. Splash the mushrooms with 1 tablespoon of the white wine.

3. Add the chicken broth and the remainder of the white wine. Bring to a boil.

4. Stir in the salt, white pepper, and parsley.

5. Turn the heat down to medium-low. Simmer, uncovered, for 5 minutes. Serve hot.

Italian Ground Beef Soup

Briefly browning the meatballs prior to adding them to the soup adds extra flavor and ensures that they are cooked through.

Serves 4

Preparation time:
10 minutes
Cooking time:
12–15 minutes

1 pound lean ground beef
½ cup crushed bread
    crumbs
¼ cup grated Parmesan
    cheese
½ teaspoon dried
    oregano leaves
½ teaspoon dried basil
    leaves
2 tablespoons minced
    onion
½ teaspoon bottled
    minced garlic
3 tablespoons milk
1 tablespoon olive oil
5 cups chicken broth
½ teaspoon salt
¼ teaspoon black pepper

1. In a medium bowl, combine the ground beef, bread crumbs, Parmesan cheese, oregano, basil, minced onion, minced garlic, and milk. Form into small meatballs about the size of golf balls.

2. Heat the olive oil in a skillet on medium-high heat. Add the meatballs. Brown the meatballs for 5 minutes, turning at least once.

3. While the meatballs are browning, bring the chicken broth to a boil in a large saucepan.

4. Add the salt, pepper, and meatballs.

5. Return to a boil. Cook for 5 to 7 minutes, until the meatballs are cooked through. Serve the soup hot.

Warming Wonton Soup

Don't have time to fill and wrap wontons to make authentic wonton soup? This recipe takes the ingredients normally used to make the wontons and combines them with Chinese vegetables in a seasoned broth.

1. Bring the chicken broth to a boil over medium-high heat.

2. Add the ground pork, breaking it up with a spatula.

3. Add the wonton wrappers, bamboo shoots, and water chestnuts. Return to a boil.

4. Stir in the salt, sugar, white pepper, and green onions. Stir in the oyster sauce.

5. Turn the heat down slightly and simmer for 5 minutes to soften the wonton wrappers and combine all the flavors. Serve hot.

Serves 4

Preparation time:
5 minutes
Cooking time: 10 minutes

5 cups chicken broth
½ pound leftover cooked
    ground pork
18 wonton wrappers
½ cup canned bamboo
    shoots
½ cup canned sliced
    water chestnuts
¼ teaspoon salt
½ teaspoon granulated
    sugar
⅛ teaspoon white pepper,
    or to taste
2 green onions, chopped
1 tablespoon oyster sauce

Leftover Meatball Soup

Add extra flavor by using canned tomatoes with herbs, or replacing the dried oregano with an equivalent amount of Italian seasoning.

1. Heat the olive oil in a saucepan over medium heat. Add the onion and garlic. Sprinkle the paprika and oregano on top of the onion. Sauté until the onion is shiny and softened (about 4 minutes).

2. Add the canned tomatoes, stirring to mix in with the onion and garlic. Add the broth and bring to a boil.

3. Add the meatballs. Stir in the pepper and turmeric. Return to a boil.

4. Turn the heat down to medium-low and simmer until the meatballs are cooked through. Serve hot.

Serves 6

Preparation time:
5 minutes
Cooking time: 15 minutes

1 tablespoon olive oil
½ cup chopped onion
1 teaspoon bottled
    minced garlic
1 teaspoon paprika, or to
    taste
½ teaspoon dried
    oregano leaves
1 cup canned tomatoes
6 cups canned or
    packaged beef broth
24 frozen meatballs,
    thawed
¼ teaspoon black pepper
1 teaspoon turmeric

Easy Oyster Bisque

Serves 4

Preparation time:
5–10 minutes
Cooking time: 15 minutes

24 canned Pacific oysters
2 teaspoons olive oil
2 teaspoons bottled
    minced garlic
2 shallots, finely chopped
2 teaspoons dried parsley
2 cups light cream
1 cup clam juice
1 teaspoon salt
¼ teaspoon black pepper,
    or to taste
2 tablespoons seafood
    cocktail sauce
8 slices sourdough bread

Seafood cocktail sauce, a spicy mixture that includes horseradish and Worcestershire, adds spice to this simple seafood bisque. It's fine to chop the shallots ahead of time and store them in a resealable plastic bag in the refrigerator until needed.

1. Drain the oysters and chop into thin pieces.

2. Heat the olive oil in a saucepan over medium-high heat. Add the garlic and shallots and sprinkle the dried parsley over them. Sauté for 2 to 3 minutes, until the shallots are softened.

3. Add the light cream and clam juice. Bring to a boil.

4. Add the oysters. Stir in the salt, pepper, and cocktail sauce.

5. Reduce the heat to medium-low. Simmer for 5 minutes. Serve hot, with the bread for dipping.

Chapter 5
Salads

Instant Mashed Potato Salad

For a more tart flavor, feel free to increase the amount of white wine vinegar to 1 tablespoon.

Serves 4

Preparation time:
10 minutes

*4 cups boiling water
8 ounces instant flavored
    mashed potatoes
⅔ cup mayonnaise
3 tablespoons sour cream
2 teaspoons white wine
    vinegar
1 teaspoon dried dill
4 hard-boiled eggs,
    peeled, chopped
2 ribs celery, thinly sliced*

1. Pour the boiling water into a large bowl. Add the instant flavored mashed potatoes, stirring with a fork to make sure they are completely covered. Cover and let sit for 5 minutes while preparing the mayonnaise dressing.

2. In a medium bowl, stir together the mayonnaise, sour cream, white wine vinegar, and dried dill.

3. In a large salad bowl, combine the mashed potatoes with the mayonnaise dressing, chopped eggs, and celery.

4. Chill until ready to serve.

Greek Bean Salad

You can serve the bean salad with a good crusty bread that has been rubbed with a bit of leftover juice from chopping the tomato.

Serves 4

Preparation time:
10 minutes

*2 tablespoons olive oil
2 tablespoons lemon juice
2 teaspoons water
1 teaspoon granulated
    sugar
2½ cups drained canned
    chickpeas
1 medium tomato, cut into
    chunks
½ sweet onion, cut into
    rings
½ teaspoon salt
Black pepper, to taste*

1. In a small bowl, whisk together the olive oil, lemon juice, water, and sugar.

2. Combine the chickpeas, tomato, and onion.

3. Toss with the lemon juice dressing.

4. Sprinkle with the salt and pepper. Serve immediately.

Classic Greek Salad

For an extra touch, cut a garlic clove in half and rub it over the salad bowl. You can use Greek oregano if it is available.

1. In a large salad bowl, combine the lettuce, red onion, tomatoes, cucumber, and bell pepper.

2. In a small bowl, whisk together the olive oil, red wine vinegar, sugar, pepper, sea salt, garlic, and oregano.

3. Drizzle the olive oil dressing over the salad.

4. Sprinkle the crumbled feta on top.

5. Add the olives. Serve immediately.

Greek Salad

A staple on Greek restaurant menus around the world, traditional Greek salad (horiatiki) is made with tomatoes, cucumbers, Greek oregano, and an olive oil dressing. Although they are popular additions, feta cheese and plump kalamata olives are optional.

Serves 4

Preparation time:
20 minutes

4 romaine lettuce leaves, washed, drained, and torn
½ red onion, peeled, cut into thin rings
12 cherry tomatoes, cut in half
1 English cucumber, thinly sliced
1 green bell pepper, seeded, cut into chunks
3 tablespoons extra-virgin olive oil
2 tablespoons red wine vinegar
1 teaspoon granulated sugar
¼ teaspoon black pepper
½ teaspoon sea salt
½ teaspoon bottled minced garlic
¼ teaspoon dried oregano, or to taste
1 cup crumbled feta cheese
12 whole olives, chopped and pitted

Five-Ingredient Taco Salad

Taco shells are found in the refrigerated section of many super-markets; look for hot chipotle salsa with the other sauces.

Serves 1

Preparation time:
7–10 minutes

1 (14-ounce) can black
    beans, drained
1 taco salad shell
1 cup packaged salad
    mix
¼ cup chipotle salsa
½ cup shredded Cheddar
    cheese
¼ cup canned, chopped
    pitted olives

1. In a small saucepan, quickly heat the black beans, stirring.

2. Line the taco shell with the salad greens.

3. Spoon the beans on top.

4. Stir in the salsa.

5. Sprinkle the shredded cheese and olives on top.

Taco Salad History

A Mexican-inspired dish, taco salads first began appearing in Mexican takeout restaurants in the 1960s. (It is possible that the idea originated at a Taco Bell restaurant.) The traditional taco salad is made with ground beef, tomatoes, chilies, and cheese, and is served with corn chips.

Cottage Cheese and Fruit Salad

*This simple salad makes an easy side dish for 4,
or a quick midday meal for 2.*

Serves 4

Preparation time:
5 minutes

2 cups cottage cheese
1 teaspoon ground
    cinnamon
½ teaspoon ground
    nutmeg
1 large green apple, thinly
    sliced
2 tablespoons apple juice
Black pepper, to taste

Combine all ingredients. Chill until ready to serve.

Tropical Fruit Salad with Pecans

A rich source of vitamin C and several B vitamins, papayas are available year round in many supermarkets. Canned litchis can be found in the canned fruit section, or at ethnic supermarkets.

Serves 4

Preparation time:
10–15 minutes

2 papayas
¼ cup tropical fruit punch
1 teaspoon granulated
    sugar
1 cup drained canned
    pineapple chunks
1 cup drained canned
    litchis
2 bananas, peeled, thinly
    sliced
½ cup pecan pieces

1. Cut the papayas in half and use a spoon to remove the seeds. Remove the peel from each half of the papaya with a paring knife. Lay the papayas flat, scooped side downward, and cut crosswise into thin strips.

2. In a small bowl, stir together the fruit punch and sugar.

3. Combine the fruit in a large salad bowl.

4. Sprinkle the juice over the top and toss gently. Garnish with the pecans.

5. Serve immediately, or cover and chill until ready to serve.

How to Pick a Papaya

When choosing a papaya, look for one that is neither too firm nor too soft, but yields to gentle pressure. The skin should be smooth and firm, and the color mainly yellow. Avoid papayas that have a wrinkled skin or a strong smell.

Basic Garden Salad

Serves 6

4 large iceberg lettuce
    leaves
2 ribs celery, thinly sliced
¼ cup chopped green
    onion
2 carrots, peeled and
    chopped
1 tomato, thinly sliced
⅓ cup Italian salad
    dressing

A simple garden salad makes a quick and easy side dish on a busy weeknight. Feel free to replace the Italian dressing with your favorite salad dressing.

1. Separate the lettuce leaves. Rinse, drain, and tear loosely.

2. In a large salad bowl, combine the lettuce, celery, green onion, carrots, and tomato.

3. Pour the dressing over the vegetables and toss gently.

Mandarin Orange Salad

Serves 4

Preparation time:
10 minutes

¼ teaspoon black pepper
¼ teaspoon salt
1 cup low-fat cottage
    cheese
¼ cup reserved mandarin
    orange juice
1 teaspoon granulated
    sugar
1 head romaine lettuce
    leaves, washed,
    drained, torn
2 green onions, finely
    chopped
½ medium red onion,
    peeled and chopped
2 (10-ounce) cans
    mandarin oranges,
    drained

The sweet taste of mandarin oranges adds something extra to a plain cottage cheese salad. For a special touch, top the salad with walnuts halves or candied (sugared) walnuts.

1. In a medium bowl, stir the pepper and salt into the cottage cheese. Stir in the mandarin orange juice and sugar.

2. Put the torn romaine lettuce leaves in a salad bowl. Toss with the onions.

3. Add the cottage cheese and the mandarin oranges on top.

4. Serve immediately, or chill until ready to serve.

Make-Ahead Salads

Many of the vegetables found in a typical salad, including lettuce, can be prepared ahead of time. Wrap the cut vegetables in paper towels and store in a resealable plastic bag in the crisper section of your refrigerator until ready to use.

Chicken and Strawberry Salad

A simple yogurt dressing jazzes up this salad made with fresh strawberries and leftover chicken.

Serves 4

Preparation time:
10–15 minutes

2 leftover cooked chicken breasts
1¼ teaspoons Dijon mustard
½ teaspoon salt
⅛ teaspoon black pepper
1 cup vanilla yogurt
1 pint strawberries, washed, hulled
4 cups packaged salad greens

1. Cut the chicken breasts into thin strips.

2. In a medium bowl, stir the mustard, salt, and pepper into the yogurt.

3. Stir in the chicken and strawberries.

4. Arrange the greens in a salad bowl. Spoon the yogurt, fruit, and chicken mixture over the greens.

5. Serve the salad immediately or cover and chill until ready to serve.

Delicious Dijon Mustard

Originating in the Dijon region in southeastern France, Dijon mustard gets its sharp taste from brown or black mustard seeds. Although mustard has been cultivated in France since ancient times, Dijon mustard was invented in the mid-1800s by Jean Naigeon, who came up with the idea of replacing the vinegar used to make mustard with verjuice, the sour juice from unripe grapes. Today, Dijon-style mustard is produced throughout the world.

Asian Chicken Noodle Salad

Serves 4

Preparation time:
10–15 minutes

1 pound cooked chicken
    breast meat
3 tablespoons red wine
    vinegar
1 tablespoon olive oil
2 tablespoons soy sauce
2 tablespoons Asian
    sesame oil
1 teaspoon granulated
    sugar
1 head romaine lettuce,
    washed, drained, torn
4 green onions, finely
    chopped
1 (11-ounce) can
    mandarin oranges,
    drained
1 cup chow mein noodles

This is a California classic—chow mein noodles, mandarin oranges, and salad vegetables, all topped with a tart vinegar and sesame oil dressing.

1. Cut the chicken into thin strips.

2. In a small bowl, whisk the red wine vinegar, olive oil, soy sauce, sesame oil, and sugar.

3. Place the salad dressing in the bottom of a large salad bowl. Stir in the romaine lettuce, green onions, and chicken strips.

4. Add the mandarin oranges and the chow mein noodles on top.

Salad Basics

Always make sure lettuce is drained thoroughly—wet, soggy lettuce can affect the salad's flavor. Shred the lettuce leaves instead of cutting them with a knife. Unless the recipe states otherwise, if preparing a salad ahead of time, add the dressing just before serving. Toss the salad gently with the dressing, taking care not to overstir.

Marinated Vegetable Salad

This simple salad requires little preparation and has a (comparatively) short marinating time. It makes a nice salad, or you could serve it as a side dish in place of cooked vegetables or over cooked pasta.

1. In a small bowl, whisk together the olive oil, apple cider vinegar, chopped basil, salt, and pepper.

2. Place the vegetables in a salad bowl and gently toss with the vinegar dressing.

3. Cover the salad and chill for one hour. Stir again gently before serving.

Serves 2

Preparation time:
15 minutes
Marinating time: 1 hour

⅓ cup olive oil
3 tablespoons apple cider
    vinegar
1 tablespoon chopped
    fresh basil
¼ teaspoon salt
⅛ teaspoon black pepper,
    or to taste
2 medium cucumbers,
    thinly sliced
2 tomatoes, chopped into
    chunks
½ red onion, peeled,
    sliced

Basic Spinach Salad

Using low-fat yogurt provides a light alternative to mayonnaise in this easy recipe. Both the salad and the dressing can be prepared ahead of time and refrigerated, but don't toss the salad with the dressing until you're ready to serve.

1. Wash the spinach leaves and drain in a colander or salad spinner.

2. In a medium bowl, stir together the yogurt, mustard, dill, salt, and pepper.

3. Combine the spinach leaves, mushrooms, chopped peppers, and bacon bits in a salad bowl.

4. Toss the vegetables with the yogurt dressing. Serve.

Serves 6

Preparation time:
10 minutes

4 cups packed fresh
    spinach leaves
¾ cup plain low-fat yogurt
1 teaspoon Dijon mustard
1 teaspoon dried dill
½ teaspoon salt
Black pepper, to taste
1 cup sliced fresh
    mushrooms
2 Roasted Red Peppers
    (page 221), chopped
½ cup bacon bits

Meal-Size Salad with Herbed Chicken

Serves 6

Preparation time:
15 minutes

1 deli rotisserie smoked
    chicken
4 cups mixed salad
    greens
1 cup drained mandarin
    oranges
1 cup golden raisins
1 cup Italian salad
    dressing

Instead of Italian salad dressing, you could also use the yogurt dressing in Basic Spinach Salad (page 71)—increase the yogurt to 1 cup and stir in 1¼ teaspoons Dijon mustard and dried dill, adding salt and pepper to taste.

1. Shred the chicken meat, breaking it into bite-size pieces.

2. In a salad bowl, combine the salad greens, chicken, mandarin oranges, and raisins.

3. Toss the salad with the Italian salad dressing. Serve.

Caesar Turkey Salad

Serves 3

Preparation time:
5 minutes
Cooking time: 15 minutes

2 cups ground turkey
¼ teaspoon salt
¼ teaspoon black pepper
1 teaspoon bottled
    minced garlic
1 head romaine lettuce,
    washed, drained, torn
2 cups croutons
⅓ cup bacon bits
¾ cup Caesar salad
    dressing
¼ cup Parmesan cheese

Ground turkey turns a standard Caesar salad into a high-protein meal. To increase the health benefits, replace the bacon bits with chopped nuts.

1. Brown the turkey in a skillet over medium-high heat.

2. Sprinkle the salt and pepper over the turkey. Stir in the minced garlic.

3. Continue cooking the turkey until it is cooked through and there is no pinkness (about 10 minutes).

4. While the turkey is cooking, in a salad bowl, combine the romaine lettuce leaves, croutons, and bacon bits.

5. Drain the turkey and add it to the salad. Toss the salad with the Caesar dressing. Sprinkle the cheese on top and serve.

Classic Three-Bean Salad

You can dress up this salad by serving it on a bed of romaine lettuce leaves.

Serves 6

Preparation time:
10 minutes

¼ cup olive oil
⅓ cup white wine vinegar
1 teaspoon Dijon mustard
½ teaspoon salt, or to
    taste
⅛ teaspoon black pepper,
    or to taste
1 teaspoon minced onion
2 cups drained, rinsed
    canned green beans
1 (15-ounce) can kidney
    beans, drained, rinsed
1 (15-ounce) can yellow
    beans, drained, rinsed

1. In a small bowl, whisk together the olive oil, white wine vinegar, Dijon mustard, salt, pepper, and minced onion.

2. Place all the beans in a salad bowl and toss gently with the dressing.

3. Serve the salad immediately, or cover and chill until ready to serve.

Bean Salad Basics
Beans are an excellent choice for salads, as they easily absorb the dressing. When using canned beans, always drain and rinse them to remove any "tinny" taste. Rinsing the beans also removes excess sodium.

Colorful Pasta Salad

Fusilli vegetable pasta adds color and flavor to this simple salad. To speed up the preparation time even further, use leftover cooked pasta.

Serves 4

Preparation time:
5 minutes
Cooking time: 15 minutes

Water to cook pasta, as
    needed
3 cups fusilli vegetable
    pasta
½ cup low-fat mayonnaise
½ cup plain yogurt
1 tablespoon Dijon honey
    mustard
1 cup green seedless
    grapes

1. Bring a large saucepan with the water to a boil. Cook the pasta according to the package directions, or until it is tender but still firm. Drain.

2. In a medium mixing bowl, stir together the mayonnaise, yogurt, and honey mustard.

3. Put the cooked pasta and grapes in a large salad bowl.

4. Toss gently with the yogurt and mayonnaise dressing.

Spicy Mexican Potato Salad

This quick and easy potato salad is perfect for a romantic picnic for two. Feel free to adjust the amount of jalapeño peppers according to your own taste.

Serves 2

Cooking time: 10 minutes
Preparation and assembly time:
10 minutes

2 medium red potatoes
½ medium tomato,
    seeded and chopped
½ red onion, chopped
½ cup drained canned
    Mexican-style corn
1 tablespoon bottled
    chopped jalapeño
    peppers
¼ cup Orange-Cilantro
    Marinade (page 247)

1. Wash the potatoes, peel if desired, and cut into chunks. Place the potatoes in a large, microwave-safe bowl with enough water to cover. Cover the dish with microwave-safe plastic wrap. Microwave the potatoes on high heat for 8 minutes, give the bowl a quarter turn, and then continue cooking for 1 minute at a time until the potatoes are fork-tender (total cooking time should be about 10 minutes). Drain.

2. While the potatoes are boiling, prepare the vegetables: seed and chop the tomato and chop the onion.

3. Combine the potatoes and other vegetables (including the corn and chopped peppers) in a large salad bowl.

4. Whisk the Orange-Cilantro Marinade (page 247). Add it to the salad and toss to mix thoroughly.

What Makes a Dish Microwave-Safe?

The main material that makes a dish unsuitable for microwaving is metal. During cooking, microwaves bounce off the metal instead of harmlessly passing through. This causes sparks that may damage the oven or blacken the dish. Today, most microwave-safe dishware is clearly marked.

Chapter 6
Chicken and Other Poultry

Cashew Chicken

A salty liquid made from fermented fish, fish sauce is a staple ingredient in Southeast Asian cooking. If fish sauce is unavailable, substitute one tablespoon of soy sauce.

Serves 3

Preparation time:
5 minutes
Cooking time:
8–10 minutes

¾ pound boneless, skinless chicken breast
2 tablespoons vegetable or peanut oil
1 tablespoon red curry paste
2 cloves garlic, chopped
1 yellow onion, cut into thin slices
¼ cup chicken broth
2 tablespoons oyster sauce
1 tablespoon fish sauce
2 scallions, chopped
1 teaspoon granulated sugar
½ cup roasted cashews
1 bunch cilantro sprigs, optional garnish

1. Cut the chicken into bite-size pieces.

2. Heat the oil in a wok or heavy skillet. Add the red curry paste and the garlic. Stir-fry until the garlic is aromatic. Add the chicken and stir-fry at high heat for 4 to 5 minutes, until the chicken is white and nearly cooked.

3. Add the onion to the pan. Stir-fry for 2 minutes, then stir in the chicken broth, oyster sauce, and fish sauce. Stir in the scallions and the sugar. Stir in the cashews.

4. Continue cooking for another minute to combine all the ingredients and make sure the chicken is cooked through. To serve, garnish with the cilantro sprigs.

Chicken with Salsa Verde

Flavorful salsa verde makes an excellent accompaniment to chicken. Serve with Mexican Fried Rice (page 148) or crusty bread.

Serves 4

Preparation time:
5 minutes
Cooking time:
15–20 minutes

Pre-made Simple Salsa Verde (page 248) or store-bought
1½ pounds chicken thighs

1. Preheat the broiler. Spray a broiling rack with nonstick cooking spray.

2. Broil the chicken thighs, 9 inches from the heat source, for 15 to 20 minutes until cooked through. Turn the chicken over every 5 minutes.

3. Serve the chicken with the Simple Salsa Verde.

Tomato Turkey Cutlets

This healthy dish is loaded with cancer-fighting foods, from turkey and tomatoes to mushrooms and garlic.

1. Heat the oil on medium-high heat. Add the garlic, onion, and turkey cutlets. Sprinkle the sage and ground cumin on top of the cutlets.

2. Add the mushrooms, splashing with the red wine vinegar. Cook for 5 to 7 minutes, until the cutlets have browned and the mushrooms are softened.

3. Add the tomatoes and the water. Stir in the salt and pepper.

4. Cook, stirring occasionally, for 5 to 7 minutes, until the turkey is cooked through.

Check the Packaging

When purchasing chicken, be sure to check the "sell by" date on the package. Poultry purchased on the "sell by" date should be used within two days.

Serves 4

Preparation time:
5–8 minutes
Cooking time: 15 minutes

2 teaspoons olive oil
2 cloves garlic, minced
1 medium onion, peeled, chopped
1 pound turkey breast cutlets
1 teaspoon sage
2 teaspoons ground cumin
1½ cups sliced fresh button mushrooms
1 tablespoon red wine vinegar
1 cup canned tomatoes
¼ cup water
¼ teaspoon salt
⅛ teaspoon black pepper

Lemon Chicken in a Rice Cooker

Steaming chicken breasts helps make them extra tender.

1. Cut any excess fat from the fillets. Cut the chicken breasts into bite-size cubes.

2. Place the chicken in the steamer and sprinkle the rosemary on top. Steam the chicken for 20 minutes, or according to the steamer directions.

3. While the chicken is steaming, bring the lemon juice, brown sugar, oyster sauce, soy sauce, and chicken broth to a boil over medium heat, stirring to dissolve the sugar.

4. Remove the chicken from the steamer. Pour the sauce over the chicken. Garnish with the chopped scallions.

Serves 2

Preparation time:
10 minutes
Cooking time:
20–30 minutes

1¼ pounds chicken breast fillets
1 tablespoon dried rosemary
2 tablespoons lemon juice
2 tablespoons brown sugar
1 tablespoon oyster sauce
1 tablespoon soy sauce
2 tablespoons chicken broth
2 scallions, chopped

Chicken with Orange-Cilantro Marinade

On weekends or evenings when you have more time, add even more flavor to this dish by increasing the marinating time to 2 hours.

Serves 4

Preparation time:
15 minutes
Cooking time: 15 minutes

2 portions Orange-
  Cilantro Marinade
  (page 247)
1½ pounds boneless,
  skinless, chicken
  thighs

1. Prepare the Orange-Cilantro Marinade (page 247). Reserve ¼ cup to use as a basting sauce.

2. Place a few diagonal cuts on the chicken so that the marinade can penetrate. Place the chicken in a large resealable plastic bag and add the marinade. Marinate the chicken for at least 5 minutes.

3. Preheat the broiler.

4. Place the chicken on a rack that has been sprayed with nonstick cooking spray. Brush some of the reserved marinade on top. Broil the chicken, 9 inches from the heat source, for about 15 minutes, until the chicken is cooked through. Every 5 minutes, turn the chicken over and brush with the reserved marinade.

The Difference Between Grilling and Broiling

What separates grilling and broiling is more than whether or not the food is cooked indoors or outside on the grill. The main difference between these two cooking methods is the location of the heat source. In broiling, heat is applied to the food from the top, whereas in grilling the heat comes from the bottom. Both methods rely upon an intense direct heat that sears the food, giving it a rich flavor.

Lemon Chicken with Broccoli Stir-Fry

Sweet brown sugar balances the tart flavor of lemon in this simple stir-fry. For extra flavor, add chicken or vegetable broth to the steaming water for the broccoli.

Serves 2

Preparation time:
5 minutes
Cooking time: 15 minutes

1 pound chicken breast
   fillets
¼ teaspoon salt, or to
   taste
¼ teaspoon black pepper,
   or to taste
1 tablespoon oyster sauce
1 tablespoon soy sauce
2 tablespoons lemon juice
2 tablespoons chicken
   broth
2 teaspoons brown sugar
2 tablespoons olive oil
1 pound broccoli florets

1. Cut the chicken fillets into thin strips. Rub the salt and pepper over them to season.

2. In a small bowl, combine the oyster sauce, soy sauce, lemon juice, chicken broth, and brown sugar. Set aside.

3. Heat the olive oil in a skillet and add the chicken. Cook the chicken, turning once, for about 10 minutes, until it is browned and nearly cooked through. Remove the chicken from the pan.

4. While the chicken is cooking, steam the broccoli: place the broccoli florets on a metal steamer tray and steam in a medium saucepan over boiling water for 6 to 8 minutes, until they are tender but still crisp. Remove and drain.

5. Add the cooked broccoli to the pan. Add the sauce and bring to a boil. Return the chicken to the pan. Stir to heat through and serve immediately.

Lemon Chicken Around the World

Nearly every cuisine has its own recipe for pairing tender chicken with a tart lemony sauce. Stir-fried lemon chicken is a popular Chinese restaurant dish, while in Greece the chicken is basted with an oil and lemon sauce during grilling. Thai lemon chicken recipes frequently include a sweet-and-sour fish sauce for dipping.

Chili Chicken with Peanuts

Serves 2

Preparation time:
5–8 minutes
Cooking time: 10 minutes

*1 pound boneless,
    skinless chicken
    thighs
3 tablespoons reduced-
    sodium chicken broth
1 tablespoon red wine
    vinegar
1 teaspoon sugar
4 teaspoons vegetable oil,
    divided
¼ teaspoon salt
⅛ teaspoon black pepper
1 tablespoon bottled,
    chopped jalapeño
    peppers
1 shallot, peeled and
    chopped
1 teaspoon minced ginger
½ cup skinless, unsalted
    peanuts*

*To make this simple stir-fry even easier, use bottled minced
ginger, available at most supermarkets.*

1. Cut the chicken into 1" cubes. In a small bowl, stir together the chicken broth, red wine vinegar, and sugar.

2. Heat 2 teaspoons vegetable oil in a heavy skillet over medium-high heat. Add the chicken cubes. Cook for about 5 minutes, stirring constantly, until they turn white and are nearly cooked. Stir in the salt and pepper while the chicken is cooking. Remove the chicken from the pan.

3. Heat 2 teaspoons oil in the pan. Add the chopped jalapeño peppers, shallot, and ginger. Cook, stirring for about 2 minutes, until the shallot is softened.

4. Stir the chicken broth mixture, pour into the pan, and bring to a boil.

5. Return the chicken to the pan. Add the peanuts. Cook for 1 to 2 more minutes to finish cooking the chicken and combine the ingredients. Serve hot.

Stir-Fried Chicken Cacciatore

Normally a slow simmered dish, this recipe transforms Italian chicken cacciatore into a quick stir-fry that is perfect for busy weeknights.

Serves 4

Preparation time:
8 minutes
Cooking time: 12 minutes

1 pound boneless,
   skinless chicken
   thighs
3½ tablespoons dry white
   wine, divided
1 teaspoon dried oregano
Black pepper, to taste
2 teaspoons cornstarch
1 shallot, peeled and
   chopped
¼ pound sliced fresh
   mushrooms
1 red bell pepper,
   seeded, cut into thin
   strips
3 tablespoons low-sodium
   chicken broth
3 tablespoons diced
   tomatoes with juice
½ teaspoon granulated
   sugar
3 tablespoons olive oil,
   divided
1 tablespoon chopped
   fresh oregano

1. Cut the chicken into thin strips about 2" to 3" long. Place the chicken strips in a bowl and add 2½ tablespoons white wine, oregano, pepper, and cornstarch, adding the cornstarch last. Let the chicken stand while preparing the other ingredients.

2. While the chicken is marinating, cut the vegetables. In a small bowl, combine the chicken broth, diced tomatoes, and sugar. Set aside.

3. Heat 1 tablespoon oil in a preheated wok or heavy skillet. When the oil is hot, add the chopped shallot. Stir-fry for a minute, until it begins to soften, then add the sliced mushrooms. Stir-fry for a minute, then add the red bell pepper. Stir-fry for another minute, adding a bit of water if the vegetables begin to dry out. Remove the vegetables from the pan.

4. Heat 2 tablespoons oil in the wok or skillet. When the oil is hot, add the chicken. Let the chicken brown for a minute, then stir-fry for about 5 minutes, until it turns white and is nearly cooked through. Splash 1 tablespoon of the white wine on the chicken while stir-frying.

5. Add the chicken broth and tomato mixture to the middle of the pan. Bring to a boil. Return the vegetables to the pan. Stir in the fresh oregano. Cook, stirring, for another couple of minutes to mix everything together. Serve immediately.

Stir-Fry Tips

When stir-frying, always make sure the oil is hot before adding the food. Stir vegetables continually, to keep them from sticking to the bottom of the pan. When stir-frying meat, allow it to brown briefly before you begin stirring.

Simple Steamed Chicken Dinner

Serves 4

Preparation time:
10 minutes
Cooking time:
20–25 minutes

Water, as needed
3 tablespoons dry white
*   wine*
1 teaspoon minced ginger
1 teaspoon granulated
*   sugar*
1 green onion, finely
*   chopped*
⅛ teaspoon black pepper,
*   or to taste*
2 pounds boneless,
*   skinless chicken*
*   breast halves*
2 zucchini, cut diagonally
*   into thin slices*
2 cups baby carrots

The exact amount of water needed for steaming will depend upon the size and type of equipment you are using to steam the food.

1. Prepare the equipment you are using for steaming and bring the steaming water to a boil.

2. In a small bowl, combine the white wine, ginger, sugar, green onion, and pepper. Rub the mixture over the chicken breasts.

3. Place the chicken, zucchini, and carrots in a heatproof dish or directly in the steamer tray if you are using a rice steamer/cooker.

4. Steam for 20 to 25 minutes, until the chicken is just cooked through.

5. Chop the chicken into bite-size pieces and serve with the cooked vegetables.

Three-Ingredient Drunken Chicken

This is an easy way to add extra flavor to leftover cooked chicken. Serve with cooked rice and a salad for a quick meal for one.

Serves 1

Preparation time:
10 minutes
Refrigerate: Overnight

*1 cup leftover Simple
    Steamed Chicken
    Dinner (page 82)
1 cup pale dry sherry
1 cup chicken broth*

1. Place the leftover chicken in a jar. Pour the sherry and chicken broth on top.

2. Refrigerate overnight. Serve cold.

Sherry with Extra Flavor

If you use dry sherry regularly in cooking, feel free to season it with a few slices of fresh peeled gingerroot. Store the sherry with the ginger in the refrigerator. Besides making the ginger last longer (just replace the sherry-soaked ginger with a fresh slice as needed), it imparts a nice gingery flavor to the sherry.

One-Dish Baked Chicken and Potatoes

Serves 4

Preparation time:
5 minutes
Cooking time:
15–18 minutes

2 (10-ounce) cans cream
    of celery soup
¼ cup milk
½ teaspoon paprika
⅛ teaspoon black pepper
1 pound leftover cooked
    chicken or deli
    chicken, cubed
1½ cups drained canned
    sweet potatoes
1 tablespoon curry
    powder

You can turn the heat up or down on this dish by using a milder or hotter curry powder, as desired.

1. Preheat the oven to 250°F.

2. Heat the soup and milk in a saucepan over medium heat until it is just boiling. Stir in the paprika and pepper.

3. Place the chicken and sweet potatoes in a deep-sided casserole dish. Sprinkle the curry powder on top.

4. Add the soup, stirring.

5. Bake for 10 to 15 minutes, until the chicken is heated through.

Chicken with Havarti

Serves 4

Preparation time:
5 minutes
Cooking time: 15 minutes

4 tablespoons lemon juice
½ teaspoon garlic salt
¼ teaspoon black pepper
2 teaspoons fresh dill
    weed
4 boneless, skinless
    chicken breast halves
½ cup crumbled Havarti
    cheese

Feel free to use either plain Havarti or Havarti with dill in this recipe. Serve the chicken with steamed vegetables and cooked pasta.

1. Preheat the broiler.

2. In a small bowl, combine the lemon juice, garlic salt, pepper, and dill weed. Use a pastry brush to brush the chicken breasts with the lemon juice mixture.

3. Spray a rack with nonstick cooking spray. Broil the chicken for 15 minutes or until cooked through, turning every 5 minutes. Brush any leftover lemon juice mixture on the chicken while broiling.

4. Sprinkle the crumbled cheese over the cooked chicken.

Five-Spice Roast Chicken

Roasting chicken breasts at high heat shortens the cooking time and makes the skin turn out extra crispy. Leftovers would work very well in Leftover Coconut Chicken (page 200).

(page 200)

1. Preheat the oven to 500˚F. Spray a roasting rack with nonstick cooking spray.

2. In a small bowl, whisk together the olive oil, red wine vinegar, five-spice powder, garlic, salt, pepper, and brown sugar.

3. Rub the five-spice mixture over the chicken breasts.

4. Place the seasoned chicken in a large roasting pan with foil, skin side up.

5. Roast the chicken for about 25 to 30 minutes, or until it is cooked through and the juices run clear.

Freezing Poultry

Leftover cooked chicken (and turkey) freezes very well. Wrap the chicken tightly in plastic wrap or freezer paper and mark with the date (frozen poultry should be used within three months). A handy time-saving idea is to divide the leftover poultry into individual serving portions to use in sandwiches or wraps.

Serves 6

Preparation time:
5 minutes
Cooking time:
25–30 minutes

3 tablespoons olive oil
2 tablespoons red wine
   vinegar
2 teaspoons five-spice
   powder
½ teaspoon bottled
   minced garlic
½ teaspoon salt
¼ teaspoon black pepper
½ teaspoon brown sugar
3 pounds chicken breast
   halves, bone-in

Skillet Chicken with Peaches

Be sure to use firm peaches that aren't overripe, or they may fall apart and become mushy during cooking.

Serves 4

Preparation time:
5–10 minutes
Cooking time:
10–15 minutes

1½ pounds chicken breast
  halves
⅓ cup orange juice
1 tablespoon white or
  cider vinegar
1 tablespoon brown sugar
2 tablespoons vegetable
  oil
½ teaspoon paprika
3 large peaches, thinly
  sliced
½ teaspoon ground
  allspice

1. Chop the chicken breasts into bite-size pieces.

2. In a small bowl, combine the orange juice, vinegar, and brown sugar.

3. In a large skillet, heat the oil on medium-high heat. Turn the heat down to medium, add the chicken, and cook, stirring frequently, until the cubes turn white and are nearly cooked through. Stir in the paprika while the chicken is cooking.

4. Add the peaches and cook, stirring, for about 2 minutes. Stir in the allspice.

5. Add the orange juice mixture. Bring to a boil. Turn down the heat and simmer for 5 more minutes. Serve hot.

Easy Tandoori Chicken

Traditionally, tandoori chicken is marinated overnight in a spicy mixture of yogurt and seasonings. In this quick and easy variation, the chicken is pan-fried with the seasonings and served with the heated yogurt dressing.

1. Combine the spices, sugar, and garlic powder in a small bowl. Rub over the chicken breasts to season.

2. In a small bowl, combine the yogurt and lemon juice. Set aside (do not refrigerate).

3. Heat the oil in a skillet on medium-high heat. Add the garlic and the chicken. Pan-fry for 3 to 4 minutes on one side until browned.

4. Add the shallot. Turn over the chicken and cook the other side until the chicken is cooked through (8 to 10 minutes total cooking time). Remove the chicken to a serving plate.

5. While the chicken is cooking, briefly heat the yogurt in a saucepan over medium heat. Remove and spoon over the chicken.

Perfectly Cooked Chicken Breasts

One way to tell if a chicken breast is cooked is to press on it. Properly cooked chicken has a "springy" texture. If the chicken is too soft it is not done, while chicken meat that is tough has been overcooked.

Serves 4

Preparation time:
5 minutes
Cooking time:
10–15 minutes

1½ teaspoons ground
   coriander
1½ teaspoons ground
   cumin
1½ teaspoons ground
   cayenne pepper
½ teaspoon ground
   ginger
¼ teaspoon sugar
½ teaspoon garlic
   powder, or to taste
4 boneless, skinless
   chicken breast halves
¾ cup natural yogurt
2 tablespoons lemon juice
2 tablespoons vegetable
   oil
1 clove garlic, peeled,
   thinly sliced
1 shallot, peeled and
   chopped

Curried Chicken and Rice

Serves 4

Preparation time:
5–10 minutes
Cooking time:
25–30 minutes

2 tablespoons lemon juice
1½ pounds boneless,
    skinless chicken
    breast halves
1 cup long-grain white
    rice
1½ cups water
2 tablespoons olive oil
½ teaspoon garlic powder
1 medium onion, chopped
1 tablespoon curry
    powder
1 tomato, thinly sliced
1 cup chicken broth
½ cup raisins
¼ teaspoon salt
⅛ teaspoon black pepper

Instead of regular cooked rice, you can, of course, use instant rice or reheat leftover cooked rice in the microwave.

1. In a medium bowl, combine the lemon juice with the chicken breasts, turning to coat them. Begin cooking the rice in the 1½ cups water (see How to Cook Long-Grain Rice, page 148).

2. Heat the olive oil in a skillet over medium-high heat. Add the chicken breasts. (Discard any excess lemon juice.) Sprinkle the garlic powder on top. Cook for 4 to 5 minutes, until the chicken is browned on both sides, turning over halfway during cooking. Remove the chicken from the pan.

3. Add the onion to the pan. Add the curry powder, stirring to mix it in with the onion. Add the tomato. Cook, stirring occasionally, until the onion is shiny and has softened (4 to 5 minutes total cooking time for the onion).

4. Add the broth to the pan. Bring to a boil.

5. Return the chicken to the pan. Stir in the raisins. Turn down the heat and simmer, covered, until the chicken is cooked through (10 to 15 minutes). Season with salt and pepper. Serve with the rice.

Using Leftover Chicken

Always store leftover cooked chicken in a sealed container in the refrigerator (if it is not being frozen). Use the chicken within three to four days.

Turkey Meat Loaf

You can add extra flavor by using Italian seasoned bread crumbs in this recipe.

1. In a large bowl, combine all the ingredients and stir, but do not overmix.

2. Spoon the mixture into a microwave-safe casserole dish and shape into a loaf.

3. Microwave on high heat for 10 minutes, and then for 5 minutes or as needed until the turkey is cooked and the juices run clear (total cooking time should be about 15 minutes).

4. Let stand for 5 minutes.

5. Pour any fat off the dish and serve.

Serves 4

Preparation time:
10 minutes
Cooking time:
10–15 minutes

1 pound lean ground
    turkey
¼ cup ketchup
¼ cup water
½ medium onion,
    chopped
2 tablespoons instant
    basil and tomato soup
    mix
1 egg, beaten
½ teaspoon black pepper
¾ cup bread crumbs

Easy Roast Turkey Breast

Roasting a turkey breast is a great alternative to cooking a whole turkey.

1. Preheat the oven to 325°F.

2. In a small bowl, stir together the vegetable oil, salt, pepper, garlic powder, and dried thyme. Use a pastry brush to brush the mixture over the turkey breast.

3. Wrap the turkey in aluminum foil and roast until the internal temperature reaches 170°F (about 2¼ to 2½ hours).

4. Baste the turkey with the drippings during the last minutes of cooking.

5. Let the turkey stand for 15 minutes, then slice and serve.

Serves 4

Preparation time:
15 minutes
Cooking time:
2½ – 2¾ hours

4 tablespoons vegetable
    oil
½ teaspoon salt
¼ teaspoon black pepper
¼ teaspoon garlic powder
2 teaspoons dried thyme
1 (6-pound) turkey breast

Pan-Fried Garlic Chicken Thighs
with Sun-Dried Tomatoes

Serves 2

Preparation time:
2–3 minutes
Cooking time:
17–20 minutes

1 pound (6 to 8 small)
   boneless, skinless
   chicken thighs
⅛ teaspoon garlic salt
¼ teaspoon black pepper
2 teaspoons olive oil
½ medium onion, thinly
   sliced
2 tablespoons sun-dried
   tomato strips
½ cup chicken broth
2 teaspoons lemon juice
1 tablespoon chopped
   fresh basil leaves

There's almost no preparation required to make this flavorful chicken dish. Ready-to-use sun-dried tomatoes, such as Mariani's, are a great timesaver, since they don't need to be softened before using.

1. Rinse the chicken thighs and pat dry. Rub the garlic salt and pepper over the chicken to season.

2. Heat the olive oil in a skillet over medium heat. Add the chicken. Cook for 5 to 6 minutes, until browned on both sides, turning over halfway during cooking. Stir the chicken occasionally to make sure it doesn't stick to the pan.

3. Push the chicken to the sides of the pan. Add the onion and sun-dried tomato strips. Cook in the oil for about 3 minutes, until the onion is browned.

4. Add the chicken broth. Stir in the lemon juice.

5. Simmer for 8 to 10 minutes, until the liquid is nearly absorbed and the chicken is just cooked through. Stir in the basil leaves during the last 2 minutes of cooking.

Cooking with Olive Oil

Loaded with heart-healthy monounsaturated fats, olive oil is a great choice for pan-frying, sautéing, and stir-frying. Just be sure to stick with the olive oils that don't break down at high heats (such as pure olive oil) and leave the extra-virgin olive oil for salads. Always wait until the olive oil is fully heated before adding the food.

Ground Turkey Burgers with Havarti

Using Havarti cheese instead of bread crumbs adds a sweet, buttery flavor to these healthy burgers made with ground turkey.

1. In a large bowl, combine the ground turkey with all other ingredients except the vegetable oil, using your fingers to mix.

2. Form the ground turkey mixture into eight patties.

3. Heat the oil in a skillet over medium heat.

4. Carefully place the patties into the pan. Cook for a total of 10 to 15 minutes, turning once, until the patties are thoroughly cooked through.

How to Broil Burgers

Burgers can also be broiled or grilled. Place the burgers on a rack or grill that has been brushed with nonstick cooking spray. (If broiling, place the rack approximately 4 inches from the heat source.) Broil or grill for about 10 minutes, turning over halfway through cooking, until the burgers are heated through.

Serves 8

Preparation time:
10 minutes
Cooking time:
10–15 minutes

1½ pounds ground turkey
1½ tablespoon
    Worcestershire sauce
2½ tablespoons ketchup
2 green onions, minced
¼ teaspoon black pepper,
    or to taste
½ teaspoon salt, or to
    taste
¼ teaspoon dried
    oregano leaves
¼ cup crumbled Havarti
    cheese
2 teaspoons vegetable oil

Turkey Sloppy Joes

Serves 4

Preparation time:
5–8 minutes
Cooking time: 25 minutes

1½ pounds ground turkey
1 medium onion, chopped
1 green bell pepper,
    chopped into chunks
½ cup water
1 cup ketchup
3 tablespoons brown sugar
3 tablespoons red wine
    vinegar
¾ teaspoon ground
    cumin, or to taste
¼ teaspoon black pepper
4 hamburger buns
⅓ cup crumbled Havarti
    cheese

Not a fan of hamburger buns? You can also make the sloppy joes with sandwich buns, on a loaf of French or Italian bread, or even with tortilla or nacho chips.

1. Brown the ground turkey in a skillet over medium-high heat.

2. Add the onion and bell peppers. Cook for 4 to 5 more minutes, until the onion is softened. Drain the fat out of the pan.

3. Add the water, ketchup, brown sugar, and red wine vinegar. Stir in the cumin and pepper. Turn the heat down to low and simmer, uncovered, for 15 minutes.

4. Spoon the turkey mixture over the hamburger buns. Sprinkle the crumbled cheese on top.

Chapter 7
Beef Dishes

Beef and Broccoli Stir-Fry

Serves 3

Preparation time:
15–20 minutes
Cooking time: 8 minutes

1 pound flank steak
1½ tablespoons soy
    sauce
1 tablespoon apple juice
2 teaspoons cornstarch
2 cups broccoli florets
¼ cup water
1 tablespoon oyster sauce
1 teaspoon granulated
    sugar
1 tablespoon vegetable oil

Apple juice provides a convenient substitute for the rice wine or dry sherry that is normally used in Chinese marinades.

1. Cut the beef into thin strips about 2" long. (It's easiest to do this if the beef is partially frozen.) In a medium bowl, combine the beef with the soy sauce, apple juice, and cornstarch. Let the beef marinate for 15 minutes.

2. In a large saucepan with enough water to cover, blanch the broccoli for 2 to 3 minutes, until it is tender but still crisp. Remove the broccoli and rinse under cold running water. Drain.

3. In a small bowl, combine the water, oyster sauce, and sugar. Set aside.

4. Heat the oil in a heavy skillet over medium-high heat. Add the beef. Let brown for a minute, and then stir-fry until it loses its pinkness and is nearly cooked through.

5. Add the broccoli to the pan. Stir the sauce and pour it into the pan. Cook, stirring, to mix everything together and heat through. Serve immediately.

Speedy Stir-Frying

Stir-frying is one of the quickest cooking methods—it's easy to prepare a stir-fry meal in under 30 minutes. While it may seem time-consuming to marinate the meat, marinating helps tenderize the meat and adds extra flavor. And you can prepare the vegetables and sauce while the meat is marinating.

Tex-Mex Chili

This is an excellent recipe for nights when you want a quick and easy recipe that's also quite filling. Add extra protein by sprinkling shredded cheese over the chili before serving.

Serves 4

Preparation time: 5 minutes
Cooking time: 20 minutes

1 pound ground beef
2 tablespoons chili powder
¼ teaspoon ground cumin
1 teaspoon salt
1 tablespoon butter or margarine
½ medium onion, peeled and chopped
½ cup drained canned corn
2 (15-ounce) cans red kidney beans, drained
1 (28-ounce) can crushed tomatoes
1 cup canned mild green chilies

1. In a large bowl, combine the ground beef with the chili powder, ground cumin, and salt, using your fingers to mix in the seasonings.

2. Place the butter or margarine and onion in a microwave-safe casserole dish. Microwave on high heat for 2 minutes, or until the onion is tender.

3. Add the ground beef. Cover the dish with microwave-safe wax paper. Microwave on high heat for 5 minutes, give the dish a quarter turn, and then microwave for 3 more minutes (the ground beef should be nearly cooked). Remove and drain off the excess fat.

4. Stir in the remaining ingredients. Microwave for 7 minutes, stir, and microwave for 7 minutes more; then microwave for 1 or 2 minutes at a time until the other ingredients are heated and the beef is cooked through.

5. Let stand for 5 minutes. Serve hot.

Chili Condiments

Preparing chili for a crowd? Make it last longer by serving it with a variety of condiments, from taco chips, shredded cheese, and sour cream to cooked spaghetti or cornbread muffins.

Kung Pao Chili con Carne

The spices and seasonings that make Chinese cooking so popular add heat to south-of-the-border chili in this fun fusion recipe. If Sichuan peppercorn is unavailable, feel free to use freshly ground black, white, or lemon peppercorns.

Serves 3

Preparation time:
10 minutes
Cooking time: 10 minutes

¾ pound coarsely ground beef
½ teaspoon salt
½ teaspoon black pepper
5 teaspoons vegetable oil, divided
2 cloves garlic, chopped
1 medium onion, chopped
2 teaspoons Sichuan peppercorn, or to taste
1 tablespoon chopped jalapeño peppers, or to taste
1 medium tomato, diced
1 cup drained canned kidney beans
¾ cup tomato sauce
¼ cup roasted cashews
1 teaspoon hot sauce, optional

1. In a medium bowl, combine the ground beef with the salt and pepper.

2. Heat 2 teaspoons oil in a heavy saucepan on medium-high heat. Add the ground beef and stir-fry until the pinkness is gone. Remove the ground beef from the pan. Drain the fat and wipe pan clean with paper towels.

3. Heat 1 tablespoon oil in the pan. Add the garlic and onion. Stir in the Sichuan peppercorn and chopped peppers. Cook, stirring, until the onion begins to soften.

4. Stir in the diced tomato. Stir in the kidney beans and tomato sauce. Bring to a boil.

5. Return the ground beef to the pan. Stir-fry for 1 to 2 more minutes to mix the flavors together. Stir in the cashews. Stir in the hot sauce. Serve hot.

Herbed Steak with Marinated Vegetables

Not a fan of artichokes? You can use the basic marinade in Marinated Artichoke Hearts (page 229) to marinade other vegetables, such as baby carrots, to serve with the herbed steak.

Serves 4

Preparation time:
5 minutes
Cooking time:
15–20 minutes

¼ cup honey mustard
1½ teaspoons fresh
    chopped oregano
1½ teaspoons fresh thyme
½ teaspoon salt
½ teaspoon cayenne
    pepper
4 boneless sirloin steaks
Marinated Artichoke
    Hearts (page 229)

1. Preheat the broiler.

2. In a small bowl, stir together the mustard, oregano, thyme, salt, and cayenne pepper.

3. Rub the spice mixture over the steaks.

4. Spray a rack with nonstick cooking spray. Place the steaks on the rack, about 4 inches from the heat source. For a medium-rare steak, broil for 12 minutes, turning over halfway during cooking

5. Let the steak stand for 5 minutes. Serve with the Marinated Artichoke Hearts (page 229).

Tender Beef

To ensure that beef remains tender during broiling, it's important not to overcook it. If the beef is not being marinated, lightly brush it with oil before placing it on the broiling pan. Turn the steak once during cooking.

Lemon Beef

Serves 4

Preparation time:
10 minutes
Cooking time:
10–12 minutes

1 pound skirt or flank
    steak
2½ teaspoons lemon
    pepper seasoning
2 tablespoons lemon juice
2 tablespoons soy sauce
1 teaspoon sugar
3 tablespoons vegetable
    oil, divided
1 teaspoon minced ginger
1 cup fresh sliced
    mushrooms

Feel free to replace the mushrooms with a quick-cooking green vegetable such as snow peas, or with 1 cup of packaged stir-fry vegetables.

1. Cut the beef into thin strips about 2½" long. (It's easiest to do this if the beef is still partially frozen.) Rub the lemon pepper seasoning over the beef.

2. In a small bowl, combine the lemon juice, soy sauce, and sugar.

3. Heat 2 tablespoons oil in a large skillet or wok. Add half the beef. Let sear for about 30 seconds, then stir-fry for 3 to 4 minutes, until the steak is nearly cooked. Remove the beef from the pan. Repeat with the remaining half of the beef.

4. Heat 1 tablespoon oil in the pan. Add the minced ginger and the mushrooms. Stir-fry for about 2 minutes, adding 1 tablespoon water if the mushrooms dry out.

5. Stir the lemon juice and soy sauce mixture. Pour into the pan. Add the beef to the pan. Cook for 1 to 2 minutes to finish cooking the beef and mix everything together. Serve hot.

Quick Fried Beef with Onion-Cilantro Relish

Onion-cilantro relish is an easy side dish with a bit of spice that pairs nicely with plain fried beef. You can jazz it up a bit by adding a few slices of tomato or cucumber, or to quickly heat it in 2 teaspoons of pure olive oil. Not a fan of cilantro? You can substitute chopped fresh parsley.

Serves 4

Preparation time:
10 minutes
Cooking time:
10–12 minutes

1¼ pounds flank steak
1½ tablespoons white
    wine vinegar
1½ tablespoons soy
    sauce
2 teaspoons cornstarch
1 medium sweet onion,
    minced
4 tablespoons minced
    green onion
1 cup chopped fresh
    cilantro
2 tablespoons lemon juice
½ teaspoon Asian chili
    sauce
½ teaspoon salt
2 tablespoons vegetable
    oil
1 garlic clove, thinly
    sliced

1. Cut the beef across the grain into thin strips, about 2½" to 3" long. (It's easiest to do this if the beef is still slightly frozen.) Place in a large bowl, and stir in the white wine vinegar, soy sauce, and cornstarch, mixing in the cornstarch with your fingers. Let the beef stand while preparing the relish.

2. In a medium bowl, combine the onion, green onion, and cilantro. Stir in the lemon juice, chili sauce, and salt.

3. Heat the oil in a heavy skillet. Add the garlic and half the steak. Let sear for about 30 seconds, then stir-fry, moving the beef around the pan until it loses its pinkness and is cooked through. Remove the beef from the pan and drain.

4. Repeat with the remaining half of the beef.

5. Serve the beef with the onion-cilantro relish.

Or Broil It

This Onion-Cilantro Relish would also pair very nicely with broiled steak. Instead of cutting the steak into thin strips, prepare it for broiling by rubbing with a garlic clove cut in half. Place on a rack and broil for 10 to 15 minutes, turning halfway through cooking, until the steak is cooked through and the juices run clear. Sprinkle the steak with salt and pepper during broiling.

Quick Microwave Lasagna

*With flavorful marinara sauce, this dish doesn't really need any
extra seasoning. But if you like, you can add a pinch of dried
oregano, basil, or parsley.*

Serves 2

Preparation time:
5 minutes
Cooking time: 25 minutes
(with standing time)

½ pound ground beef
1 cup crushed tomatoes
1½ cups marinara sauce
1½ cups grated
*   mozzarella cheese*
1½ cups ricotta cheese
12 oven-ready lasagna
*   noodles*

1. Crumble the ground beef into a microwave-safe bowl. Microwave the
    beef on high heat for 5 minutes. Give the dish a quarter turn and micro-
    wave on high heat for 4 more minutes. Make another quarter turn and
    microwave for 1 minute at a time until the beef is cooked through.
    Remove from the microwave and drain the fat.

2. Combine the ground beef with the crushed tomatoes and marinara
    sauce. Stir in the cheeses.

3. Lay out four of the lasagna noodles in a large bowl or a 1-quart
    microwave-safe casserole dish. (Break the noodles if needed to fit into
    the container.) Spoon one-third of the sauce mixture over the noodles,
    spreading evenly. Add two more layers of the noodles and sauce.

4. Cover the dish with wax paper. Microwave on high heat for 7 to 8 min-
    utes, until the cheeses are cooked. Let the lasagna stand for 10 minutes
    before serving.

Sloppy Joes

*Invented to cope with a meat shortage during World War II,
sloppy joes are a favorite with kids, who like its soupy texture.*

Serves 4

Preparation time:
5–8 minutes
Cooking time: 25 minutes

1½ pounds ground beef
½ yellow onion, chopped
½ green bell pepper,
    diced
1 cup water
1 cup tomato paste
2 tablespoons brown
    sugar
¼ teaspoon paprika, or to
    taste
¼ teaspoon garlic powder
¼ teaspoon black pepper,
    or to taste
4 hamburger buns
⅓ cup shredded Cheddar
    cheese

1. Place the ground beef in a large skillet and brown over medium heat. After the beef is halfway cooked, add the onion and bell pepper. Continue cooking until the beef is browned and the onion is softened.

2. Add the water. Stir in the tomato paste. Stir in the brown sugar, paprika, garlic powder, and pepper.

3. Bring to a boil. Turn down the heat, cover, and simmer for about 10 minutes, until the mixture is heated through and reaches desired thickness.

4. Spoon the beef mixture over the hamburger buns. Sprinkle with shredded cheese and serve.

Sloppy Joes with Sizzle

Feel free to jazz up this basic recipe for Sloppy Joes by replacing the tomato paste with your favorite prepared salsa, or the water with tomato soup.

Microwave Irish Stew for Two

Serves 2

2 leftover Honey Mustard
    Pork Chops (page
    119)
4 baby onions
1 tablespoon margarine
1 (8-ounce) can peas,
    with liquid
¼ teaspoon dried thyme
¼ teaspoon salt
¼ teaspoon black pepper,
    or to taste

Leftover cooked pork chops make a handy substitute for lamb in this quick and easy variation on Irish stew. For extra flavor, add a few sprigs of fresh parsley or ½ teaspoon of dried parsley.

1. Cut the pork chops into bite-size chunks. Peel the baby onions and cut in half.

2. Place the margarine and baby onions in a microwave-safe casserole dish. Microwave on high heat for 1 minute. Stir and then microwave for 1 minute at a time until the baby onions are tender (total cooking time should be 2 to 3 minutes).

3. Add the canned peas. Stir in the dried thyme, salt, and pepper. Microwave on high heat for 30 seconds.

4. Stir in the pork.

5. Use a reheat setting, or microwave at 70 percent power for 2 minutes and then for 1 minute at a time, until the pork is heated. Serve hot.

Five-Ingredient Meat Loaf

Parmesan cheese and tomato sauce are both good sources of umami, the meaty or savory flavor that is the secret ingredient in MSG (monosodium glutamate).

Serves 4

Preparation time:
5 minutes
Cooking time:
15 – 20 minutes

1½ pounds ground pork
¾ cup plus 2 tablespoons
    tomato sauce
¼ cup chopped onion
1 tablespoon balsamic
    vinegar
½ cup Parmesan cheese

1. In a large bowl, combine all the ingredients. For the tomato sauce, add ¾ cup and then add the remaining 2 tablespoons of sauce if needed.

2. Shape into a loaf and place in a microwave-safe casserole dish. Cover with microwave-safe wax paper.

3. Microwave on high heat for 15 minutes, 5 minutes at a time, rotating the dish a quarter turn between each cooking period. If the meat loaf is not cooked after 15 minutes, continue to cook for 1 minute at a time until done. (Total cooking time should be about 15 minutes.) The meat loaf is cooked when the internal temperature reaches 160°F.

4. Let stand for 5 minutes.

5. Pour any fat off the dish and serve.

Speedy Meat Loaf Muffins

Looking for an easy way to speed up cooking on nights when you're baking the meat loaf in the oven? Instead of shaping the meat loaf mixture into one big loaf, place individual portions in muffin tins. This reduces baking time and makes serving easy. Better still, leftover muffins can be frozen, making a quick and easy snack or midday meal. Bake the muffins at 350°F. for 25–30 minutes until the muffins are cooked through.

Sweet-and-Sour Meat Loaf

Be sure not to overmix the meat loaf or it can dry out during cooking. Place an instant-read kitchen thermometer in the center of the meat loaf to check for doneness.

Serves 4

Preparation time:
5–8 minutes
Cooking time:
15 – 20 minutes

1½ pounds ground beef
1 (5.5-ounce) can tomato
    paste
¼ cup milk
3 tablespoons brown
    sugar
3 tablespoons vinegar
2 teaspoons soy sauce
1 egg, beaten
½ cup crushed bread
    crumbs
2 tablespoons minced
    onion
¼ teaspoon salt, or to
    taste
¼ teaspoon black pepper,
    or to taste

1. In a large bowl, combine all the ingredients.

2. Shape into a loaf and place in a microwave-safe casserole dish. Cover with microwave-safe wax paper.

3. Microwave on high heat for 15 minutes, 5 minutes at a time, rotating the dish a quarter turn between each period. If the meat loaf is not cooked after 15 minutes, continue to cook for 1 minute at a time until done (total cooking should be about 15 minutes). The meat loaf is cooked when the internal temperature reaches 160°F.

4. Let stand for 5 minutes.

5. Pour any fat off the dish and serve.

Steak and Marinated Artichoke Hearts

This is a great choice for busy weeknights—prepare the sauce and artichoke hearts ahead of time on the weekend, and serve the steak over reheated cooked rice.

Serves 4

Preparation time:
10 minutes
Cooking time: 10 minutes

¾ *pound flank steak*
2 tablespoons vegetable oil
1 teaspoon minced fresh gingerroot
Marinated Artichoke Hearts (page 229)
Simple Stir-Fry Sauce (page 244)

1. Cut the flank steak across the grain into thin strips. (It's easiest to do this if the beef is still slightly frozen.)

2. Heat the oil in a heavy skillet or wok over medium-high heat. Add the ginger and cook for 10 seconds, then add the beef. Let the beef brown for about 30 seconds and then cook, stirring constantly, until it is no longer pink. Remove the beef from the pan. Drain on paper towels.

3. Add the artichokes to the pan. Stir-fry for 1 minute. Pour in the sauce and bring to a boil.

4. Return the beef to the pan. Cook for another minute, stirring to mix everything together. Serve hot.

Going Against the Grain

Cutting beef across or against the grain shocks the muscle fibers and relaxes them. It's a great way to tenderize leaner cuts of meat such as flank steak. To cut beef across the grain, find the muscle fibers by looking for the lines or "grains" running across the cut of beef. Cut the beef perpendicular to the grains.

Steak with Brown Sauce

Serves 2

Preparation time:
5–8 minutes
Cooking time:
15–18 minutes

½ teaspoon seasoned salt
½ teaspoon black pepper
4 beef tenderloin steaks
    (3 to 5 ounces each)
2 tablespoons vegetable
    oil
1 shallot, chopped
¼ cup red wine
Quick and Easy Brown
    Sauce (page 252)

Making the sauce ahead of time takes much of the work out of preparing this flavorful dish. You can also prepare the sauce while the steak is cooking.

1. Rub the salt and pepper over the steaks to season.

2. Heat the oil in a skillet over medium-high heat. Add the steaks. Cook for 4 to 5 minutes, until the steak is browned on the bottom.

3. Add the shallots to the pan. Turn the steak over and cook for another 4 to 5 minutes. Remove the steak and shallots from the pan. Pour off any excess fat.

4. Add the red wine to the pan and bring to a boil. Deglaze the pan by using a rubber spatula to scrape up any browned bits from the meat (do not remove the browned bits: they add extra flavor to the liquid).

5. Add the brown sauce to the pan and cook, at low-medium heat, until it is heated through. Pour the sauce over the steak.

Perfectly Done Steak

The best way to tell whether a steak is cooked the way you like it is to check the texture and appearance. Rare-cooked steak has a soft texture, and is completely pink in the center. Steak that is cooked to a medium level of doneness has a firm texture that will give a bit when you touch it. The very middle will be pink, gradually fading to a grayish-brown. Well-done steak should be quite taut and have no pinkness at all.

Easy Pepper Steak with Rice

Don't have a large skillet? Stir-fry the vegetables in a separate pan, and then combine with the beef and the broth.

Serves 4

Preparation time:
5–10 minutes
Cooking time: 10 minutes

1½ pounds beef sirloin
¼ cup beef broth
1½ tablespoons soy
sauce
1 teaspoon Worcestershire
sauce
½ teaspoon granulated
sugar
1 teaspoon cornstarch
2 tablespoons olive oil
1 garlic clove, thinly
sliced
1 onion, cut into wedges
1 red bell pepper,
seeded, cut julienne-
style
1 green bell pepper,
seeded, cut julienne-
style
1 cup sliced fresh
mushrooms

1. Cut the beef into thin strips 2½" to 3" long. (It's easiest to do this if the steak is still slightly frozen.) In a small bowl, stir together the beef broth, soy sauce, Worcestershire sauce, and sugar. Whisk in the cornstarch.

2. In a large skillet, heat the oil over medium-high heat. Add the garlic, cook for a few seconds, then add the beef to the pan. Let sear for 30 seconds, and then stir-fry for 4 to 5 minutes, until the pinkness has gone.

3. Push the steak to the sides and add the onion, bell peppers, and mushrooms to the pan. Stir-fry for 2 to 3 minutes, until the onion and peppers are softened.

4. Stir the beef broth mixture and pour it into the middle of the pan, stirring quickly to thicken.

5. Let simmer for 5 minutes. Serve hot.

Beef Burgundy Stew

Don't have leftover beef on hand? Brown 1 pound of cubed stewing beef over medium-high heat until nearly cooked through. This will add 5 to 10 minutes to the cooking time.

Serves 2

Preparation time:
5–10 minutes
Cooking time:
12–15 minutes

1 tablespoon vegetable oil
2 baby onions, cut in half
4 ounces sliced fresh
   mushrooms
1 zucchini, thinly sliced
¼ teaspoon dried oregano
2 cups leftover cooked
   beef, cubed
¼ cup burgundy
½ cup beef broth
1 tablespoon tomato paste
1 tablespoon
   Worcestershire sauce
⅛ teaspoon black pepper

1. Heat the oil in a skillet on medium heat. Add the onions, mushrooms, and zucchini. Stir in the dried oregano. Sauté for about 5 minutes, until the vegetables are softened.

2. Add the beef. Cook for 2 to 3 minutes to heat through.

3. Add the burgundy and beef broth. Stir in the tomato paste and Worcestershire sauce. Bring to a boil.

4. Stir in the pepper. Turn down the heat and simmer for about 5 minutes. Serve hot.

Chili con Queso Dinner

Adding sausage to classic Chili con Queso ingredients turns this into a complete meal. Serve with tortilla chips, or spoon onto crusty French or Italian bread.

Serves 4

Preparation time:
5 minutes
Cooking time:
10–15 minutes

1 pound smoked pork
   sausage
1 medium onion, chopped
2 cups canned chopped
   tomatoes, with juice
1 cup canned whole
   green chilies
1 cup packaged
   shredded Monterey
   Jack cheese
¼ teaspoon black pepper
½ teaspoon salt, or to
   taste
¼ cup sour cream

1. Cook the sausage and onion in a skillet for about 5 minutes on medium heat, stirring occasionally, until the sausage is browned and the onion is softened.

2. Add the tomatoes and green chilies. Cook for a couple of minutes, until the tomato is softened.

3. Add the cheese and cook until the cheese is melted.

4. Stir in the salt and pepper. Taste and adjust seasoning if desired.

5. Stir in the sour cream. Serve hot.

Skillet Shepherd's Pie

*If canned or packaged beef broth isn't available, you can use
2 beef bouillon cubes dissolved in 1 cup of boiling water.*

1. Brown the ground beef in a skillet on medium heat, using a spatula to break it up. Sprinkle the salt and pepper over the beef while it is cooking.

2. After the beef has been cooking for 5 minutes, add the onion. Cook for another 5 minutes, until the pinkness is gone from the beef and the onion is softened. Drain excess fat from the pan.

3. Add the green beans and corn to the pan.

4. Add the mashed potatoes. Stir in the paprika.

5. Add the beef broth. Simmer for 5 minutes, stirring, to heat everything through. Serve hot.

Make-Ahead Mashed Potatoes

You don't have to wait until you're preparing a dish such as Skillet Shepherd's Pie to use leftover mashed potatoes—they can also be served alone as a side dish. Reheat the potatoes by frying them in 1 or 2 teaspoons of oil, or cook in the microwave with a bit of liquid, using the microwave's reheat setting or at 70 percent power.

Serves 4

Preparation time:
5–10 minutes
Cooking time:
15–20 minutes

1 pound ground beef
½ teaspoon salt
¼ teaspoon black pepper
½ medium onion, peeled and chopped
1 cup drained canned green beans
1 cup canned corn
1 portion Garlic Mashed Potatoes (page 232)
½ teaspoon paprika
1 cup beef broth

Skillet Beef Jerky

Serves 2

Preparation time:
5–10 minutes
Cooking time:
10–12 minutes

1 pound sirloin steak
2 tablespoons soy sauce
1 teaspoon
    Worcestershire sauce
1 teaspoon brown sugar
2 tablespoons
    vegetable oil

Frying the beef for longer than usual gives it a chewy texture similar to beef jerky, but this is much quicker to make. It would go very nicely with rice and steamed vegetables, such as Simple Steamed Mushrooms (page 229).

1. Cut the beef into thin strips 2" to 3" long. (It's easiest to do this if the beef is still slightly frozen.)

2. In a small bowl, stir together the soy sauce, Worcestershire sauce, and brown sugar.

3. In a heavy skillet, heat the oil on medium-high heat.

4. Add the beef, laying it flat in the pan. Let sear for a minute, and then stir-fry for about 10 minutes, until the beef is crisp and chewy. Keep stirring and moving the beef around the pan as it is cooking.

5. Stir the soy sauce mixture and swirl it into the pan. Stir to mix with the beef and serve.

Chapter 8
Pork and Lamb Dishes

Plum Pork Stir-Fry

Serves 4

Preparation time:
20 minutes
Cooking time: 10 minutes

1 pound pork tenderloin
2½ tablespoons soy
    sauce, divided
1 tablespoon apple cider
2 teaspoons cornstarch
¼ cup plum sauce
2 teaspoons brown sugar
3 tablespoons water
2 tablespoons vegetable
    or peanut oil
2 slices fresh gingerroot

Apple cider or apple juice takes the place of Chinese rice wine, which can be hard to find outside of Asian supermarkets, in this recipe. You can also use dry sherry if desired. (Drinking quality Chinese rice wine is not widely available in North America.)

1. Cut the pork into cubes. Place the pork in a bowl and add 1½ tablespoons soy sauce, apple cider, and cornstarch. Let the pork marinate for at least 15 minutes (if you have time, marinate the pork for 30 minutes).

2. In a small bowl, combine the plum sauce, 1 tablespoon soy sauce, brown sugar, and water.

3. Heat a wok or heavy skillet and add the oil. When the oil is hot, add the ginger slices. Let the ginger cook for 2 to 3 minutes, until browned (this is to flavor the oil).

4. Add the pork. Let sit briefly, then stir-fry, moving the pork cubes around the pan, until the pork turns white and is nearly cooked through.

5. Stir the plum sauce mixture, then pour into the pan and bring to a boil. Turn down the heat and simmer for 2 to 3 more minutes, stirring to mix the pork with the sauce. Serve hot.

Robust Rice Wine

Made from fermented sweet rice, rice wine is a staple ingredient in Chinese cooking. Besides using it in marinades, Chinese cooks frequently splash meat or poultry with rice wine during stir-frying. While dry sherry is the preferred substitute for rice wine, you can also use gin, or even apple cider, as in this recipe. For a nonalcoholic substitute, use apple juice.

Rosemary Lamb Chops

This recipe can easily be doubled to serve four people. Lamb cooked medium rare will be pink on the inside and have a slightly firm texture.

Serves 4

Preparation time:
5 minutes
Cooking time: 15 minutes

4 lamb loin chops, about
   1" thick, 3 ounces
   each
¼ teaspoon salt
⅛ teaspoon black pepper
2 teaspoons dried
   rosemary
2 tablespoons olive oil,
   divided
2 shallots, chopped
1 tablespoon red wine
   vinegar

1. Pat lamb chops dry with paper towels. Rub salt and pepper over the lamb chops to season. Rub the rosemary into the lamb chops.

2. Heat 1 tablespoon olive oil in a skillet over medium-high heat. Add the lamb chops. Cook for 5 minutes, then turn over (turn the heat down if the lamb chops are cooking too quickly). Push to the sides of the skillet.

3. Heat 1 tablespoon oil in the middle of the skillet and add the shallots. Sauté the shallots while the lamb chops finish cooking (total cooking time for the lamb chops should be about 10 minutes). Drain any excess fat out of the pan while cooking.

4. Splash the lamb chops with the red wine vinegar during the last few minutes of cooking.

Ground Pork Stroganoff

*If you like, you can replace the chicken broth with dry white wine.
Serve the stroganoff over cooked rice or noodles.*

Serves 4

Preparation time:
5 minutes
Cooking time: 10 minutes

2 cups ground pork
2 tablespoons margarine
1 medium onion, peeled
  and chopped
1 cup sliced fresh
  mushrooms
⅛ teaspoon nutmeg, or to
  taste
½ teaspoon dried basil
½ cup chicken broth
Salt and pepper, to taste
½ cup natural yogurt

1. Brown the ground pork in a skillet over medium heat. Remove to a plate. Drain the excess fat from the pan.

2. While the ground pork is browning, melt the margarine in a separate skillet. Add the onion and sauté for a couple of minutes, until it begins to soften.

3. Add the mushrooms and cook for about 2 minutes, until the vegetables are softened. Stir in the nutmeg and dried basil.

4. Add the chicken broth and ground pork to the pan. Cook, stirring, for a minute to heat through. Taste and season with salt and pepper if desired.

5. Stir in the yogurt. Serve immediately over the cooked rice.

Using Chicken Bouillon for Broth

Chicken bouillon cubes are a handy substitute for store-bought or home-made chicken broth. To use, dissolve one bouillon cube in ½ cup of boiling water.

Pork with Peaches

*Be sure to use peaches that are not overripe
and won't fall apart during stir-frying.*

1. Cut the pork into 1" cubes. Place the pork in a medium bowl and toss with the soy sauce and apple juice. Let stand for 5 minutes.

2. In a small bowl, dissolve the cornstarch in the water.

3. Heat 2 tablespoons oil in a skillet on medium-high heat. Add the pork and half the ginger. Cook, stirring constantly, until the pork is no longer pink and is nearly cooked through.

4. Push the pork to the sides of the pan. Add 1 teaspoon oil in the middle. Add the remainder of the ginger and the curry powder. Stir for a few seconds until aromatic. Add the sliced peaches. Cook for a minute, stirring continually, and add the chicken broth. Add the cornstarch and water mixture, stirring to thicken.

5. Season with the pepper. Cook for another minute, stirring to mix everything together. Serve hot.

Serves 4

Preparation time:
5 minutes
Cooking time: 7 minutes

¾ pound pork tenderloin
1 tablespoon soy sauce
1 tablespoon apple juice
1½ teaspoons cornstarch
1 tablespoon water
2 tablespoons plus 1
    teaspoon vegetable
    oil, divided
1 teaspoon minced
    ginger, divided
2 teaspoons curry powder
2 large peaches, thinly
    sliced
½ cup chicken broth
Black pepper, to taste

Quick Fried Minted Lamb

Serves 4

Preparation time:
5 minutes
Cooking time: 10 minutes

8 lamb rib chops, 1" thick
½ cup mint jelly, or as
needed

Traditionally, mint jelly is paired with roast leg of lamb, but it also goes nicely with quicker-cooking lamb cuts. You can spice up the mint jelly by adding a pinch of cayenne pepper.

1. Preheat the broiler. Spray a broiling rack with nonstick cooking spray.

2. Place the lamb chops on a rack about 4 inches from the heat source. Broil the chops for 8 to 10 minutes, turning once, until they are cooked through.

3. Serve the lamb with the mint jelly.

Make Your Own Mint Sauce

Instead of mint jelly, you can make your own mint sauce for this Quick Fried Minted Lamb. Simply process fresh mint leaves with a small amount of apple juice, white wine vinegar, and sugar to taste until you have a thick sauce. Season the sauce with salt and pepper to taste. For best results, prepare the mint sauce one hour ahead of time to give the flavors a chance to blend.

Skillet Sausage with Pasta and Marinara Sauce

Using leftover cooked pasta saves the time you'd spend waiting for the water to come to a boil and then cooking the pasta. If you don't have any leftover pasta on hand, or just prefer to cook your pasta in the traditional way, start preparing the other ingredients at about the same time as you add the dried pasta to the boiling water.

Serves 4

Preparation time:
5 minutes
Cooking time:
12–15 minutes

2 tablespoons olive oil, divided
8 ounces precooked pork sausage, thinly sliced
2 garlic cloves, finely chopped
1 (1-pound) bag fresh spinach, washed and drained
1 teaspoon salt
1½ cups jarred tomato marinara sauce
12 ounces leftover cooked spaghetti or linguine
4 tablespoons grated Parmesan cheese

1. Heat 1 tablespoon olive oil in the skillet on medium heat. Cook the sausages in the skillet on medium heat for 3 to 5 minutes, until they are heated through. Remove the sausages from the pan and drain on paper towels. Wipe out the pan.

2. Heat the remaining olive oil in the skillet. Add the garlic cloves and the spinach. Sprinkle the salt over the spinach and cook for 2 to 3 minutes, just until spinach leaves have wilted.

3. Add the marinara sauce and bring to a boil. Return the sausage to the pan. Cook for another minute to combine all the ingredients.

4. Place the leftover pasta in a colander and quickly run hot water over it to heat. Drain.

5. Add the pasta to the skillet and combine with the other ingredients. Sprinkle with the cheese before serving.

Orange-Flavored Pork Chops

Serves 4

Preparation time:
5 minutes
Cooking time: 15 minutes

¼ cup orange juice
1 tablespoon cider
    vinegar
1 tablespoon brown sugar
2 tablespoons soy sauce
½ teaspoon salt
¼ teaspoon black pepper
4 boneless pork chops,
    loin center (about 1¼
    pounds)
1 tablespoon vegetable oil
½ medium onion, peeled,
    finely chopped
1 teaspoon bottled
    minced garlic

Flavorful orange sauce is a great way to liven up plain pork chops. For extra heat, add a pinch of paprika or other hot spice to the orange juice mixture. You'll want to pair the pork chops with less strongly flavored side dishes, such as simple steamed vegetables and cooked rice.

1. In a small bowl or measuring cup, combine the orange juice, cider vinegar, brown sugar, and soy sauce. Set aside.

2. Rub salt and pepper over the pork chops to season.

3. Heat the oil over medium-high heat. Add the onion, garlic, and pork chops. Cook for about 10 minutes, until the pork chops are browned on both sides, turning the pork chops halfway through cooking. (Turn the heat down if the pork chops are cooking too quickly.) Remove the pork chops from the pan.

4. Stir the orange juice mixture and pour into the pan. Use a spatula to scrape up any browned bits and drippings from the cooked pork. Bring the orange mixture to a boil.

5. Return the pork to the skillet. Cook for 5 to 6 minutes, stirring occasionally and turning the pork chops so that they are covered with the sauce. Serve hot.

Two Meals in One

To save time during the week, use leftover pork chops and cooked rice from Orange-Flavored Pork Chops to make Pork Fried Rice (page 147). Just be sure to store the pork in a sealed bag in the refrigerator, and use within four to five days.

Honey Mustard Pork Chops

For extra flavor, stir 1 to 2 teaspoons curry powder into the heated honey mustard and margarine.

1. Rub the garlic salt and pepper over the pork chops. Melt the margarine and honey mustard in a saucepan over low heat. Stir in the sugar, red wine vinegar, and dried thyme.

2. Heat the olive oil in a skillet on medium-high heat. Add the garlic and the pork chops. Use a pastry brush to brush half of the melted butter mixture over the pork chops. Cook for 5 minutes, or until the underside is browned.

3. Turn the pork chops over and brush with the remaining half of the mustard mixture. Cook for 5 more minutes. (Adjust the temperature to medium as needed if the chops are cooking too quickly.)

4. Add the Burgundy and apple juice to the pan and bring to a boil.

5. Cook for about 2 more minutes, until the juices in the pork run clear. Serve immediately.

Serves 4

Preparation time:
5 minutes
Cooking time:
12–15 minutes

1 teaspoon garlic salt
¼ teaspoon black pepper, or to taste
4 pork loin chops, boneless, 1" thick (about 1¼ pounds)
4 tablespoons margarine
1 tablespoon Dijon honey mustard
1 teaspoon granulated sugar
2 teaspoons red wine vinegar
¼ teaspoon dried thyme
1 tablespoon olive oil
1 garlic clove, finely chopped
¼ cup Burgundy
3 tablespoons apple juice

One-Dish Sausage and Rice

Serves 2

Preparation time:
5 minutes
Cooking time: 15 minutes

1 cup chicken broth
1 cup long-grain instant rice
2 tablespoons olive oil
1 shallot, peeled and chopped
1 teaspoon paprika
8 ounces cooked smoked sausage, thinly sliced
2 sprigs fresh parsley
Salt and pepper, to taste

Using instant rice speeds up the cooking time of this simple, warming dish, while using chicken broth instead of water to cook the rice adds extra flavor.

1. Bring the chicken broth to a boil. Stir in the rice, making sure all the grains are moistened. Remove from the heat, cover, and let stand for 5 minutes.

2. While the rice is cooking, prepare the other ingredients: Heat the olive oil in a skillet over medium-high heat. Add the shallot. Sauté until softened (turn the heat down if the shallot is cooking too quickly). Stir in the paprika.

3. Stir in the sausage and parsley. Cook for a minute until the sausage is heated.

4. After the rice has been heating for 5 minutes, uncover and use a fork to fluff.

5. Stir the sausage and parsley into the cooked rice. Season with salt and pepper if desired.

Or Use Regular Rice

On evenings when you have a bit more time, try preparing One-Dish Sausage and Rice with regular long-grain rice. In a medium saucepan, bring the water and rice to a boil over medium heat. Let the rice cook until the water is nearly evaporated, add the sausage and parsley, reduce the heat, cover, and simmer until the liquid is absorbed and the rice is cooked. Let the rice sit for 5 minutes, then use a fork to fluff it up and mix in the sausage and parsley. The total cooking time will be about 25 minutes.

Personal Pizza

Chunky garden salsa is available in many local supermarkets. You can also use a homemade salsa in this recipe if desired.

1. Spread the garden salsa over one side of the pita pocket.

2. Lay the mushrooms on top of the salsa. Add the diced ham.

3. Sprinkle the shredded cheese on top.

4. Place the pita pocket on a microwave-safe plate. Microwave on high for 2 minutes, then for a few seconds at a time if needed until the cheese is fully melted.

Serves 1

Preparation time:
5 minutes
Cooking time:
2–4 minutes

¼ cup chunky garden salsa
1 pita pocket
½ cup fresh sliced mushrooms
¼ cup diced cooked ham
3 tablespoons shredded mozzarella or Parmesan cheese

Leftover Sausage and Potato Casserole

Leftover Instant Mashed Potato Salad (page 64) would work well in this dish. For a quick and easy dinner, serve the casserole with Basic Spinach Salad (page 71).

1. Place the onion and butter or margarine in a 1-quart microwave-safe casserole dish. Microwave on high heat until the onion is softened.

2. Add the sliced sausage. Spoon the potatoes on top.

3. In a medium bowl, stir together the tomato sauce, balsamic vinegar, basil, oregano, and pepper. Pour over the sausage and potatoes.

4. Cover the casserole loosely with plastic wrap, leaving an opening on one end for steam to vent.

5. Microwave on high heat for 4 minutes. Rotate the dish and microwave on medium-high heat for 3 to 4 more minutes, or until heated through.

Serves 2

Preparation time:
2–3 minutes
Cooking time: 10 minutes

2 tablespoons chopped red onion
2 teaspoons butter or margarine
2 cooked sausages, thinly sliced
¾ cup leftover mashed potatoes
¾ cup canned tomato sauce
2 teaspoons balsamic vinegar
¼ teaspoon dried basil leaves
¼ teaspoon dried oregano
⅛ teaspoon black pepper, or to taste

Preparation time:
5 minutes
Cooking time: 15 minutes

2 tablespoons olive oil
2 cloves garlic, chopped
½ medium onion,
    chopped
1 tablespoon creole
    seasoning
2 stalks celery, thinly
    chopped
½ pound smoked
    sausage, thinly sliced
½ cup cooked ham, diced
½ cup chicken broth
½ cup stewed tomatoes
1 cup cooked rice
1 green onion, finely
    chopped
Salt and pepper, to taste

Ham and Sausage Jambalaya

Jambalaya is the southern U.S. version of the famous Spanish dish paella. A spicy blend made with paprika, dried onion, and other ingredients, creole seasoning is available in the spice section of many supermarkets. If you don't have any on hand, a simple way to season the dish is to add 1 teaspoon paprika and ¼ teaspoon dried thyme, or to taste.

1. Heat the oil in a skillet on medium heat. Add the garlic and onion. Sprinkle the creole seasoning over the onion and garlic. Cook for about 2 minutes, then add the celery. Cook for 2 to 3 more minutes, until the onion is softened.

2. Stir in the sausage. Cook for a minute until it is heated. Stir in the cooked ham.

3. Add the chicken broth and stewed tomatoes. Bring to a boil.

4. Stir in the rice and green onion.

5. Turn the heat down and simmer for 5 minutes to heat everything through. Season with salt and pepper if desired.

Mexican-Style Lamb Chops

To cook to a medium level of doneness, remove the lamb when its internal temperature reaches 155°F and let stand for 5 minutes before serving.

Serves 4

Preparation time:
5 minutes
Cooking time:
10–12 minutes

8 lamb sirloin or rib chops
2 tablespoons olive oil
1 teaspoon ground cumin
1 teaspoon chili powder,
*   or to taste*
Simple Salsa Verde
*   (page 248)*

1. Preheat the broiler on high heat. Spray the broiling rack with nonstick cooking spray.

2. Trim most of the fat from the lamb chops. In a small bowl, combine the olive oil, ground cumin, and chili powder.

3. Place the lamb chops on the broiling rack and brush with half the olive oil mixture. Place the rack 3 inches from the heat source.

4. Broil the lamb chops for 8 to 10 minutes, until they are cooked to the desired level of doneness, turning halfway through and brushing with the remainder of the olive oil mixture.

5. To serve, spoon the Salsa Verde on the lamb chops.

Make-Ahead Salsa

Salsa ingredients can be prepared up to one day ahead of time. Be sure to store the salsa in a sealed container in the refrigerator. Unfortunately, the tomato content in salsa doesn't let it freeze very well.

Lamb with Artichokes

Serves 2

Preparation time:
5 minutes
Cooking time: 15 minutes

Salt and pepper, to taste
2 lamb chops
4 teaspoons olive oil
1 shallot, chopped
1 tomato, sliced
4 canned artichoke
    hearts, halved
½ cup low-sodium
    chicken broth

To add extra flavor to this dish, use artichoke hearts that have been marinated in olive oil and seasonings. Be sure to squeeze any excess water from the artichoke hearts before using.

1. Rub salt and pepper over the lamb chops to season.

2. Heat 2 teaspoons olive oil over medium-high heat. Add the lamb chops and the shallot. Cook for 5 minutes, then turn the lamb chops over. Drain any excess fat out of the pan.

3. Heat 2 teaspoons oil in the middle of the skillet. Add the tomato and artichokes, pressing down on the tomato so that it releases its juices. Cook for about 3 minutes.

4. Add the chicken broth. Bring to a boil. Turn down the heat, cover, and simmer on low heat for 2 to 3 minutes, until the lamb chops are cooked. Serve hot.

Amazing Artichokes

A member of the thistle family, artichokes have been prized as a digestive aid since ancient times. Until the twentieth century, medical practitioners believed that a regular diet of artichokes could help improve liver function. While studies have not borne this out, it is believed that artichokes may aid in lowering cholesterol and improve blood sugar levels in diabetics, reducing the need for insulin (see www.swedish.org/110799. cfm and www.pjbs.org/pjnonline/fin419.pdf).

Easy Lamb Chops with Green Onions

Feel free to replace the chicken broth with other types of soup or stock, such as ¼ cup of Easy Microwave Onion Soup (page 52).

1. Season the lamb chops with the salt and pepper.

2. Heat 1 tablespoon olive oil in a skillet over medium-high heat. Add the lamb chops. Cook for 5 minutes, then turn over (turn the heat down if the lamb chops are cooking too quickly). Push to the sides of the skillet.

3. Heat 1 tablespoon oil in the middle of the skillet and add the garlic and shallots. Stir in the paprika. Sauté while the lamb chops finish cooking (total cooking time for the lamb chops should be about 10 minutes).

4. Remove the lamb chops from the pan. Add the chicken broth and balsamic vinegar to the pan and bring to a boil. Deglaze the pan, using a spatula to scrape up the browned bits of meat.

5. Return the lamb chops to the pan. Add the green onion. Cook for another minute and serve hot.

Serves 4

Preparation time:
5–8 minutes
Cooking time:
12–15 minutes

4 lamb chops
Salt and pepper, as needed
2 tablespoons olive oil, divided
2 garlic cloves, finely chopped
2 shallots, chopped
1 teaspoon paprika, or to taste
¼ cup chicken broth
2 teaspoons balsamic vinegar
¼ cup green onions

Curried Lamb with Wild Rice

Serves 4

Preparation time:
5–8 minutes
Cooking time: 12 minutes

2 tablespoons vegetable
   oil
1 pound lean boneless
   lamb, cut into ½"
   cubes
2 garlic cloves, crushed
½ onion, peeled and
   chopped
¼ teaspoon red pepper
   flakes, or to taste
2 teaspoons curry
   powder, or to taste
1 tomato, thinly sliced
¼ cup beef broth
1 tablespoon chopped
   cilantro leaves
1 tablespoon tomato
   paste
Salt and pepper to taste
2 cups leftover cooked
   wild rice

This recipe can easily be adapted according to what ingredients you have on hand: you can use beef or chicken instead of lamb, or serve with scented basmati or jasmine rice instead of wild rice.

1. Heat the oil in a skillet on medium-high heat. Add the lamb. Let the meat brown for a minute, then turn down the heat to medium and cook, stirring, for 4 to 5 minutes, until it loses its pinkness. Remove the lamb from the pan.

2. Add the garlic, onion, red pepper flakes, and curry powder. Sauté for 2 to 3 minutes, until the onion begins to soften.

3. Add the tomato slices. Cook for a minute, pressing down on the tomato so that it releases its juices.

4. Add the beef broth and cilantro. Stir in the tomato paste. Return the lamb to the pan.

5. Cook, stirring, for another minute to mix everything together. Taste; season with salt and pepper if desired. Serve hot over the cooked rice.

Long-Lasting Cilantro

It's frustrating when a large bundle of fresh cilantro wilts before you've had a chance to use it all. To make fresh cilantro last longer, place it in a cup of water, cover with a plastic bag and store in the refrigerator. Cilantro stored in this way will last up to two weeks.

Chapter 9
Fish and Seafood

Coconut Shrimp Tempura

Serves 4

Preparation time:
15 minutes
Cooking time:
15–20 minutes

*1 cup unsweetened
    coconut flakes
2 eggs, refrigerated
2 cups ice cold water
2 cups rice flour
1 pound (about 24) large
    shrimp, peeled,
    deveined, tail on*

*Baking the battered shrimp instead of deep-frying takes much of
the work out of this classic appetizer. These taste delicious on
their own, or you can serve them with a spicy dipping sauce,
such as Asian chili sauce.*

1. Preheat the oven to 450°F. Spray a baking sheet with nonstick cooking spray. Place the coconut flakes in a bowl.

2. In a medium bowl, beat the eggs and then stir in the ice water.

3. Stir in the flour until the batter has a runny consistency similar to pancake batter. Add more flour or ice water if needed.

4. Coat each shrimp in the batter, using your fingers to do so. Dip the shrimp into the coconut, holding it by the tail, and then lay it on the baking sheet. Continue with the remainder of the shrimp.

5. Bake the shrimp until it is golden brown on the bottom. Turn over and cook the other side until done.

Terrific Tempura Batter

*Few fried foods are as irresistible as Japanese tempura, consisting of
seafood or vegetables coated in a light, crispy batter. It's easy to make
this restaurant favorite at home—just remember to use ice water and a
cold egg, and to not overbeat the batter.*

Easy Oyster Stew

Serve this simple stew with oyster crackers. For a richer dish, melt 2 tablespoons of butter over low heat before adding the liquid, and replace the milk with light cream or half-and-half.

Serves 4

Preparation time:
5 minutes
Cooking time: 10 minutes

½ cup reserved juice from
    canned oysters
2 cups milk
1 teaspoon salt
¼ teaspoon black pepper
1 teaspoon dried thyme
1 tablespoon lemon juice
½ teaspoon Tabasco
    sauce
24 canned Pacific oysters
1 cup drained canned
    corn

1.   In a medium saucepan, bring the reserved juice and milk to a boil over medium-high heat, stirring.

2.   When the liquid is just starting to bubble, stir in the salt, pepper, thyme, lemon juice, and Tabasco sauce. (Turn the heat down if needed so that the liquid is just simmering.)

3.   Add the oysters and bring to a boil.

4.   Add the canned corn.

5.   Turn down the heat and simmer for 3 or 4 minutes to give the flavors a chance to blend. Serve hot.

Baked Fish Fillets

Cooking the vegetables with the fish means they are flavored with the natural fish juices and lemony soy sauce mixture. Cooked rice is all that's needed to turn this into a complete meal.

Serves 4

Preparation time:
5–10 minutes
Cooking time:
15–20 minutes

1 tablespoon soy sauce
1 tablespoon lemon juice
2 teaspoons bottled
    minced ginger
Black pepper, to taste
½ teaspoon Asian chili
    sauce, or to taste
1 teaspoon salt
1 pound fish fillets, fresh
½ pound broccoli florets
10 baby carrots, cut in
    half

1. Preheat oven to 375°F.

2. In a small bowl, stir together the soy sauce, lemon juice, ginger, pepper, and chili sauce. Rub the salt over the fish fillets to season.

3. Cut four sheets of foil, each at least 12" square. Place each fish fillet in the middle of a sheet of foil and brush the fillet with a portion of the lemon juice mixture. Place one-quarter of the broccoli and carrots around the fish.

4. Fold the foil over the fish and vegetables, crimping the edges to seal. Continue with the remainder of the fish fillets.

5. Bake at 375°F for 15 to 20 minutes, until the fish is cooked through and flakes easily (be careful not to overcook the fish).

Selecting Fresh Fish

When choosing fish fillets, look for a clean smell and a firm texture, without any discoloration or brown spots. Avoid fish that have a strong fishy smell, or yield to gentle pressure. When selecting whole fish, check for bright eyes and a shiny skin.

Easy Seafood Rice Pilaf

Microwaving the rice considerably shortens the cooking time in this simple shrimp and rice dish.

Serves 4

Preparation time:
5 minutes
Cooking time: 15 minutes

1½ cups long-grain white rice
3 cups chicken broth
1 tablespoon olive oil
1 onion, peeled, chopped
2 cloves garlic, finely chopped
½ teaspoon paprika, or to taste
1 teaspoon salt
¾ pound large shrimp, shelled, deveined
1 tablespoon lemon juice

1. Place the rice and broth in a microwave-safe casserole dish. Cover with microwave-safe plastic wrap. Cook the rice on high heat for 8 minutes.

2. Check and continue microwaving until the rice is cooked (about 10 minutes). Do not stir the rice. Once the rice is finished cooking, let it stand for 5 minutes.

3. While the rice is cooking, heat the olive oil in a skillet on medium-high heat. Add the onion and garlic. Sprinkle the paprika over the onion. Sauté for 4 to 5 minutes, until the onion is softened (turn the heat down to medium if needed).

4. Sprinkle the salt over the shrimp and add to the pan. Splash the shrimp with the lemon juice and sauté until they turn pink, taking care not to overcook.

5. Fluff the rice with a fork. Stir in the shrimp mixture. Serve hot.

Four-Ingredient Baked Ginger Fish Fillets

Serves 4

Preparation time:
10 minutes
Cooking time:
15–20 minutes

2 tablespoons soy sauce
2 tablespoons lemon juice
1 tablespoon chopped
    fresh gingerroot
Freshly ground black
    pepper, to taste
1½ pounds fish fillets,
    fresh or frozen

*Baking fish in foil is a great way to add extra flavor to mild fish
such as red snapper and halibut.*

1. Preheat the oven to 375°F.

2. In a small bowl, stir together the soy sauce, lemon juice, ginger, and
    pepper.

3. Cut four sheets of foil, each at least 12" square. Place a fish fillet in the
    middle of a sheet of foil. Brush with one-quarter of the lemon juice
    mixture.

4. Fold the foil over the fish, crimping the edges to seal. Continue with the
    remainder of the fish fillets.

5. Bake at 375°F for 15 to 20 minutes, until the fish is cooked through and
    flakes easily (be careful not to overcook the fish).

Cooking with Frozen Fish

*In many cases, frozen fish can be taken straight from the freezer and
cooked without thawing, as long as you allow for extra cooking time. If
you do thaw the fish before cooking, always thaw it in the refrigerator.
Frozen fish should be used within three months.*

Easy Oysters Rockefeller on French Bread

*Don't have any cooked bacon on hand? The microwave is
perfect for cooking crisp bacon quickly: just place the
bacon on a plate lined with paper towels, cover with
another paper towel, and microwave on high heat
for 2 to 3 minutes until the bacon is cooked.*

1. Preheat the broiler. Spray the broiling rack with nonstick cooking spray.

2. Combine the spinach, bread crumbs, bacon, cream, reserved oyster juice, nutmeg, salt, garlic powder, chili sauce, and Worcestershire sauce in a blender. Process until smooth, stopping and scraping the bottom and sides if needed.

3. Add the oysters and process again until smooth.

4. Cut the French bread into 1-inch pieces. Spread a heaping tablespoon of the spinach/oyster dip on the bread. Sprinkle 1 to 1½ tablespoons of Parmesan cheese on top. Continue with the remainder of the bread.

5. Broil on high 9 inches from the heat source for about 2 minutes, until the cheese is bubbling and the bread is golden. Be careful not to burn the bread.

Serves 6

Preparation time:
5 minutes
Cooking time: 25 minutes

10 ounces frozen spinach,
   thawed, drained
6 tablespoons crushed
   bread crumbs
4 slices cooked bacon,
   chopped
¼ cup light cream
3 tablespoons reserved
   canned oyster juice
¼ teaspoon ground
   nutmeg
½ teaspoon salt
¼ teaspoon garlic powder
½ teaspoon chili sauce
1 tablespoon
   Worcestershire sauce
12 canned Pacific oysters,
   drained
1 loaf French bread
1 cup shredded
   Parmesan cheese

Shrimp Pad Thai Stir-Fry

Serves 4

Preparation time:
15 minutes
Cooking time:
7–10 minutes

8 ounces rice stick
   noodles
2 tablespoons lemon juice
2 tablespoons white
   vinegar
1½ tablespoons tomato
   sauce
2 tablespoons brown
   sugar
2 tablespoons vegetable
   oil
2 teaspoons bottled
   minced garlic
1 tablespoon bottled
   chopped red jalapeño
   peppers
20 large shrimp, peeled,
   deveined
2 eggs, beaten
1 cup mung bean sprouts
1 cup chopped fresh
   cilantro leaves
⅓ cup chopped peanuts

Boiling the soaking water for the noodles shortens the amount of time it takes for them to soften. If you purchase shrimp that is already peeled and deveined, and soften the noodles ahead of time, the pad thai will be ready in under 15 minutes.

1. In a microwave-safe bowl, bring 4 cups of water to a boil (this will take 3 to 5 minutes). Remove the bowl from the microwave. Place the noodles in the boiling water to soften. In a small bowl, stir together the lemon juice, vinegar, tomato sauce, and brown sugar.

2. Heat the vegetable oil in a wok or skillet. When the oil is hot, add the garlic and chopped jalapeños. Stir-fry for a few seconds, then add the shrimp. Cook until the shrimp turn pink (about 2 minutes).

3. Push the shrimp to the side and add the beaten egg in the middle. Scramble the egg in the pan.

4. Add the softened noodles. Stir the lemon juice and tomato sauce mixture and pour over the noodles.

5. Stir in the mung bean sprouts. Stir in the cilantro leaves. Stir-fry for a couple of minutes to combine the ingredients. Garnish with the chopped peanuts.

A Southeast Asian Specialty

Thailand's signature noodle dish, pad thai—literally meaning Thai fried dish or mixture—has a universal appeal. The distinguishing characteristic of pad thai is the intriguing mixture of sweet-and-sour and spicy flavors. For an extra touch, serve the pad thai with an assortment of lime wedges, red chilies, and extra peanuts.

Sicilian-Style Swordfish

Lemon juice tenderizes the fish while olive oil disperses the flavor of the herbs in this easy recipe. If you don't have bottled minced garlic on hand, you can substitute ¼ teaspoon garlic powder or 2 minced garlic cloves.

Serves 4

Preparation time:
15 minutes
Cooking time:
8–10 minutes

⅓ cup olive oil
⅓ cup lemon juice
2 teaspoons bottled
    minced garlic
½ teaspoon dried
    oregano
2 teaspoons dried parsley
¼ teaspoon black pepper
4 swordfish steaks

1. Preheat the broiler. Spray the broiling rack with nonstick spray.

2. In a bowl, whisk together the olive oil, lemon juice, garlic, oregano, parsley, and pepper.

3. Pour the marinade into a large resealable plastic bag. Add the swordfish and close up the bag. Marinate for 10 minutes, turning once or twice to make sure the steaks are coated.

4. Place the swordfish on the broiling rack approximately 4 inches from the heat source. Broil for 4 minutes, turn, and cook for 4 to 6 minutes more, until the swordfish is just done.

Quick Fettuccine and Tuna with Marinara Sauce

Serves 4

Preparation time:
10 minutes
Cooking time: 10 minutes

1 (28-ounce) can plum
    tomatoes with juice
1 tablespoon bottled
    minced garlic
2 tablespoons minced
    onion
1 tablespoon red wine
    vinegar
¼ cup chopped fresh
    basil leaves
¼ cup extra-virgin olive oil
1 teaspoon salt
¼ teaspoon black pepper
1 rib celery, cut diagonally
    into thin slices
2 (6-ounce) cans tuna,
    drained
1 pound leftover cooked
    fettuccine

Using the blender takes most of the work out of making tomato-based marinara sauce, which is then enriched with tuna. You can, of course, cook a fresh batch of pasta instead of reheating leftover cooked pasta if desired.

1. Combine the tomatoes, garlic, onion, red wine vinegar, basil, olive oil, salt, and pepper in a blender or food processor. Process until it forms a thick sauce.

2. Add half the celery and process again. Add the remaining half.

3. Pour the pasta sauce into a large skillet. Add the tuna, using a spatula to break it up. Bring to a boil, turn down the heat and simmer, uncovered, for 5 minutes.

4. Reheat the cooked pasta (see Serving Leftover Pasta, page 169).

5. Place the pasta in a bowl and toss with the sauce.

Fish—Perfect For Low-Fat Diets

Fish is an excellent choice for a low-fat diet. Lean fish such as cod and turbot have a fat content of under 3 percent. Oily fish such as salmon and trout are a good natural source of healthy omega-3 fatty acids. Both types of fish should be included in any diet plan, including a low-fat one.

Seafood au Gratin

If using frozen fish fillets, thaw before cooking. You can spice up the dish by adding a pinch of paprika to the white sauce.

Serves 4

Preparation time:
5 minutes
Cooking time: 25 minutes

1 portion White Sauce for
    Seafood (page 245)
1 pound fish fillets
1 teaspoon salt
½ cup grated Cheddar
    cheese

1. Preheat the oven to 375°F. Spray an 8" x 8" baking dish with nonstick cooking spray.

2. In a pan or the microwave, reheat the White Sauce for Seafood (page 245).

3. Rub the salt over the fish to season. Lay the fish fillets out in the baking dish.

4. Pour the white sauce over the fish. Sprinkle the cheese on top.

5. Bake the fish for 25 minutes, or until it is cooked through.

Teriyaki Shrimp

A combination of sweet and spicy flavors, Asian sweet chili sauce is available in the ethnic or international section of most supermarkets.

Preparation time:
5 minutes
Cooking time:
7–10 minutes

1 pound large shrimp,
   shelled, deveined, tail
   on
½ teaspoon salt
3 tablespoons vegetable
   oil, divided
1 teaspoon minced garlic
1 teaspoon minced ginger
1 teaspoon Asian sweet
   chili sauce
½ pound snow peas
½ portion Teriyaki Sauce
   (page 245)
2 green onions, chopped
   into thirds

1. Place the shrimp in a bowl and toss with the salt.

2. Heat 2 tablespoons oil in a large skillet over medium-high heat. Stir for a few seconds, then add the shrimp. Stir-fry the shrimp, stirring constantly, until they turn pink (about 2 minutes). Remove the shrimp from the pan.

3. Heat 1 tablespoon oil in the pan. Add the garlic, ginger, and chili sauce. Stir for a few seconds, then add the snow peas. Stir-fry for 2 minutes, stirring constantly. (Splash the snow peas with 1 tablespoon of water if they begin to dry out.)

4. Add the teriyaki sauce to the pan and bring to a boil.

5. Return the shrimp to the pan. Stir in the green onion. Stir-fry for a minute to combine all the ingredients. Serve hot.

Quick-Cooking Seafood

Speedy cooking times make seafood the perfect choice for busy weeknights. In fact, the main concern when preparing fish and shellfish is not to overcook it. Overcooked seafood loses its natural juiciness and can be rather tough. Cook fish until the skin flakes easily with a fork. For shrimp and prawns, cook until the skin just turns pink.

Simple Seafood Ratatouille

Precooking the eggplant in water helps prevent it from soaking up too much oil when it is combined with the other ingredients.

Serves 4

Preparation time:
10 minutes
Cooking time: 20 minutes

1 large eggplant, thinly
    sliced
1 tablespoon olive oil
1 medium onion, peeled,
    chopped
1 zucchini, thinly sliced
1 pound large shrimp,
    peeled, tail on
1 (28-ounce) can crushed
    tomatoes with herbs,
    drained
1 tablespoon red wine
    vinegar
½ teaspoon salt
¼ teaspoon black pepper

1. Place the eggplant in a microwave-safe dish and cover with water. Cover the dish with microwave-safe plastic. Microwave on high heat for 2 minutes. Continue microwaving for 30 seconds at a time, if needed, until the eggplant is softened.

2. Heat the olive oil in a skillet on medium-high heat. Add the onion. Sauté for 2 minutes, then add the zucchini. Sauté for 2 to 3 more minutes, until the vegetables are softened.

3. Add the shrimp. Sauté for 3 to 5 minutes, or until they turn pink.

4. Add the tomatoes and bring to a boil. Stir in the red wine vinegar, salt, and pepper.

5. Add the eggplant. Simmer for 2 to 3 minutes, to combine all the flavors. Serve hot.

Foil-Wrapped Fish Fillets with Dill

Serves 4

Preparation time:
5–10 minutes
Cooking time:
15–20 minutes

1½ teaspoons salt
4 (5-ounce) fish fillets
¾ cup plain yogurt
1½ teaspoons granulated
   sugar
1½ teaspoons Dijon
   mustard
1 tablespoon lemon juice
2 teaspoons fresh dill
⅛ teaspoon black pepper

This sauce would go well with more strongly flavored fish, such as salmon. Serve the fish with sliced tomato and lemon wedges.

1. Preheat the oven to 375°F. Rub the salt over the fish to season.

2. In a small bowl, stir together the yogurt, sugar, mustard, lemon juice, dill, and pepper.

3. Cut four sheets of foil, each at least 12" square. Place each fish fillet in the middle of a sheet of foil. Lightly brush each fillet with a small portion of the yogurt mixture. Fold the foil over the fish, crimping the edges to seal.

4. Bake at 375°F for 15 to 20 minutes, until the fish is cooked through and flakes easily (be careful not to overcook).

5. While the fish is baking, heat the remainder of the sauce on low heat. Keep warm while the fish is cooking. Serve the fish with the heated sauce.

Storing Fresh Fish

Since fish is highly perishable, it's important to place it in cold storage as soon as you arrive home from the store. Remove the fish from its packaging and rinse under cold water. Rewrap the fish loosely in plastic wrap or wax paper. Store the fish in the coldest part of the refrigerator and use within two days.

Pan-Fried Mussels in Coconut Curry Sauce

Canned mussels take the work out of cleaning and cooking mussels in this simple curry dish. Use leftover coconut milk to make Steamed Coconut Rice (page 153) to serve with the mussels.

Serves 4

Preparation time:
5–10 minutes
Cooking time: 15 minutes

2 teaspoons olive oil
½ cup chopped onion
*1 teaspoon chopped
    garlic*
2 teaspoons curry powder
*2 plum tomatoes,
    chopped*
2 cups canned mussels
¾ cup coconut milk
¼ cup chicken broth
½ cup raisins
¼ teaspoon salt
*⅛ teaspoon black pepper,
    or to taste*

1. Heat the olive oil in a skillet over medium-high heat. Add the onion and garlic. Add the curry powder, stirring to mix it in with the onion.

2. Add the tomato. Cook for 1 minute, then add the canned mussels. Cook, stirring occasionally, until the onion is shiny and has softened (4 to 5 minutes total cooking time for the onion).

3. Add the coconut milk and chicken broth to the pan. Bring to a boil.

4. Stir in the raisins. Turn down the heat and simmer, covered, for 10 minutes. Season with the salt and pepper.

Mussels Simmered in White Wine

Serves 3

Preparation time:
15 minutes
Cooking time: 15 minutes

30 mussels
1 tablespoon olive oil
1 clove garlic, finely
    chopped
2 shallots, chopped
2 teaspoons dried parsley
1 teaspoon dried thyme
1 tomato, chopped
¼ teaspoon red pepper
    flakes
1 cup dry white wine
⅓ cup light cream

Be sure to discard any mussels that haven't opened after cooking. Serve the mussels with a good crusty bread for dipping into the wine and cream mixture.

1. Clean and debeard the mussels (don't remove the shells).

2. Heat the olive oil in a large skillet over medium-high heat. Add the garlic and shallots. Sprinkle the parsley and thyme over the shallots. Sauté for 2 to 3 minutes, until the shallots turn golden. Add the tomato and cook for a minute. Stir in the red pepper flakes.

3. Add the wine and bring to a boil. Add the mussels. Cook, covered, on high heat until the mussels start to open (4 to 6 minutes). Using a slotted spoon, remove the mussels as soon as they open.

4. Add the cream to the pan. Bring to a boil. Stir to mix everything together and serve over the mussels.

5. Place the mussels in a large bowl or individual serving bowls. Spoon the cream mixture on top.

How to Clean Mussels

Cleaning mussels is easy and only takes a few minutes. Rinse the mussels under cold running water, scrubbing with a stiff brush to remove any dirt. Grab and remove the "beard" (the fibers sticking out of the shell). Soak the mussels in cold water for 5 minutes and rinse again before using.

Fish Stick Casserole

*Here's a way to put leftover pasta
and sauce to use. Simple Linguine with Tomato Sauce
(page 166) would work well in this recipe.*

Serves 2

Preparation time:
5 minutes
Cooking time: 30 minutes

1 cup frozen peas
2 cups leftover pasta with
    sauce
12 fish sticks
1 (10-ounce) can cream
    of mushroom soup

1. Preheat the oven to 425°F. Grease a 8"×8" baking dish.

2. Place the frozen peas in a microwave-safe bowl. Cover with microwave plastic wrap, leaving one corner open to vent steam. Microwave the peas on high heat for 2 minutes, and then for 30 seconds at a time, until cooked (total cooking time should be 2 to 3 minutes).

3. Spread 1 cup of the leftover pasta over the bottom of the baking dish. Carefully arrange the fish sticks on top. Stir together the soup and microwaved peas. Spoon over the fish sticks.

4. Spread the remaining cup of leftover pasta on top. Bake for 30 minutes, or until the fish sticks are fully cooked. Serve hot.

Indian Seafood Curry

If fresh cooked shrimp is unavailable, you can cook the shrimp by stir-frying until they turn pink, or boil them in a large saucepan with 6 cups water for 2 minutes.

Serves 4

Preparation time:
5 minutes
Cooking time: 15 minutes

2 tablespoons vegetable
   oil
1 teaspoon bottled
   minced ginger
1 medium onion, chopped
1 tablespoon curry
   powder
1 medium zucchini, thinly
   sliced
¾ cup coconut milk
1½ cups chicken broth
1 tablespoon lime juice
¼ teaspoon black pepper,
   or to taste
2 cups instant rice
1 pound cooked peeled,
   deveined fresh shrimp

1. Heat the oil in a skillet over medium heat. Add the ginger and onion. Stir in the curry powder. Add the zucchini. Cook for 3 to 4 minutes, until the onion is softened.

2. Add the coconut milk and chicken broth and bring to a boil. Stir in the lime juice and pepper. Stir in the instant rice, making sure it is completely wet.

3. Cover the saucepan and let sit for 4 minutes.

4. Add the cooked shrimp and let sit for another minute, or until the rice has completely absorbed the liquid.

Chapter 10
Rice and Other Grains

Basic Cooked Instant Rice

Using instant rice (also called quick-cooking rice) considerably speeds up the cooking time. While these general instructions should work for most types of instant long-grain cooked rice, be sure to follow the package directions if they are different.

Serves 2

Preparation: 2 minutes
Cooking time:
8–10 minutes

¾ cup water
¾ cup cooked instant
    long-grain rice
⅛ teaspoon salt, or to
    taste
Black pepper, to taste

1. Bring the water to a boil in a medium saucepan.

2. Stir in the rice, making sure it is thoroughly wet. Stir in the salt and pepper.

3. Remove the rice from the heat. Cover the saucepan and let stand for 5 minutes, or until the water is absorbed.

4. Fluff up the rice with a fork and serve.

Easy Flavored Rice

Cooking rice in broth, juice, or another liquid is a great way to add extra flavor. Feel free to load up the rice by stirring in ½ cup of golden Sultana raisins.

Serves 4

Cooking time:
10–12 minutes

¾ cups chicken broth
¾ cup coconut milk
½ teaspoon curry powder
1½ cups cooked instant
    long-grain rice
2 teaspoons margarine
¼ teaspoon salt, or to
    taste
Black pepper, to taste

1. Bring the chicken broth, coconut milk, and curry powder to a boil in a medium saucepan.

2. Stir in the rice, making sure it is thoroughly wet. Stir in the margarine, salt, and pepper.

3. Remove the saucepan from the heat.

4. Cover the saucepan and let stand for 5 minutes. Fluff up with a fork and serve.

Pork Fried Rice

Tamari soy sauce and sweet chili sauce are available in the ethnic or international section of many supermarkets. If you're using leftover pork that was marinated (for example, leftover Orange-Flavored Pork Chops, page 118), you can leave them out altogether if desired, or simply use 1 tablespoon of regular soy sauce.

2 large eggs
⅛ teaspoon freshly
    ground black or white
    pepper
2 tablespoons vegetable
    oil
2 teaspoons chopped
    garlic
1 teaspoon sweet chili
    sauce
½ medium onion,
    chopped
1 cup diced leftover
    cooked pork or ham
3 cups cold cooked rice
1 red bell pepper, cut into
    thin strips
1 tablespoon tamari soy
    sauce, or to taste

1. In a small bowl, lightly beat the egg. Stir in the pepper.

2. Heat the oil in a skillet on medium-high heat. Add the garlic, chili sauce, and onion. Stir until the onion begins to soften. Push the onion to the sides of the pan. In the middle of the pan, add the beaten egg. Stir quickly to scramble, then mix with the onion.

3. Push the egg to the sides of the pan. Add the diced pork or ham in the middle and stir for a minute to heat through.

4. Add the rice to the pan. Cook, stirring constantly, for 2 to 3 minutes, until the rice is heated through and mixed with the other ingredients.

5. Stir in the bell pepper and the tamari soy sauce. Stir for another minute to cook the bell pepper and mix all the ingredients. Serve hot.

Perfect Rice for Fried Rice

Fried rice tastes best with cooked rice that is at least one day old. Before cooking, wet your fingers and run them through the rice to remove any clumps. This will ensure that the rice cooks more evenly.

Mexican Fried Rice

Serves 4

Preparation time:
5–8 minutes
Cooking time: 10 minutes

3 tablespoons vegetable
  oil, divided
½ medium yellow onion,
  finely chopped
1 tablespoon jarred
  chopped jalapeño
  peppers
1 tomato, diced
1 cup canned corn niblets
3 cups cold cooked rice
½ teaspoon ground cumin
2 green onions, finely
  sliced
¼ teaspoon salt, or to
  taste
⅛ teaspoon black pepper,
  or to taste

*This spicy side dish would go nicely with a less highly seasoned
main dish, such as Simple Steamed Chicken Dinner (page 82).*

1. Heat 1½ tablespoons oil in a nonstick skillet on medium heat. Add the
    onion. Cook for 4 to 5 minutes, until the onion is softened.

2. Stir in the chopped jalapeño peppers. Stir in the tomato. Cook for a min-
    ute and stir in the canned corn. Remove the vegetables from the pan.

3. Heat 1½ tablespoons oil in the pan. Add the rice. Cook, stirring, for 1 to
    2 minutes, until heated through. Stir in the ground cumin.

4. Return the vegetables to the pan. Stir in the green onions. Stir to mix
    everything together. Season with the salt and pepper. Serve hot.

How to Cook Long-Grain Rice

*Cooking rice the traditional way gives you an alternative to always
having to use instant rice on nights when time is limited. To cook the
rice, bring the rice and water to boil in a medium saucepan, using 2
cups water for every cup of rice. When the water is boiling, turn the heat
down to medium-low and partially cover. Continue cooking until "holes"
start to appear in the rice. Cover fully, turn the heat down to low. Let the
rice steam for at least 15 minutes more, until the water is fully
absorbed.*

Easy Apple Risotto

Traditionalists insist that the only way to make risotto is to stand over the pot, painstakingly stirring the liquid into the rice. However, simply letting the rice simmer in broth and apple juice does a reasonably good job, leaving you free to prepare the rest of the meal.

1. Heat the olive oil in a skillet on medium-high heat. Add the apple and cinnamon. Cook, stirring, for about 2 minutes, until the apples start to become crisp.

2. Add the rice and cook for about 2 minutes, until the grains start to become shiny and translucent. Stir in the raisins.

3. Add the chicken broth and apple juice.

4. Turn the heat down to low, cover, and simmer for 20 minutes.

5. Stir in the cheese and serve.

Rustic Risotto

A classic dish from northern Italy, risotto is famous for its rich, creamy texture. The distinctive flavor and texture of risotto come from using a super-absorbent rice with grains that stick together when cooked. Arborio is the most popular rice for making risotto in North America, but other varieties of Italian rice, such as carnaroli, can also be used.

Serves 4

Preparation time: 5 minutes
Cooking time: 25 minutes

2 tablespoons olive oil
1 medium red apple, cored and sliced
1 teaspoon cinnamon, or to taste
1 cup arborio short-grain rice
2 tablespoons golden raisins
1½ cups chicken broth
1 cup apple juice
3 tablespoons shredded Cheddar cheese

Creamy Risotto Side Dish

Serves 4

Preparation time:
5–10 minutes
Cooking time:
17–18 minutes

1 cup frozen baby peas
1 cup arborio or other
    short-grain rice
2 cups chicken broth,
    divided
½ teaspoon dried basil
    leaves
½ teaspoon dried
    oregano
½ teaspoon garlic powder
⅛ teaspoon black pepper,
    or to taste
1 teaspoon salt, divided
⅓ cup shredded
    Parmesan cheese

This won't have quite the same texture and flavor as authentic risotto, but it's a good stand-in for nights when you're in a hurry.

1. Place the frozen peas in a microwave-safe casserole dish. Cover with microwave plastic wrap, leaving one corner open to vent steam. Microwave the peas on high heat for 2 minutes, and then for 30 seconds at a time until cooked (total cooking time should be 2 to 3 minutes).

2. Add the rice and 1½ cups broth. Stir in the basil, oregano, garlic powder, pepper, and ½ teaspoon salt. Cover the dish with microwave-safe plastic wrap and microwave for 5 minutes.

3. Stir in ½ cup broth and ½ teaspoon salt. Microwave on high for 5 more minutes.

4. Stir, cover, and microwave for 5 minutes, or until the liquid is mainly absorbed and the rice grains are tender.

5. Stir in the Parmesan cheese. Serve hot.

Healthy Brown Rice

While instant brown rice is a quick and easy alternative to making regular brown rice, it can be hard to find. Another option is to make brown rice ahead of time and reheat it later.

Serves 4

Preparation time:
5 minutes
Cooking time:
50–55 minutes

1 cup brown rice
2¼ cups water

1. Bring the rice and water to boil in a medium saucepan.

2. Reduce the heat to low-medium.

3. Cook the rice, uncovered, until the water is absorbed (40 to 45 minutes).

4. Let stand for 10 minutes. Fluff and serve.

Rice Reheating Tips

For safety's sake, it's important to cool down and refrigerate the cooked rice within 2 hours after cooking. To reheat, combine the rice with 1 to 2 tablespoons water in a saucepan and cook over low heat, or heat in the microwave (follow your microwave's instructions for reheating food).

Jambalaya

This stir-fry allows you to enjoy the flavors in slow simmered jambalaya during busy weekdays. If you like, replace the spices with store-bought creole seasoning.

Serves 4

Preparation time:
5 minutes
Cooking time: 15 minutes

1½ cups Basic Cooked
   Instant Rice (page
   146)
2 tablespoons olive oil,
   divided
1 garlic clove, finely
   chopped
½ medium onion, finely
   chopped
1 red bell pepper, thinly
   sliced
2 cups cooked shrimp
⅛ teaspoon salt, or to
   taste
⅛ teaspoon black pepper,
   or to taste
¼ teaspoon Tabasco
   sauce, or to taste
1 cup canned chopped
   tomatoes with juice
1 teaspoon chopped fresh
   thyme leaves

1. Prepare the Basic Cooked Instant Rice (page 146). Heat 1 tablespoon oil in a large heavy skillet or wok over medium-high heat. Add the garlic and onion. Stir-fry for about 2 minutes, until the onion begins to soften.

2. Add the red bell pepper. Stir-fry for 1 minute until it becomes tender. Add the cooked shrimp. Cook for 1 minute.

3. Heat 1 tablespoon oil in a medium saucepan. Add the cooked rice, stirring for a minute until it begins to turn light brown. Stir the salt, pepper, and Tabasco sauce into the rice.

4. Add the tomatoes and thyme leaves to the rice. Bring to a boil.

5. Add the shrimp and vegetables to the pan. Cook for another minute, stirring to mix everything together. Serve hot.

Steamed Coconut Rice

*Microwave basmati rice takes less time to make and still has the
rich nutty flavor of regular boiled scented rice.*

Serves 6

Preparation time:
5–10 minutes
Cooking time: 22 minutes

1½ cups scented rice
1 tablespoon margarine
2 shallots
1¼ cups coconut milk
1¾ cups water
½ teaspoon salt

1. Rinse the rice in cold water and drain.

2. Place the margarine and chopped shallots in a microwave-safe 3-quart
    casserole dish. Microwave on high heat for 1½ minutes, stir, then micro-
    wave for 30 seconds at a time until the shallots are tender.

3. Add the coconut milk, water, rice, and salt. Microwave on high for
    10 minutes.

4. Stir the rice. Cover the dish with microwave-safe wax paper. Micro-
    wave for 3 minutes and then for 1 minute at a time until the liquid is
    absorbed.

5. Remove the dish from the heat. Let stand for 5 minutes. Fluff
    and serve.

Or Cook it the Regular Way

*Another way to cut down on the time it takes to prepare rice for dinner
is to boil the rice in advance so that it just needs to be reheated. To cook
basmati rice on the stovetop, sauté the margarine and shallots in a
skillet until the shallots are softened. Add the rice, coconut milk, water,
and salt and bring to a boil, uncovered. Turn down the heat to medium
and boil, uncovered, until the liquid is nearly absorbed (10 to 12 minutes). Continue cooking for a few more minutes until the water is
absorbed.*

Spanish Rice Side Dish

Serves 4

Preparation time:
5 minutes
Cooking time: 10 minutes

⅔ cup tomato juice
1⅓ cups water
2 cups instant rice
½ teaspoon salt, or to
     taste
⅛ teaspoon black pepper
1 tablespoon olive oil,
     divided
2 cloves garlic, chopped
1 onion, chopped
1 teaspoon paprika, or to
     taste
1 green bell pepper,
     chopped into chunks

*This simple side dish is incredibly easy to make. To turn it into a
main meal, simply add 2 cups of cooked shrimp or leftover
cooked chicken.*

1. In a saucepan, bring the tomato juice and water to a boil. Stir in the
    rice, salt, and pepper. Remove from the heat, cover, and let stand for 5
    minutes.

2. While the rice is cooking, prepare the vegetables: Heat the olive oil in
    a heavy skillet or wok on medium-high heat. Add the garlic and onion.
    Sprinkle the paprika over the onion and sauté for about 2 minutes, until
    the onion begins to soften.

3. Add the green pepper and continue cooking until the vegetables are
    softened.

4. Stir the cooked vegetables into the rice. Stir with a fork before serving.

Microwave Rice Pilaf

Feel free to dress up this easy side dish by adding a few slices of apple with the onion. On the other hand, when you're in a hurry you can leave out the onion—stir in the cinnamon and margarine after removing the rice from the microwave.

Serves 4

Preparation time:
5 minutes
Cooking time:
20–22 minutes

½ medium onion,
   chopped
1 tablespoon margarine
½ teaspoon ground
   cinnamon
1 cup long-grain white
   rice
1 cup orange juice
1 cup water
¼ cup raisins

1. Place the onion and margarine in a microwave-safe 2-quart casserole dish. Sprinkle the ground cinnamon on top. Microwave on high heat for 1½ minutes. Stir and microwave for 30 seconds at a time until the onion is tender.

2. Add the white rice, orange juice, and water. Microwave on high heat for 10 minutes. Stir the rice and microwave for short periods (first 2 minutes, then 1 minute) at a time until the water is absorbed and the rice is cooked (total cooking time for the rice should be 14 to 15 minutes).

3. Remove the rice from the microwave. Stir in the raisins.

4. Let the cooked rice stand for 5 minutes. Fluff and serve.

Know Your Rice

The main difference between long- and short-grain rice isn't the length of the grains but rather the type of starch each one contains. Long-grain rice is high in amylase, which makes it turn out light and fluffy. Short-grain rice (like the arborio rice) contains a higher ratio of amylopectin, which makes the rice grains sticky. If you like your rice light and fluffy, always use long-grain rice when making plain rice to serve as a side dish.

Easy Italian Rice Pilaf

This comforting dish is full of flavor without being too heavy. Reduced-sodium chicken broth is available in resealable cartons in many supermarkets.

Serves 4

Preparation time:
10 minutes
Cooking time:
13–15 minutes

1 tablespoon olive oil
2 shallots, peeled and
    chopped
1 teaspoon bottled
    minced garlic
1 tablespoon chopped
    sun-dried tomato
    strips
1 cup chopped red bell
    pepper
1 cup drained canned
    mushrooms
¼ teaspoon cayenne
    pepper
1 tablespoon balsamic
    vinegar
2¼ cups reduced-sodium
    chicken broth
2 cups instant white rice

1. Heat the olive oil in a skillet on medium heat. Add the shallots, garlic, and sun-dried tomato strips. Sauté for 3 to 4 minutes, until the shallots are softened.

2. Add the chopped bell pepper and the mushrooms. Sprinkle the cayenne pepper on top. Splash the vegetables with the balsamic vinegar. Cook until the vegetables are softened (total cooking time is about 5 minutes).

3. Add the chicken broth. Bring to a boil.

4. Stir in the instant rice. Cover and let stand for 5 minutes. Serve hot.

Polenta Chips

The polenta should be poured into a large baking sheet after cooking. If you're not comfortable with deep-frying, bake the chips in a 450°F oven for 20 minutes, or until they turn golden.

Serves 6

Preparation time:
10 minutes
Cooking time: 20 minutes

4 cups vegetable oil
1 cup cooked quick-
  cooking polenta,
  cooled
½ cup cornstarch
1 teaspoon cayenne
  pepper

1. In a large saucepan or deep-fat fryer, preheat the oil to 360°F.

2. Cut the polenta into thin strips, julienne-style.

3. In a small bowl, combine the cornstarch and cayenne pepper. Coat the polenta strips with this mixture.

4. When the oil is hot, carefully lower about 7 or 8 polenta chips into the hot oil (it's easiest to do this if you have a mesh basket). Deep-fry the chips until they turn golden brown (about 4 minutes).

5. Carefully remove the chips from the oil (if not using a mesh basket, lift the chips out with a slotted spoon). Drain the chips on paper towels. Continue with the remainder of the polenta chips. Serve immediately.

All about Polenta

Made from boiled cornmeal, polenta makes an interesting alternative to a side dish of rice, bread, or pasta. Although polenta is frequently boiled, it can also be baked. Taking only five minutes to make, quick-cooking polenta is available in many supermarkets. So is premade polenta, which comes packaged in tubes.

Savory Rice with Portobello Mushrooms

Preparation time:
5–10 minutes
Cooking time:
10–12 minutes

2 cups instant white rice
2 cups vegetable stock
1 tablespoon margarine
1 medium onion, chopped
4 ounces portobello
    mushrooms, thinly
    sliced
2 teaspoons dried parsley
    flakes
1 teaspoon dried oregano
½ teaspoon salt

This simple side dish goes very nicely with chicken or other poultry. You can replace the white rice with instant brown rice or leftover Healthy Brown Rice (page 151).

1. Cook the instant rice in the vegetable stock according to package directions or the instructions in Basic Cooked Instant Rice (page 146) (replace the water with vegetable stock).

2. Heat the margarine in a skillet on medium-high heat. Add the chopped onion.

3. Sauté the onions for 2 minutes, then add the portobello mushrooms.

4. Sauté for about 2 minutes until the onion is softened (turn down the heat to medium if the onion is cooking too quickly). Stir in the dried parsley, oregano, and salt while the onion is cooking.

5. Combine the mushrooms and onion with the cooked rice. Fluff with a fork and serve hot.

Chapter 11
Perfect Pasta

Angel Hair Pasta with Shrimp

Serves 4

Preparation time:
15 minutes
Cooking time: 15 minutes

3 quarts water
1½ teaspoons salt
¾ pound angel hair pasta
1 tablespoon olive oil
2 cloves garlic, minced
2 shallots, chopped
1 teaspoon dried basil
1 teaspoon dried oregano
1 tomato, chopped
1 pound peeled, deveined
    shrimp
2 tablespoons lemon juice
¼ cup light cream
¼ teaspoon black pepper

You can sprinkle ½ cup Parmesan cheese over the cooked shrimp and pasta. To reduce the preparation time, feel free to use leftover cooked pasta.

1. Bring a large pot with the water to a boil with the salt. Add the pasta to the boiling water. Cook until the pasta is cooked al dente. (Prepare the vegetables and shrimp while the pasta is cooking.)

2. Heat the olive oil in a skillet. Add the garlic and shallots. Sprinkle the dried basil and oregano over the shallots. Sauté for 3 to 4 minutes, until softened.

3. Add the tomato and the shrimp. Sauté the shrimp until they turn pink.

4. Add the lemon juice and cream. Cook until thickened. Stir in the pepper. Keep warm.

5. Drain the cooked pasta in a colander. Place in a large bowl. Toss the pasta with the sauce.

Pasta Cooking Tips

The key to making perfect pasta is to use plenty of water, giving the pasta room to move around, and stirring it to separate the strands. Ideally, pasta should be cooked until it reaches the al dente stage (an Italian term meaning "to the tooth"). Pasta that is cooked al dente is neither over- nor undercooked, but firm, slightly chewy, and offering a bit of resistance.

Basic Stir-Fried Noodles

Linguine and spaghetti both make handy substitutes for Chinese egg noodles. If you like, stir-fry one-half pound of fresh spinach leaves with the noodles.

1. Bring a large pot with 2 quarts of water to a boil with the salt. Add the linguine to the boiling water. Cook for 3 to 4 minutes, until the linguine is cooked al dente. Drain in a colander.

2. In a small bowl, stir together the soy sauce, sugar, and red wine vinegar.

3. Heat the oil in a skillet over medium-high heat. Add the minced garlic. Stir for a few seconds, then add the noodles.

4. Stir for 1 minute, then pour in the sauce.

5. Stir-fry for 1 to 2 more minutes, until the noodles are heated through. Serve hot.

Marvelous Mian

They may not have the same intriguing shapes as Italian pasta, but there are many varieties of Chinese noodles, called mian. Delicate rice noodles, made from rice flour and water, are frequently added to soups and sometimes salads. Made with wheat flour, egg, and noodles, thick fresh Shanghai noodles are more than able to hold their own in stir-fries, absorbing the flavors of the sauce they are cooked with.

Serves 4

Preparation time:
15 minutes
Cooking time: 8 minutes

2 quarts water
1 teaspoon salt
½ pound linguine
2 teaspoons soy sauce
½ teaspoon granulated
    sugar
1 tablespoon red wine
    vinegar
2 tablespoons vegetable
    oil
1 teaspoon bottled
    minced garlic

Colorful Pasta Primavera

Serves 4

Preparation time:
5–10 minutes
Cooking time: 10 minutes

2 tablespoons olive oil
1 white onion, peeled,
    chopped
1 zucchini, chopped
1 teaspoon dried basil
1 teaspoon dried oregano
1 cup drained canned
    asparagus tips
1 cup roasted red
    peppers
½ cup tomato sauce
½ cup light cream
½ teaspoon salt, or to
    taste
¼ teaspoon black pepper,
    or to taste
½ pound leftover cooked
    whole-wheat spaghetti
½ cup shredded
    Parmesan cheese

Traditionally, pasta primavera is loaded with fresh spring vegetables (the word primavera means "spring") but using canned vegetables helps you enjoy this Italian specialty on busy weeknights. Feel free to use homemade Roasted Red Peppers (page 221) or store-bought bottled roasted peppers.

1. Heat the olive oil in a skillet over medium-high heat. Add the onion. Sauté for a couple of minutes, then add the zucchini. Sprinkle the basil and oregano over the onion while it is cooking. Sauté until the vegetables are softened (turn the heat down to medium if needed).

2. Add the canned asparagus and the red peppers. Cook for a minute on medium heat.

3. Add the tomato sauce and cream. Cook, stirring, until it begins to bubble and thicken slightly. Stir in the salt and pepper. Turn down the heat and keep warm.

4. Reheat the cooked pasta (see Serving Leftover Pasta, page 169).

5. Place the pasta in a bowl and toss with the primavera sauce. Sprinkle with the Parmesan cheese.

Weeknight Linguine with Alfredo Sauce

Traditionally, this creamy sauce is served with fettuccine, a ribbon-shaped pasta made with egg, flour, and water. However, any dried pasta made with eggs will do.

Serves 4

Preparation time: 10 minutes
Cooking time: 20 minutes

3 quarts water
1½ teaspoons salt
¾ pound whole-wheat
   linguine
4 tablespoons margarine
3 tablespoons flour
1½ cups milk
⅔ cup grated Parmesan
   cheese
½ teaspoon dried
   oregano
½ teaspoon dried basil
½ teaspoon ground
   nutmeg, or to taste
Black pepper, to taste
1 (4.25-ounce) can
   crabmeat

1. Bring a large pot containing the water and salt to a boil. Add the pasta to the boiling water. Cook until the pasta is cooked al dente. (Prepare the Alfredo sauce while the pasta is cooking.)

2. In a small saucepan, melt the margarine on very low heat. Add the flour and stir continually to make a roux.

3. Add the milk and heat until it is nearly boiling, stirring with a whisk.

4. Add the Parmesan cheese and continue stirring with a whisk until the mixture has thickened. Stir in the oregano, basil, nutmeg, and pepper. Stir in the crabmeat and cook for another minute. Keep the sauce warm.

5. Drain the cooked pasta in a colander. Place in a large bowl. Toss the pasta with the sauce.

Pairing Pasta with Sauce

Timing is everything when it comes to combining pasta with a sauce. Ideally, the pasta should be sauced as soon as possible after it is cooked. If you are using dried pasta, start preparing the sauce after adding the pasta to the cooking water. Keep the sauce warm while cooking the pasta. Place the pasta in a warm bowl and toss thoroughly with the sauce.

Eggplant Penne

Serves 4

Preparation time:
5 minutes
Cooking time: 30 minutes

1 eggplant, about 1
  pound
5 tablespoons olive oil,
  divided
1 (28-ounce) can plum
  tomatoes, no salt
  added, with juice
1 tablespoon bottled
  minced garlic
2 tablespoons minced
  onion
1 tablespoon red wine
  vinegar
¼ cup chopped fresh
  basil leaves
1 teaspoon salt
¼ teaspoon black pepper
¾ pound penne
3 quarts water
1½ teaspoons salt

The necessary interval needed to cool the eggplant makes this dish a perfect candidate for advance prep work. Prepare the eggplant and sauce earlier in the day, and then they'll be ready when it comes time to cook the pasta.

1. Pierce the eggplant several times with a fork. Brush 1 tablespoon olive oil over the eggplant. Place in a large microwave-safe bowl and cover the dish with microwave-safe plastic wrap.

2. Microwave the eggplant for 2 minutes. Turn over, re-cover, and microwave for 2 minutes, or as needed until the eggplant has softened. Remove from the microwave and cool.

3. While the eggplant is cooling, prepare the sauce. Combine the tomatoes with juice, garlic, onion, red wine vinegar, basil, 4 tablespoons olive oil, salt, and pepper in a blender or food processor. Process until it forms a thick sauce. Chill for 15 minutes to blend the flavors.

4. When the eggplant is cool enough to handle, chop it into bite-size chunks. Pour the pasta sauce into a large skillet. Add the eggplant. Bring to a boil, turn down the heat and simmer, uncovered, for 5 minutes.

5. Bring a large pot with 3 quarts salted water to a boil. Add the penne to the boiling water. Cook until the pasta is cooked al dente. Drain in a colander. Toss the pasta with the eggplant and sauce.

Linguine with Marinated Artichoke Hearts

A combination of lemon, pepper, garlic, basil, and other season-ings, lemon pepper adds flavor to seafood and pasta dishes.

Serves 4

Preparation time:
5 minutes
Cooking time:
7–10 minutes

2 teaspoons olive oil
1 tablespoon bottled
   minced garlic
1 medium white onion,
   peeled, chopped
1 teaspoon lemon pepper,
   or to taste
Marinated Artichoke
   Hearts (page 229)
1 (28-ounce) can
   tomatoes, juice
   discarded
¾ pound leftover cooked
   linguine

1. Heat the olive oil in a skillet on medium-high heat. Add the garlic and onion. Sprinkle the lemon pepper over the onion. Sauté for 4 to 5 minutes, until the onion is softened.

2. Add the marinated artichoke hearts. Cook for 1 minute, stirring occasionally.

3. Add the canned tomatoes. Bring to a boil. Cook, stirring for a minute to heat through.

4. Reheat the pasta (see Serving Leftover Pasta, page 169). Place the pasta in a bowl and toss with the artichoke and tomato mixture.

Storing Leftover Pasta

Preparing pasta ahead of time cuts down substantially on cooking time, since you don't need to wait for the water to boil. To store cooked pasta for later use, toss the pasta with a small amount of vegetable oil (this keeps the cooled noodles from sticking together) and place in a reseal-able plastic bag in the refrigerator.

Simple Linguine with Tomato Sauce

Here's a classic pasta dish using leftover cooked pasta. For best results, chill the sauce for at least 15 minutes to give the flavors a chance to blend before pairing with the pasta.

Serves 4

Preparation time:
10 minutes
Chill time: 15 minutes

1 (28-ounce) can plum tomatoes, no salt added, with juice
1 tablespoon bottled minced garlic
2 tablespoons minced onion
1 tablespoon red wine vinegar
¼ cup chopped fresh basil leaves
¼ cup extra-virgin olive oil
1 teaspoon salt
¼ teaspoon black pepper
1 pound leftover cooked linguine

1. Combine the tomatoes and their juice, garlic, onion, red wine vinegar, basil, olive oil, salt, and pepper in a blender or food processor. Process until it forms a thick sauce.

2. Reheat the cooked pasta (see Serving Leftover Pasta, page 169).

3. Place the pasta in a bowl and toss with the tomato sauce.

Plum Tomatoes

A plump, oval-shaped tomato with few seeds, plum tomatoes are born to be used in a sauce. If you can't find canned plum tomatoes, look for them by their other name, Roma tomatoes.

Leftover Pasta and Burgundy Beef Casserole

This simple dish could also be cooked in the microwave: use a reheat setting or cook at 70 percent power for 1 minute, and then for 1 minute at a time until heated through.

1. Preheat the oven to 325°F. Run the pasta under warm running water to reheat.

2. Bring the brown sauce to a boil in a medium saucepan with the Burgundy.

3. Spread 1 cup of the leftover pasta over the bottom of a baking dish. Spoon the beef over the pasta.

4. Spoon the sauce over the beef. Spread the remaining cup of pasta on top.

5. Cook for 10 to 15 minutes to heat through. Serve immediately.

Serves 2

Preparation time:
5 minutes
Cooking time:
15–20 minutes

2 cups leftover cooked
    pasta
½ portion leftover Quick
    and Easy Brown
    Sauce (page 252)
3 tablespoons Burgundy
½ pound leftover cooked
    steak

Five-Ingredient Spaghetti and Meatballs

There are a number of good pre-made tomato sauces on the market—choose your favorite. Use your preferred frozen vegetables in this recipe—spinach, cauliflower, and a frozen stir-fry vegetable mix are all good choices.

Serves 4

Preparation time:
5 minutes
Cooking time:
10–15 minutes

24 frozen meatballs
3 cups frozen vegetables
¾ pound leftover cooked spaghetti
3 cups pre-made tomato sauce
¾ cup grated Parmesan cheese

1. Place the frozen meatballs in a microwave-safe dish. Microwave on high heat for 2 minutes, and then for 30 seconds at a time if needed until the meatballs are cooked.

2. Place the frozen vegetables in a microwave-safe dish. Cover and microwave on high heat for 3 minutes, and then for 1 minute at a time until cooked.

3. Reheat the pasta (see Serving Leftover Pasta, page 169).

4. Heat the pre-made tomato sauce in a saucepan over medium heat.

5. Toss the pasta with the tomato sauce. Stir in the meatballs and vegetables. Sprinkle the Parmesan cheese on top.

Cooking Pasta in the Microwave

Don't have leftover pasta on hand and there's no time to cook a new batch? You can quickly cook pasta in the microwave. First, heat the water in a microwave-safe dish. Add the noodles—stirring to make sure they are completely covered with the water—and cook on high heat until tender. The exact cooking time will depend on the amount of pasta to be cooked—count on at least 4 minutes for 8 ounces of dried egg noodles.

Garlic Noodles with Bacon

Here is a quick and easy way to jazz up leftover pasta. You can use other types of long pasta in the recipe, such as linguine or angel hair pasta.

Serves 4

Preparation time:
5 minutes
Cooking time: 10 minutes

8 ounces leftover cooked
   spaghetti
3 slices bacon
3 tablespoons margarine
2 tablespoons cream
   cheese
2 teaspoons bottled
   minced garlic, or to
   taste
1 cup half-and-half
⅓ cup grated Parmesan
   cheese
½ teaspoon dried basil,
   or to taste
½ teaspoon dried
   oregano, or to taste
Black pepper, to taste

1. Reheat the spaghetti (see Serving Leftover Pasta below).

2. Place the bacon on a plate covered with a paper towel. Lay two more paper towels over the bacon. Microwave on high heat for 2 minutes, and then for 1 minute at a time until the bacon is cooked. Remove and chop.

3. Melt the margarine in a saucepan over low heat. Whisk in the cream cheese. Stir in the garlic.

4. Turn the heat up and add the half-and-half. Add the Parmesan cheese and continue stirring with a whisk until the mixture has thickened. Stir in the oregano, basil, and pepper.

5. Place the cooked pasta in a large bowl. Toss with the sauce.

Serving Leftover Pasta

The easiest way to reheat leftover cooked pasta is to place it in a colander and quickly rinse under hot running water, moving your fingers through to separate the strands. To reheat pasta in the microwave, place in a microwave-safe bowl covered with wax paper or plastic wrap. Microwave on high heat for 1 minute, and then for 30 seconds at a time until the pasta is heated through.

Crab Pasta with Artichokes

Preparation time:
5 minutes
Cooking time: 20 minutes

2 quarts water
1 teaspoon salt
½ pound macaroni or
    other shell-shaped
    pasta
2 teaspoons olive oil
2 shallots, peeled,
    chopped
8 canned artichoke
    hearts, halved
1 tomato, thinly sliced
1½ cups drained canned
    crabmeat
2 tablespoons lemon juice
¼ cup chicken broth or
    light cream
¼ teaspoon black pepper,
    or to taste
½ teaspoon salt, or to
    taste

Try garnishing this dish with ½ cup of sliced olives. You can use unmarinated or marinated canned artichoke hearts in this recipe.

1. Bring a large pot with the water and salt to a boil. Add the pasta to the boiling water. Cook until the pasta is cooked al dente. (Prepare the remainder of the ingredients while the pasta is cooking.)

2. In a skillet, heat the olive oil. Add the shallots and sauté until softened.

3. Add the artichoke hearts. Cook for 1 minute and add the tomato, pressing down so that it releases its juice. Stir in the crabmeat and lemon juice.

4. Add the broth or light cream to the pan and bring to a boil. Season with the salt and pepper. Keep warm.

5. Drain the pasta in a colander. Place the pasta in a bowl and toss with the crabmeat and artichoke mixture. Serve hot.

Know Your Pasta!

Italian pasta comes in all sorts of shapes and sizes, from classic long pastas such as spaghetti and linguine to silky ribbons of fettuccine and tube-shaped penne and macaroni. Overall, there are over 600 types of pasta. Pasta is such an important staple worldwide that representatives of national pasta associations agreed to designate October 25th as World Pasta Day.

Shrimp Penne with Asparagus and Sun-Dried Tomatoes

Sturdy penne pasta is often paired with a thick sauce, but here it is combined with lemon-flavored shrimp and asparagus.

Serves 4

Preparation time: 10 minutes
Cooking time: 15 minutes

¾ pound penne pasta
3 quarts water
1½ teaspoons salt
½ pound fresh asparagus, cut diagonally into 1" pieces
1 tablespoon olive oil
2 shallots, peeled, chopped
2 tablespoons sun-dried tomatoes
1 pound shrimp, peeled, deveined, tail on
2 tablespoons lemon juice
¼ teaspoon black pepper
1 teaspoon dried basil leaves
¼ cup grated Parmesan cheese, optional

1. Bring a large pot with 3 quarts of water to a boil with the salt.

2. Fill a medium saucepan with enough water so that an expanding metal steamer will sit just above the water (about 1½"). Bring the water to a boil. Add the asparagus. Steam the asparagus, covered, until it is tender but still crisp (about 5 to 8 minutes). Drain.

3. In a skillet, heat the olive oil. Add the shallots and sun-dried tomato strips. Sauté the shallot until it is softened.

4. Add the shrimp. Stir in the lemon juice, pepper, and dried basil. Sauté the shrimp until it turns pink.

5. Add the noodles to the boiling water. Cook, stirring to separate the pasta, until the linguine is cooked al dente. Drain in a colander. Toss the pasta with the shrimp and asparagus. Sprinkle the Parmesan cheese over top if using.

Greek Macaroni and Cheese

Serves 3

Preparation time:
5 minutes
Cooking time: 20 minutes

½ pound leftover tubular
    pasta, cooked
4 tablespoons unsalted
    butter
3 tablespoons flour
1 teaspoon bottled
    minced garlic
1 cup whole milk
⅓ cup crumbled feta
    cheese
¼ teaspoon ground
    nutmeg, or to taste
1 teaspoon dried mint
¼ teaspoon black pepper,
    or to taste
1 teaspoon lemon juice

Here is a more adult version of the kid's favorite mac 'n' cheese, made by adding cheese and herbs traditionally used in Greek cooking to a basic white sauce and serving over pasta. You can use any small tubular shaped pasta as the macaroni, including traditional macaroni noodles.

1. Reheat the pasta (see Serving Leftover Pasta, page 169).

2. Melt the butter on very low heat. Add the flour and blend it into the melted butter, stirring continually until it thickens and forms a roux. Stir in the garlic.

3. Turn the heat up to medium low and slowly add the milk and cheese. Stir in the ground nutmeg and the dried mint. Continue stirring with a whisk until the mixture has thickened.

4. Stir in the pepper and lemon juice.

5. Toss the pasta with the sauce and serve immediately.

Pasta with Smoked Salmon

Lemon extract provides a convenient substitute for lemon zest, but if you prefer the real thing, replace the extract with 2 teaspoons of lemon zest. Be careful when adding salt, as smoked salmon and capers (even after rinsing) are both quite salty.

1. Bring a large pot containing the water and salt to a boil. Add the pasta to the boiling water. Cook until the pasta is cooked al dente. Drain in a colander.

2. Begin preparing the sauce while the pasta is cooking. Heat the olive oil over medium-high heat. Add the shallot and sauté until it begins to soften. Add the smoked salmon. Sprinkle the dried parsley over the salmon and shallot. Continue cooking for 1 to 2 more minutes, until the salmon turns a light color.

3. Stir in the whipping cream, lemon extract, and capers. Continue cooking until the cream is heated through. Do a taste test and season with the salt and pepper as needed.

4. Toss the pasta with the sauce and serve immediately.

Serves 4

Preparation time:
5–10 minutes
Cooking time:
20–25 minutes

3 quarts water
1½ teaspoons salt
¾ pound angel hair pasta
2 tablespoons olive oil
1 shallot, peeled and
    chopped
⅓ pound smoked salmon
2 teaspoons dried parsley
¾ cup whipping cream
1 teaspoon lemon extract
2 tablespoons capers,
    rinsed
¼ teaspoon salt, or to
    taste
¼ teaspoon black pepper,
    or to taste

Chapter 12
Vegetarian Entrées

Buddhist Monk's Soup

Serves 6

Preparation time:
10 minutes
Cooking time: 15 minutes

1 pound firm tofu
2 teaspoons vegetable oil
½ cup chopped sweet
   onion
1 cup sliced fresh
   mushrooms
½ teaspoon cayenne
   pepper
2 cups drained canned
   sweet potatoes
3 cups coconut milk
2 cups water
2 teaspoons lime juice
½ teaspoon salt
⅛ teaspoon black pepper,
   or to taste
¾ cup unsalted cashews

*This warming soup is traditionally served on the first day
of the New Year, when Buddhists believe that no living
thing should be killed.*

1. Drain the tofu (see How to Drain Tofu, page 186) and cut into cubes.

2. After the tofu has been draining for about 5 minutes, begin preparing the other ingredients. Heat the vegetable oil in a saucepan on medium-high heat. Add the chopped onion and mushrooms.

3. Turn the heat down to medium and sauté for about 5 minutes, until the vegetables are softened. Stir in the cayenne pepper. Add the canned sweet potatoes and cook for a minute, stirring.

4. Add the coconut milk and water. Bring to a boil. Stir in the lime juice, salt, and pepper. Add the cubed tofu.

5. Simmer for 5 minutes. Serve hot, garnished with the cashews.

Are All Buddhists Vegetarians?

Contrary to popular belief, not all Buddhists are vegetarians. While the Buddhist philosophy forbids killing animals specifically for consumption, it is permissible to eat an animal that was killed accidentally. Still, many Buddhists do follow a vegetarian diet.

Portobello Mushroom Burgers

Combining garlic and mayonnaise is a quick and easy way to make aioli, a garlicky sauce from France that complements everything from vegetables to meat, poultry, and seafood. This recipe can easily be doubled to serve 8.

1. Wipe the mushrooms clean with a damp cloth and thinly slice.

2. In a small bowl, stir together the balsamic vinegar and vegetarian chicken-flavored broth. In a separate small bowl, stir together the garlic, mayonnaise, lemon juice, and cayenne pepper. Chill the mayonnaise mixture until needed.

3. Heat the oil in a skillet over medium-high heat. Add the shallot and cook until tender. Turn the heat down to medium and add the sliced mushrooms. Stir in the vinegar and broth mixture and the black pepper. Cook for 4 to 5 minutes until the mushrooms are tender.

4. Lay out the hamburger buns in front of you. Put a lettuce leaf on the bottom of each bun. Spread 1 tablespoon of the garlic/mayonnaise mixture inside the top of each bun and spoon one-quarter of the sautéed mushroom on top of the lettuce. Serve immediately.

Serves 4

Preparation time:
5–8 minutes
Cooking time:
10–12 minutes

4 portobello mushroom caps
2 tablespoons balsamic vinegar
1 tablespoon vegetarian chicken-flavored broth
2 garlic cloves, finely chopped
¼ cup mayonnaise
1 teaspoon lemon juice
¼ teaspoon cayenne pepper, or to taste
1 tablespoon olive oil
1 shallot, chopped
¼ teaspoon black pepper, or to taste
4 romaine lettuce leaves
4 hamburger buns

French Cassoulet

Serves 4

Preparation time: 5–10 minutes
Cooking time: 10–15 minutes

2 teaspoons olive oil
2 cloves garlic, crushed
1 white onion, peeled and chopped
12 ounces Gimme Lean Sausage style meat substitute, cut into
    1" pieces
1 medium tomato, chopped
1 cup tomato sauce
2½ cups drained white cannellini beans
1 bay leaf
1 tablespoon chopped fresh parsley
1½ teaspoons chopped fresh basil
¼ teaspoon salt, or to taste
Black pepper, to taste

Canned cannellini beans take the work out of soaking dried beans overnight. On nights when you're even more rushed than usual, replace the tomato and tomato sauce with 2 cups canned diced tomatoes.

1. Heat the oil in a skillet on medium heat. Add the crushed garlic, onion, and Gimme Lean meat substitute. Sauté for a couple of minutes.

2. Add the tomato, pressing down so that it releases its juices. Continue cooking for 2 to 3 more minutes, until the onion is softened.

3. Add the tomato sauce. Bring to a boil. Add the beans.

4. Add the bay leaf. Stir in the parsley, basil, salt, and pepper.

5. Turn the heat down and simmer, uncovered, for 5 minutes. Remove the bay leaf before serving.

Substituting Herbs

Dried herbs make a handy substitute when you don't have fresh chopped herbs on hand. When substituting dried herbs for fresh, always follow the ⅓ rule: use ⅓ the amount of dried herbs as fresh herbs that are called for in the recipe. In this recipe, for example, the fresh parsley and basil leaves could be replaced with 1 teaspoon dried parsley and ½ teaspoon dried basil.

Stuffed Red Peppers with Garlic Mashed Potatoes

It's hard to overestimate the health benefits of beans—while not completely replacing the protein found in meat, they are high in fiber, low in fat, and full of flavor.

Serves 1

Preparation time:
5 minutes
Cooking time:
10–15 minutes

½ cup leftover Garlic
    Mashed Potatoes
    (page 232)
1 tablespoon vegetarian
    chicken-flavored broth
½ teaspoon granulated
    sugar
⅛ teaspoon hot sauce, or
    to taste
½ cup drained canned
    black beans
2 medium red bell
    peppers, seeded, cut
    in half

1. Heat the garlic mashed potatoes in a small saucepan with the vegetarian chicken-flavored broth. Stir in the sugar and hot sauce. Remove from the heat.

2. In a small bowl, combine the mashed potatoes and beans. Carefully spoon one-quarter of the mixture onto each bell pepper half.

3. Place the bell pepper halves in a microwave-safe baking dish. Cover with plastic wrap, leaving an opening in one corner for steam to vent. Microwave the peppers on high heat for 5 minutes.

4. Give the dish a quarter turn and microwave on high heat for 2 minutes, and then for 1 minute at a time until everything is heated through. Let stand for 5 minutes.

Tofu Cacciatore

This quick and easy stir-fry allows you to enjoy the flavors of chicken cacciatore, traditionally a slowly simmered dish, on busy weeknights.

Serves 3

Preparation time:
5 minutes
Cooking time:
7–8 minutes

16 ounces soft tofu
1½ tablespoons olive oil
1 shallot, chopped
4 ounces vegetarian
   bacon substitute (such
   as Smart Bacon)
1 tomato, thinly sliced
½ cup canned
   mushrooms
⅓ cup vegetarian
   chicken-flavored broth
2 tablespoons tomato
   sauce
1 tablespoon chopped
   fresh basil
1 teaspoon chopped fresh
   thyme
½ teaspoon salt

1. Remove the excess water from the tofu. Cut into 1" cubes.

2. Heat the olive oil in a skillet over medium heat. Add the shallot and bacon substitute. Cook for 2 minutes, then add the tofu. Cook, stirring the tofu cubes gently, for 1 to 2 minutes, until the tofu cubes are browned and the shallot is softened.

3. Push the tofu to the sides of the pan and add the tomato in the middle, pressing down so that it releases its juices. Stir in the canned mushrooms.

4. Add the vegetarian chicken-flavored broth and tomato sauce. Bring to a boil.

5. Stir in the fresh basil and thyme. Stir in the salt. Cook for another minute, stirring to combine the ingredients. Serve hot.

Replacing Meat with Tofu

Protein-rich and low in calories, tofu makes a great substitute for meat in vegetarian cooking. Always be sure to drain the tofu ahead of time so that it can fully absorb the spices and other flavors in a dish. Also, to make up for the lack of the soluble fat in meat that disperses flavor, consider marinating the tofu in a flavorful marinade before cooking.

Spicy Vegetable-Filled Tacos

The spicy combination of herbs and seasonings used to flavor the black beans are the same ones frequently used to marinade beef to make Tex-Mex fajitas.

Serves 6

Preparation time:
5 minutes
Cooking time:
10–15 minutes

6 taco shells
2 teaspoons vegetable oil
¼ cup chopped red onion
2 cups drained canned black beans
6 tablespoons vegetarian chicken-flavored broth
4 teaspoons lime juice
1 teaspoon Asian chili sauce
¼ teaspoon bottled minced garlic
¼ teaspoon ground cumin
¼ teaspoon salt
1 cup fresh shredded cabbage
¾ cup shredded Cheddar cheese

1. Preheat the oven to 350°F. Place the taco shells on an ungreased baking sheet. Bake for 5 to 10 minutes, until warm.

2. While the taco shells are heating, prepare the filling ingredients. Heat the vegetable oil in a saucepan over medium-high heat. Add the onion and sauté for 4 to 5 minutes, until softened.

3. Add the black beans. Stir in the broth, lime juice, chili sauce, minced garlic, cumin, and salt.

4. Remove the taco shells from the oven.

5. Fill each taco with a portion of the black bean mixture. Add the shredded cabbage. Sprinkle with 2 tablespoons of cheese.

Vegetarian Chili

*Nutrient-rich beans take the place of ground beef in this chili
recipe. As always, how much chili powder to use is a matter
of personal taste—feel free to add more if desired.*

1. Heat the oil in a large skillet. Add the bell pepper. Cook, stirring, for
    3 to 4 minutes, until softened.

2. Add the canned corn, kidney beans, and black beans.

3. Stir in the whole tomatoes and the tomato paste.

4. Stir in the seasonings.

5. Bring to a boil, then turn down the heat and simmer for 5 minutes or
    until heated through. Serve hot.

Vegan or Vegetarian?

*Although the terms vegan and vegetarian are both used to refer to
people who don't eat meat, there are some significant differences
between the two. While a vegetarian will not eat meat, poultry, or seafood, vegans eschew all animal products and byproducts, including
eggs, milk, and sometimes honey. So, while all vegans are vegetarian,
not all vegetarians are vegans.*

Vegetarian Fried Rice

Although scrambled egg is frequently added to fried rice dishes, it's not necessary. If you do not have a large skillet, remove the vegetables before stir-frying the rice and add them back in at the end.

1. Heat the oil in a large skillet over medium-high heat. Add the minced ginger, chopped peppers, and onion. Cook, stirring, for about 2 to 3 minutes, until the onion begins to soften. Add the peas and stir-fry for another minute.

2. Push the vegetables to the sides and add the rice in the middle. Heat through, stirring frequently to break up any clumps in the rice.

3. Stir in the soy sauce and lemon juice.

4. Stir in the green onion and cashews.

5. Stir for another minute to heat through. Serve hot.

Serves 4

Preparation time:
5 minutes
Cooking time:
7–8 minutes

2 tablespoons vegetable oil
1 teaspoon bottled minced ginger
1 tablespoon bottled chopped red jalapeño peppers
1 medium onion, peeled and chopped
½ cup frozen peas
3 cups cold cooked brown rice
1½ tablespoons soy sauce
1½ teaspoons lemon juice
2 green onions, chopped
1 cup unsalted cashews

Meal-Size Spinach Salad with Goat Cheese

If not serving the salad immediately, cover and refrigerate. Toss with the lemon juice and vinegar dressing just before serving.

Serves 4

Preparation time:
15 minutes

2 tablespoons lemon juice
1 teaspoon balsamic
vinegar
2 tablespoons olive oil
Black pepper, to taste
¼ teaspoon hot sauce
1 pound (4 cups) fresh
spinach leaves
1 cup sliced fresh
mushrooms
3 tablespoons sun-dried
tomatoes
⅓ cup grated goat
cheese

1. In a small bowl, whisk together the lemon juice, balsamic vinegar, olive oil, pepper, and hot sauce.

2. In a large bowl, combine the spinach and mushrooms.

3. Toss the vegetables with the sun-dried tomatoes and goat cheese.

4. Gently toss with the dressing.

One-Pot Beans and Rice

Feel free to use instant brown rice in this recipe. Begin cooking the instant rice just after adding the onion to the pan.

Serves 4

Preparation time:
5 minutes
Cooking time:
10–12 minutes

1 tablespoon vegetable oil
2 garlic cloves, peeled,
thinly sliced
½ medium onion,
chopped
¼ teaspoon ground
cinnamon
¼ teaspoon ground
allspice
1 tablespoon apple juice
1 (14-ounce) can black
beans, undrained
1 (14-ounce) can
chickpeas, undrained
½ cup chopped tomatoes
1½ cups cooked white or
brown rice

1. Heat the vegetable oil in a skillet on medium-high heat. Add the garlic and onion. Cook, stirring, for 2 to 3 minutes, until the onion begins to soften. Stir in the ground cinnamon, ground allspice, and apple juice while the onion is cooking.

2. Turn the heat down to medium. Add the beans and cook for 3 to 4 minutes to heat through.

3. Add the chopped tomatoes and bring to a boil (turn the heat up if needed).

4. Stir in the cooked rice. Reduce the heat and simmer, uncovered, for 2 to 3 minutes. Serve hot.

Skillet Vegetarian Shepherd's Pie

The vegetarian version of Worcestershire sauce leaves out the anchovies. If not available, you can substitute ¾ teaspoon of soy sauce mixed with ¾ teaspoon of lemon juice.

Serves 2

Preparation time:
8–10 minutes
Cooking time:
12–15 minutes

1 tablespoon margarine
2 tablespoons chopped
    onions
1 cup baby carrots, cut
    in half
1 cup meat substitute,
    such as soy crumbles
½ cup vegetarian beef-
    flavored broth
1½ teaspoons vegetarian
    Worcestershire sauce
½ teaspoon dried
    oregano
¼ teaspoon salt, or to
    taste
¼ teaspoon black pepper,
    or to taste
1 cup leftover Garlic
    Mashed Potatoes
    (page 232)

1. Heat the margarine in a skillet. Add the onion and carrots and cook for 3 to 4 minutes, until softened.

2. Add the soy crumbles, vegetarian beef-flavored broth, and Worcestershire sauce.

3. Stir in the oregano, salt, and pepper. Cook for 5 minutes, or until the soy crumbles are heated through.

4. Stir in the mashed potato. Cook for another minute to heat through. Serve hot.

Cooking with Substitute Beef

Using beef substitutes is a quick and easy way to transform a recipe into a vegetarian dish. However, you may want to make a few adaptations. All ground beef contains a certain amount of fat, which adds extra flavor. To make up for this lack when preparing a vegetarian version of the recipe, try adding extra seasonings.

Tofu Fajitas

Serves 4

Preparation time:
10 minutes
Cooking time: 10 minutes

4 tortilla wraps
1 pound firm tofu, drained
2 tablespoons lime juice
1 teaspoon chili powder
1 teaspoon salt
¼ teaspoon ground
   cumin, or to taste
½ teaspoon freshly
   ground black pepper
¼ teaspoon garlic salt
3 tablespoons extra-virgin
   olive oil, divided
1 onion, chopped
2 tablespoons jarred
   chopped red chilies
2 red bell peppers,
   seeded, cut into
   chunks

Draining tofu earlier in the week substantially reduces the preparation time, making it easier to get a meal on the table in minutes. Store the tofu in a resealable plastic bag in the refrigerator until ready to use.

1. Heat the tortillas according to package directions.

2. Cut the tofu loosely into cubes and crumble (you should have about ½ cup crumbled).

3. In a small bowl, stir together the lime juice, chili powder, salt, cumin, pepper, and garlic salt. Whisk in 2 tablespoons olive oil. Stir the crumbled tofu into the lime juice mixture.

4. Heat 2 tablespoons olive oil in a skillet on medium heat. Add the onion, chopped red chilies, and bell pepper. Sauté for 4 to 5 minutes, then add the tofu mixture. Cook, stirring gently, for another 4 to 5 minutes, until the tofu is browned.

5. Lay a tortilla out in front of you. Spoon about ½ cup of the mixture in the center of the tortilla wrap, taking care not to come too close to the edges. Fold in the left and right sides and roll up the wrap. Repeat with the remainder of the tortillas.

How to Drain Tofu

Drained tofu acts like a super-absorbent sponge, soaking up the flavors of the foods it is cooked with. To drain the tofu, place it in a bowl and weight down with a plate or other heavy object. Let the tofu sit for 15 minutes, then drain off the excess water.

Skillet "Stuffed" Eggplant

Textured vegetable protein (TVP) makes an excellent substitute for ground beef in vegetarian dishes. This dish has the flavor and taste of traditional baked stuffed eggplant, but takes less than 30 minutes to make.

1. Trim the ends from the eggplant and cut into 1" cubes. Place the chopped eggplant in a deep-sided casserole dish and cover with water. Cover the dish with microwave-safe paper, leaving one corner uncovered. Microwave the eggplant on high heat for 5 minutes, or until softened. Remove and drain the eggplant.

2. Heat the oil in a heavy saucepan on medium-high heat. Stir in the minced onion. Add the textured vegetable protein, using a spatula to break it up. Sprinkle the salt and pepper over.

3. Add the crushed tomatoes and tomato paste to the pan. Stir in the brown sugar. Simmer for a few minutes, then stir in the bread crumbs and the cubed eggplant.

4. Cook for 2 to 3 more minutes to mix everything together and heat through. Serve hot.

Serves 4

Preparation time:
5–10 minutes
Cooking time:
15–20 minutes

2 pounds eggplant (1 large eggplant)
2 teaspoons vegetable oil
1 tablespoon minced onion
1 pound textured vegetable protein
½ teaspoon salt
¼ teaspoon black pepper
½ cup crushed tomatoes
1 (6-ounce) can tomato paste
2 teaspoons brown sugar
⅔ cup bread crumbs

Skillet Tofu Stroganoff

Serves 4

Preparation time:
5 minutes
Cooking time:
12–15 minutes

1½ pounds firm tofu,
  drained earlier
2½ cups instant brown or
  white rice
1 tablespoon vegetable oil
1 medium yellow onion,
  chopped
½ teaspoon dry tarragon
1½ cups sliced fresh
  mushrooms
1½ tablespoons red wine
  vinegar
½ cup vegetarian beef-
  flavored broth
¼ teaspoon salt, or to
  taste
¼ teaspoon black pepper,
  or to taste
½ cup natural yogurt

Using natural yogurt instead of sour cream—the traditional way of finishing off beef stroganoff—turns this into a healthy low-fat dish.

1. Cut the tofu into ¾" cubes. Cook the rice according to the instructions in Basic Cooked Instant Rice (page 146) or follow the package directions.

2. While the rice is cooking, heat the oil in a skillet over medium heat. Add the onion and sauté for 3 to 4 minutes to soften. Sprinkle the dry tarragon over the onion.

3. Add the mushrooms and sauté for about 2 minutes, stirring in the red wine vinegar.

4. Add the vegetarian beef-flavored broth, salt, and pepper. Bring to a boil. Add the tofu cubes. Turn the heat down and simmer for 5 minutes.

5. Stir in the yogurt. Serve the stroganoff over the cooked rice.

Know Your Tofu

Tofu comes in a variety of textures, from soft to extra-firm. Firm and extra-firm tofus work best for pan-fried dishes, while the creamy texture of soft tofus makes them perfect for puddings and other desserts.

Microwave Garden Vegetable Lasagna

For a vegan version of this dish, replace the cottage cheese with crumbled firm tofu that has been combined with the seasonings, and the mozzarella cheese with mozzarella-flavored soy cheese.

1. In a medium bowl, stir together the crushed tomatoes and the cottage cheese. Stir in the mozzarella cheese, basil, oregano, and pepper.

2. Lay out one of the zucchini in a deep-sided casserole dish that is microwave-safe. Add half of the spinach.

3. Spoon about half of the cheese and tomato mixture over the spinach. Repeat with the remainder of the zucchini, spinach, and cheese and tomato mixture.

4. Cover the dish with microwave-safe wax paper. Microwave on high heat for 3 minutes. Give the dish a quarter turn and microwave for 2 minutes at a time until the cheese is cooked (total cooking time should be 7 to 9 minutes).

5. Sprinkle the Parmesan cheese over the top. Let stand for at least 5 minutes before serving.

Serves 4

Preparation time:
10 minutes
Cooking time: 10 minutes

2 cups crushed tomatoes
1¼ cups cottage cheese
¼ cup mozzarella cheese
¼ teaspoon dried basil
¼ teaspoon dried
   oregano
⅛ teaspoon black pepper
2 zucchini, thinly sliced
1 cup frozen spinach,
   thawed and drained
3 tablespoons Parmesan
   cheese

Tofu and Cashew Stir-Fry

Serves 4

Preparation time:
5 minutes
Cooking time:
7–8 minutes

1 pound firm tofu, drained
½ cup vegetarian
    chicken-flavored broth
¼ cup soy sauce
2 tablespoons lemon juice
1 teaspoon granulated
    sugar
1 teaspoon cornstarch
2 tablespoons vegetable
    oil
1 teaspoon minced ginger
2½ cups fresh stir-fry
    vegetables
2 tablespoons water,
    optional
½ cup unsalted cashews

Draining the tofu earlier in the day means that this simple stir-fry can go from kitchen to table in under 15 minutes.

1. Cut the tofu into ¾" cubes.

2. In a small bowl, stir together the vegetarian chicken-flavored broth, soy sauce, lemon juice, and sugar. Whisk in the cornstarch.

3. Heat the oil in a heavy skillet or wok over medium-high heat. Add the minced ginger. Stir for a few seconds, then add the stir-fry vegetables, pushing them around the pan constantly so that they don't burn. (Add 1 or 2 tablespoons water if needed to keep the vegetables from burning.) Stir-fry for 2 to 3 minutes, until they are tender but still crisp.

4. Add the tofu cubes. Cook for 1 or 2 minutes, gently stirring the cubes, until they are browned.

5. Stir the sauce and swirl into the pan. Bring to a boil and cook for about 2 more minutes to heat through. Stir in the cashews. Serve hot.

Freezing Tofu

Freezing tofu gives it a chewy, meatier texture. For best results, use firm or extra-firm tofu. Drain the tofu before freezing (see How to Drain Tofu, page 186) and wrap tightly in plastic. Use the tofu within three months.

Sweet-and-Sour Tofu

Drained tofu acts like a sponge, absorbing the flavorful sweet-and-sour sauce. For best results, be sure to use extra-firm tofu, which can hold its shape during stir-frying.

1. In a small bowl, stir together the pineapple juice, water, vinegar, brown sugar, ketchup, and soy sauce.

2. Cut the tofu into 1" cubes. Heat the oil in a heavy skillet over medium-high heat. Add the ginger and let brown for 2 minutes. Remove the ginger.

3. Add the celery. Stir-fry for 2 minutes, stirring constantly. Add the red bell peppers. Add the straw mushrooms. Cook for another minute. (Splash the vegetables with 1 to 2 tablespoons of water if they begin to dry out during stir-frying.)

4. Add the tofu cubes. Cook, stirring, for about 1 minute to brown the tofu.

5. Stir the sauce and add it to the pan. Bring to a boil, and cook for about 2 minutes, stirring, to thicken. Serve hot.

Serves 4

Preparation time:
5–10 minutes
Cooking time:
8–10 minutes

¼ cup pineapple juice
½ cup water
¼ cup vinegar
¼ cup brown sugar
2 tablespoons ketchup
2 teaspoons soy sauce
1 pound extra-firm tofu,
    drained earlier
2 tablespoons vegetable
    oil
2 thin slices ginger
2 ribs celery, sliced on the
    diagonal
1 medium red bell
    pepper, cut into
    chunks
1 cup straw mushrooms

Chapter 13

When You Only Have Ten Minutes

Fast Ground Beef Stroganoff

Traditionally, this Russian dish is made with fillet of beef, but ground beef makes a quick and easy substitute.

Serves 4
_____

Preparation time:
5 minutes
Cooking time:
5–10 minutes

2 cups leftover cooked
    noodles
1 tablespoon olive oil
½ teaspoon bottled
    minced garlic
2 cups leftover cooked
    ground beef
2 tablespoons tomato
    paste
2 tablespoons dried
    minced onion
½ teaspoon dried parsley
    flakes, or to taste
½ teaspoon dried basil
¼ teaspoon black pepper
1 cup drained canned
    mushrooms
¼ cup beef bouillon
¼ cup plain yogurt

1. Reheat the pasta (see Serving Leftover Pasta, page 169).

2. Heat the olive oil in a skillet over medium-high heat. Add the garlic and the cooked ground beef. Cook for a minute to heat through, stirring in the tomato paste, minced onion, parsley, basil, and pepper.

3. Add the mushrooms. Sauté for 1 minute and add the beef bouillon. Bring to a boil.

4. Remove the skillet from the heat and stir in the yogurt. Serve hot over the noodles.

Pan-Fried Steak with Italian Pesto

The actual cooking time for this dish will depend on how well done you like your steak.

Serves 4
_____

Preparation time:
2–3 minutes
Cooking time: 10 minutes

2 teaspoons lemon
    pepper seasoning
½ teaspoon salt
1 pound beef tenderloin
    steaks
1 tablespoon olive oil
½ cup Italian pesto

1. Rub the lemon pepper seasoning and salt over the steaks.

2. Heat the olive oil in a skillet over medium-high heat.

3. Add the steaks to the pan. To cook the steaks to medium doneness, cook for 8 to 10 minutes, turning halfway through cooking.

4. Serve the steaks with the pesto.

Pan-Fried Seafood with Tarragon Cream Sauce

A simple white sauce adds flavor to pan-fried halibut. If you like, make the sauce ahead of time and store in a sealed container in the refrigerator until ready to use. Reheat in a saucepan over low heat, stirring continually.

Serves 4

Preparation time:
3–5 minutes
Cooking time: 10 minutes

1 tablespoon olive oil
1 teaspoon bottled
    minced ginger
1 shallot, chopped
4 (5-ounce) halibut steaks
4 tablespoons unsalted
    butter
3½ tablespoons flour
½ teaspoon dried
    tarragon
¾ cup milk
¼ cup heavy cream
½ teaspoon ground
    nutmeg, or to taste
⅛ teaspoon black or white
    pepper, or to taste
1 teaspoon lemon juice

1. Heat the olive oil in a skillet over medium-high heat. Add the ginger, shallot, and halibut.

2. Cook the halibut for 5 minutes, turn, and cook for 4 to 5 minutes more, until it is cooked through.

3. While the halibut is frying, prepare the cream sauce: In a small saucepan, melt the butter on low heat. Add the flour and blend it into the melted butter, stirring continually, until it thickens and forms a roux (3 to 5 minutes). Stir in the tarragon.

4. Increase the heat to medium. Slowly add the milk and the cream, stirring with a whisk until the mixture has thickened. Stir in the nutmeg, pepper, and lemon juice.

5. Pour the cream sauce over the halibut steaks and serve.

Fast Foil-Wrapped Fish

Another great way to quickly cook fish is to wrap it in foil and bake it in the oven. This technique, called en papillote, allows the fish to steam in its own juices, locking in the flavor. Add your favorite mixed vegetables, finish with an assortment of seasonings (fresh ginger, green onion, lemon juice, or soy sauce are all good choices), and you've got a complete meal!

Orange-Glazed Fish Fillets

Serve this flavorful seafood dish with Sautéed Asparagus (page 228) or Thai-Style Creamed Corn (page 225) and cooked rice.

Serves 4

Preparation time:
2–3 minutes
Cooking time: 8 minutes

2 tablespoons olive oil
2 tablespoons orange
    juice
1 tablespoon
    Worcestershire sauce
2 teaspoons chopped
    fresh cilantro
½ teaspoon paprika
1½ pounds red snapper
    fillets

1. Spray a rack with nonstick cooking spray.

2. In a small bowl, whisk together the olive oil, orange juice, Worcestershire sauce, cilantro, and paprika.

3. Brush the marinade over the fish fillets.

4. Broil the fish for 4 minutes. Turn over, brush with the marinade and continue for another 4 to 5 minutes, until the fish is cooked through. (Be sure not to overcook the fish.)

Spicy Scallop Ceviche

Be careful not to overcook the scallops—remove them from the heat as soon as they change color. If you don't have time to thaw the frozen scallops, you can also use cooked shrimp.

Serves 2

Preparation time:
5 minutes
Cooking time: 5 minutes

1 tablespoon olive oil
1 teaspoon bottled
    minced garlic
1 pound fresh or thawed
    frozen bay scallops
2 tablespoons lime juice
3 tablespoons lemon juice
3 tablespoons ketchup
1 teaspoon chili powder
¼ teaspoon salt
⅛ teaspoon black pepper
1 teaspoon minced onion
1 medium cucumber,
    peeled, thinly sliced

1. Heat the olive oil in a skillet over medium-high heat.

2. Add the garlic and the scallops. Cook for 4 to 5 minutes, until the scallops turn opaque.

3. In a small mixing bowl, whisk together the lime juice, lemon juice, ketchup, chili powder, salt, pepper, and minced onion.

4. Place the scallops and cucumber in a salad bowl. Toss with the dressing. Serve immediately.

Meal-Size Indonesian-Style Potato Salad

The Indonesian version of potato salad, Gado Gado salad, is a popular restaurant dish. This simplified version is perfect for busy weekdays during the summer months.

Serves 3

Preparation time:
7–8 minutes

*Spicy Peanut Sauce
(page 252)*
*2 leftover cooked
potatoes, cut into
chunks*
*3½ cups packaged salad
greens*
*3 leftover hard-boiled
eggs, peeled and
sliced*

1. Start preparing the Spicy Peanut Sauce (page 252).

2. While the sauce is heating, assemble the salad ingredients on a large serving platter, with the potatoes on the outside, the greens on the inside, and the hard-boiled eggs on top.

3. Pour the peanut sauce over the salad. Serve immediately.

Make-Ahead Gado Gado Salad

If you're planning to prepare a potato salad for a picnic or other outdoor gathering, you may want to do as much work as possible ahead of time. In the case of this Meal-Size Indonesian-Style Potato Salad, the hard-boiled eggs can be prepared up to five days ahead of time, while the peanut sauce can be made up to three days ahead of time. Shell the eggs, assemble the salad, and garnish with the peanut sauce just before serving (thin the sauce with a bit of water if needed).

Veggie-Loaded Salad Rolls

Feel free to use Asian rice paper wrappers instead of tortilla wrappers to make the salad rolls if desired. Thai basil leaves can be found in the produce section of many supermarkets, or you can use regular basil.

Serves 10

Preparation time:
15 minutes

⅓ cup soy sauce
1 tablespoon white
   vinegar
1 tablespoon granulated
   sugar
1 teaspoon bottled
   minced garlic
1 tablespoon bottled
   chopped jalapeño
   peppers
1½ cups packaged salad
   greens
1 cup cooked shrimp
¼ cup chopped fresh Thai
   basil leaves
8 vegetable-flavored
   tortilla wrappers

1. In a small bowl, stir together the soy sauce, vinegar, sugar, garlic, and jalapeño peppers.

2. In a bowl, stir together the salad greens, cooked shrimp, and basil leaves.

3. Lay a tortilla wrapper on a cutting board in front of you. Place about ¼ cup of the shrimp and salad mix on the bottom half of the wrapper, being careful not to come too close to the edges.

4. Roll up the wrapper like a taco, tucking in the sides. Continue filling and rolling up the remainder of the wrappers.

5. Serve the rolls cold with the soy dipping sauce.

Glazed Ham

A flavorful orange sauce, sweetened with brown sugar, is the perfect accompaniment for cooked ham. Serve the ham with Garlic Mashed Potatoes (page 232) and Quick Green Beans Amandine (page 222).

Serves 4

Preparation time:
5 minutes
Cooking time: 5 minutes

½ pound cooked ham,
   sliced
4 tablespoons orange
   juice
3 tablespoons white wine
1 teaspoon Dijon mustard
2 tablespoons brown
   sugar
½ teaspoon bottled
   minced ginger

1. Lay out the ham slices on a plate.

2. In a small saucepan, bring the orange juice, white wine, Dijon mustard, brown sugar, and ginger to a boil, stirring to dissolve the sugar.

3. Pour the sauce over the ham slices.

Simple Shrimp Pasta

Using reserved shrimp juice adds extra flavor to this simple dish with leftover shrimp and pasta. Instead of Parmesan cheese, you can use another cheese, such as a shredded Italian cheese blend, if desired.

1. Reheat the pasta (see Serving Leftover Pasta, page 169).

2. Heat the olive oil with the garlic in a skillet over medium-high heat. Add the tomato, pressing down so that it releases its juices.

3. Add the shrimp. Sauté for a minute to heat through.

4. Add the Marinated Artichoke Hearts (page 229) and the reserved shrimp juice. Stir in the pepper.

5. Serve the shrimp over the cooked pasta. Sprinkle with the Parmesan cheese.

Serves 4

Preparation time:
2–3 minutes
Cooking time:
7–8 minutes

2 cups leftover cooked pasta
2 teaspoons olive oil
1 teaspoon bottled minced garlic
1 large tomato, thinly sliced
2 cups drained canned shrimp
Marinated Artichoke Hearts (page 229)
2 tablespoons reserved shrimp juice
⅛ teaspoon black pepper, or to taste
⅓ cup shredded Parmesan cheese

Leftover Coconut Chicken

A Southeast Asian condiment made with fermented fish, fish sauce is found in the ethnic section of many supermarkets, or you can substitute 1½ tablespoons of soy sauce. Serve this flavorful dish with steamed jasmine or basmati rice.

Serves 4

Preparation time:
5 minutes
Cooking time:
5–7 minutes

½ cup light coconut milk
3 tablespoons peanut
   butter
1 tablespoon brown sugar
1 tablespoon Asian fish
   sauce
1 tablespoon lime juice
1 teaspoon Tabasco
   sauce
1 tablespoon olive oil
1 teaspoon bottled
   minced garlic
1 pound cooked chicken
   meat
1 cup drained canned
   asparagus

1. In a medium mixing bowl, whisk together the coconut milk, peanut butter, brown sugar, fish sauce, lime juice, and Tabasco sauce.

2. Heat the olive oil in a skillet on medium-high heat. Add the garlic.

3. Add the chicken and asparagus. Cook for a minute, stirring, to heat through.

4. Whisk the coconut milk mixture one more time. Add it to the pan and bring to a boil.

5. Cook for another minute, stirring to blend all the flavors. Serve hot.

Storing Leftover Food

Always store leftover food within two hours after cooking, in shallow, sealed containers. With a few exceptions, most leftover food can be used safely for up to three days. Throw away any stored food that looks unusual or has a strange odor.

Pan-Fried Steak with Fresh Fruit

If ripe peaches aren't in season, you can substitute 1 cup of drained canned peaches. Serve the stir-fried steak over cooked rice.

1. In a medium bowl, combine the beef with the soy sauce, red wine vinegar, pepper, and cornstarch.

2. In a small bowl, stir together the orange juice, water, and honey.

3. Heat the oil in a skillet over medium-high heat. Add the minced ginger. Stir-fry for 10 seconds. Add the beef strips. Let brown for 30 seconds, then stir-fry, moving the strips around the pan. Stir-fry the beef for 3 to 5 minutes, until it loses its pinkness and is nearly cooked through.

4. Push the beef to the sides of the pan. Add the peaches to the middle of the pan. Stir-fry the peaches for a minute.

5. Stir the orange juice mixture and pour into the pan. Bring to a boil. Cook for another minute to blend all the flavors. Serve hot.

Serves 4

Preparation time:
5 minutes
Cooking time: 5 minutes

¾ pound beef stir-fry strips
1 tablespoon soy sauce
1 tablespoon red wine vinegar
Black pepper, to taste
2 teaspoons cornstarch
2 tablespoons orange juice
2 tablespoons water
1 teaspoon liquid honey
1 tablespoon vegetable oil
1 teaspoon bottled, minced gingerroot
2 large peaches, not overripe, sliced

Easy Cajun Shrimp

Serves 4

Preparation time:
5 minutes
Cooking time: 5 minutes

1 tablespoon
    Worcestershire sauce
1 tablespoon lemon juice
2 tablespoons ketchup
1 tablespoon water
1 pound shelled,
    deveined medium
    shrimp
3 tablespoons Cajun
    Spice seasoning
1 tablespoon margarine

A salt-based mixture with chili powder and other spices, Cajun Spice seasoning can be found in the spice section of most supermarkets. To turn this into a one-dish meal, add two thinly sliced ribs of celery, prepare a double portion of sauce, and serve over cooked rice.

1. In a small bowl, stir together the Worcestershire sauce, lemon juice, ketchup, and water.

2. Rinse the shrimp and pat dry with paper towels. Place the shrimp in a bowl and toss with the Cajun Spice seasoning.

3. Melt the margarine in a skillet over medium-high heat, tilting the skillet so that the margarine covers the bottom of the pan.

4. Add the shrimp to the pan. Cook for about 3 minutes, until they turn pink.

5. Add the sauce and bring to a boil. Stir to mix everything together. Serve hot.

Reheating Leftovers

Instead of simply warming the food, reheat leftovers to an internal temperature of 165°F before serving This kills any bacteria that may have formed. Be sure to bring soups, sauces, and gravies to a rolling boil before reusing.

Stir-Fried Ground Turkey Paprikash

Sweet Hungarian paprika works best in this recipe, but if it is unavailable you can use hotter Spanish paprika.

Serves 4

Preparation time:
3–4 minutes
Cooking time:
5–6 minutes

2 cups leftover cooked
    pasta
1 tablespoon vegetable oil
1 teaspoon bottled
    minced garlic
½ sweet onion, peeled
    and chopped
1 tablespoon paprika
½ teaspoon ground cumin
1 cup packaged stir-fry
    vegetables
½ cup canned or
    packaged beef broth
2 cups leftover cooked
    ground turkey
½ cup low-fat yogurt

1. Reheat the pasta (see Serving Leftover Pasta, page 169).

2. Heat the oil in a skillet over medium-high heat. Add the garlic and onion. Stir-fry for 2 minutes, sprinkling the paprika and ground cumin over the onion.

3. Add the stir-fry vegetables. Stir-fry for 2 minutes or until the vegetables begin to soften. Splash with 1 tablespoon of the beef broth if they begin to dry out.

4. Add the ground turkey and stir-fry for a minute to heat through. Add the beef broth and bring to a boil.

5. Stir in the yogurt. Serve over the reheated noodles.

Got Leftover Leftovers?

Although it may be tempting, discard any reheated leftovers that aren't consumed the second time around. There is some evidence that reheating food more than once increases the risk of foodborne illness.

Easy Cooked Shrimp Scampi with Leftover Pasta

Did you know: scampi is the Italian word for shrimp.

Serves 4

Preparation time:
5 minutes
Cooking time: 5 minutes

2 cups leftover cooked
    pasta
1 tablespoon olive oil
1 teaspoon lemon juice
½ stick unsalted butter
1 tablespoon bottled
    minced garlic
2 cups cooked shrimp
¼ teaspoon paprika
1 tablespoon chopped
    fresh parsley

1. Reheat the pasta (see Serving Leftover Pasta, page 169).

2. Heat the olive oil, lemon juice, butter, and garlic in a skillet over medium heat, stirring to melt the butter. (Turn down the heat if the butter begins sizzling.)

3. Add the shrimp. Cook for a minute, stirring to heat through and mix it in with the melted butter.

4. Stir in the paprika and fresh parsley.

5. Serve the shrimp over the reheated pasta.

Chapter 14
Grilling

Basic Grilled Steak with Barbecue Sauce

Serves 4

Preparation time:
10 minutes
Cooking time:
10 minutes

1½ pounds flank steak
½ cup store-bought
   barbecue sauce

Instead of store-bought barbecue sauce, you can also use Spicy Barbecue Sauce (page 250) in this recipe. Just prepare the sauce ahead of time and refrigerate until ready to use. How much barbecue sauce to use is a matter of personal preference; feel free to add more if desired.

1   Preheat the grill.

2.   Trim the steak of excess fat.

3.   Arrange the beef on the hottest part of the grill.

4.   Grill, turning occasionally, until the beef is cooked (about 8 minutes). Brush the steak with the barbecue sauce during the last few minutes of cooking.

5.   Let the steak rest for 2 to 3 minutes before serving.

Barbecue Sauce

Tomato-based, with brown sugar and vinegar, the classic barbecue sauce is an intriguing combination of sweet and tart flavors. Spices in the sauce frequently include cayenne pepper and garlic.

Grilled Steak and Onion Salad

*This marinade tenderizes lean flank steak, making it
perfect for grilling.*

1. Preheat the grill.

2. In a medium bowl, combine the balsamic vinegar, olive oil, Worcestershire sauce, shallots, salt, parsley, and basil.

3. Arrange the beef on the hottest part of the grill. Brush with the balsamic vinegar dressing.

4. Grill the beef, turning occasionally and basting with the dressing, until it is cooked (about 8 minutes).

5. Let the steak rest for 2 to 3 minutes. Cut into thin strips and serve with the salad greens.

Serves 4

Preparation time:
10 minutes
Cooking time:
10–12 minutes

¼ cup balsamic vinegar
¼ cup olive oil
2 tablespoons
   Worcestershire sauce
2 shallots, chopped
½ teaspoon salt
1 tablespoon fresh
   chopped parsley
1 teaspoon chopped fresh
   basil leaves
1½ pounds flank steak
3 cups packaged salad
   greens

Grilled Corn on the Cob

Serves 6

Preparation time:
25 minutes
Cooking time:
30–40 minutes

6 ears sweet corn, husks
    on
4 tablespoons olive oil, or
    as needed
¼ cup melted butter, or
    as needed

*Grilling corn on the cob takes more time than many other types
of vegetables but the results are worth it. Corn on the cob is
a natural for the grill, as the husks help protect the sweet
corn from drying out. For extra flavor, use a flavored herb
butter to brush on the corn.*

1. Remove the thin strands of silk from the corn. Fill a large saucepan with enough cold water to cover the corn. Add the corn and let it soak for 20 minutes.

2. While the corn is soaking, preheat the grill.

3. Drain the corn thoroughly. Carefully pull back the husks as far as possible without removing them. Pull off any excess silk. Brush the olive oil over the ears of corn with a pastry brush, using about 1 tablespoon per ear of corn. Smooth the husks back over the corn and tie at the ends with an extra piece of husk or with a piece of twine.

4. Grill the corn on medium heat for 30 to 40 minutes, turning occasionally, until it is tender when pierced with a fork. Remove the corn from the grill and pull off the husks. (Be sure to wear oven mitts, as the corn and husks are hot.) Serve the corn with the melted butter.

Preparing Vegetables for Grilling

As with meat, poultry, and seafood, the high heat needed for grilling can dry out vegetables. A simple way to prevent this is to soak the vegetables in cold water for 30 minutes prior to cooking. Pat the soaked vegetables dry with paper towels and brush with a bit of olive oil before placing them on the grill.

Teriyaki Chicken

Lemon juice tenderizes the meat in this acid-based marinade, while olive oil disperses the sweet teriyaki flavor through the chicken. Instead of a bowl, you can marinate the chicken in a large zip-top bag, turning occasionally to make sure the chicken is coated.

Serves 4

Preparation time:
10 minutes
Marinating time: 2 hours
Cooking time:
15–20 minutes

4 boneless, skinless
    chicken breast halves
    (about 1½ pounds)
½ cup teriyaki sauce
⅓ cup olive oil
⅓ cup lemon juice
1 teaspoon bottled
    minced ginger
Salt and pepper, to taste

1. Rinse the chicken breasts and pat dry. Cut a few diagonal slits in the chicken to allow the marinade to penetrate.

2. In a large bowl, whisk together the teriyaki sauce, olive oil, lemon juice, minced ginger, salt, and pepper. Reserve ¼ cup to use as a basting sauce.

3. Add the chicken. Marinate in the refrigerator for 2 hours, turning once to ensure the chicken is completely coated in the marinade.

4. Preheat the grill.

5. Grill the chicken until it is cooked through (10 to 15 minutes), turning every 5 minutes and basting with the reserved marinade.

Using Marinades for Basting

A flavorful marinade makes a great basting sauce. However, there are potential health risks if the marinade has sat holding raw food. Be sure to stop basting at least 5 minutes before removing the food from the grill. The safest solution is to double up the marinade recipe, reserving half to use as a basting sauce.

Thai-Style Lime Chicken

Made from tamarind fruit—a tropical fruit that is rich in antioxidants—tamarind paste can be found in many Asian or ethnic supermarkets.

Serves 4

Preparation time:
10 minutes
Cooking time: 15 minutes

⅓ cup lime juice
⅓ cup olive oil
2 tablespoons fish sauce
1 tablespoon soy sauce
2 tablespoons tamarind
  paste
1 teaspoon bottled
  minced garlic
¼ cup chopped fresh
  cilantro leaves
4 boneless, skinless
  chicken breast halves

1. Preheat the grill.

2. In a blender, process the lime juice, olive oil, fish sauce, soy sauce, tamarind paste, garlic, and cilantro until smooth.

3. Place the marinade and the chicken breasts in a large, resealable plastic bag. Marinate the chicken in the refrigerator for at least 15 minutes. Remove and drain off excess marinade.

4. Place the chicken on the grill. Grill for 15 minutes or until the chicken is cooked through, turning over halfway through cooking.

Easy Korean Bulgogi

In this quick and easy version of the popular Korean dish, a soy sauce and sesame oil dressing is brushed on the steak while it is cooking. On evenings when you have more time, you can double the amount of dressing and use it to marinate the beef for at least 15 minutes before grilling.

Serves 4

Preparation time:
10 minutes
Cooking time: 10 minutes

4 tablespoons Kikkoman
    soy sauce
2 tablespoons apple cider
    vinegar
2 tablespoons Asian dark
    sesame oil
1 teaspoon bottled
    minced garlic
2 tablespoons granulated
    sugar
2 pounds beef sirloin
    steak, thinly sliced
2 tablespoons toasted
    white sesame seeds

1. Preheat the grill. In a small bowl, stir together the soy sauce, apple cider vinegar, sesame oil, garlic, and sugar.

2. Arrange the beef on the hottest part of the grill. Brush with the dressing.

3. Grill the beef, turning occasionally and basting with the dressing, until it is cooked, about 8 minutes.

4. While the steak is grilling, toast the sesame seeds in a frying pan over medium-low heat, shaking the pan continually, until the seeds turn golden and have a nutty flavor (about 5 minutes). Pour the seeds over the steak.

5. Let the steak rest for 2 to 3 minutes. Cut into thin strips. Serve with salad greens.

Bulgogi Trimmings

Traditionally, bulgogi is served with a number of side dishes, including sticky rice, green onions, and lettuce for wrapping up the cooked meat. Condiments include a dipping sauce made with Asian sesame oil and salt, soybean paste, and spicy Korean pepper paste.

Japanese Sukiyaki

Sake, the Japanese version of rice wine, has a sweeter | flavor than Chinese rice wine. Sake can commonly be found in liquor stores.

Preparation time:
15 minutes
Cooking time: 15 minutes

1½ pounds sirloin steak
1 cup Kikkoman soy
   sauce
½ cup Japanese sake
6 tablespoons granulated
   sugar
2 green onions, thinly
   chopped
8 ounces fresh shiitake
   mushrooms, cleaned,
   stems removed

1. Preheat the grill. Cut the beef into thin strips about 3" long.

2. In a medium bowl, combine the soy sauce, sake, sugar, and chopped green onions. Pour half the mixture into a separate bowl. Add the thinly sliced beef and marinate for 10 minutes.

3. Heat the reserved half of the mixture in a saucepan over medium-low heat. Keep warm on low heat while the steak is cooking.

4. Thread the marinated beef and the mushrooms onto skewers. Cook for 5 minutes, turn, and grill for 5 more minutes.

5. Serve the beef with the reserved heated marinade to use as a dipping sauce.

Buffalo Wings

Grilling the wings and using store-bought blue cheese dressing takes most of the work out of this spicy appetizer from Buffalo, New York. Use your favorite brand of hot sauce.

Serves 5

Preparation time:
10 minutes
Cooking time: 10 minutes

1 teaspoon salt
1 teaspoon black pepper
15 chicken wings
1½ tablespoons apple
    cider vinegar
1¼ cups blue cheese
    dressing
1 stick unsalted butter
½ cup hot sauce

1. Preheat the grill. Rub the salt and pepper over the chicken wings.

2. In a medium bowl, stir the vinegar into the blue cheese dressing.

3. In a saucepan on low heat, melt the butter with the hot sauce, stirring.

4. Place the chicken wings on the grill and brush with the butter and hot sauce mixture.

5. Grill the wings for 10 minutes or until they are cooked, turning halfway and brushing frequently with the hot butter. Serve the wings with the blue cheese dressing for dipping.

Grill Your Potato Salad

Potato salad is a popular side dish for Buffalo wings, but preparing it ahead of time can lead to food safety issues. An easy way to avoid the problem is to prepare your potato salad on the grill. Partially cook the potatoes by boiling them until they can be pierced with a knife, but are not tender. Grill the potatoes on high heat for approximately 20 minutes, until tender, then combine them in a large bowl with cooked bacon, celery, onion, or whatever else you prefer. Toss the salad with your favorite mustard or red wine vinaigrette.

Grilled Tuna Steaks

Serves 4

Preparation time:
5 minutes
Cooking time: 10 minutes

½ cup olive oil
3 tablespoons lemon juice
¼ teaspoon black pepper
4 tuna steaks, 8 ounces
  each
Simple Salsa Verde (page
  248)

Not sure how long to cook tuna? For well-done tuna, grill for 9 to 10 minutes, until it is opaque right through. For medium doneness, cook the tuna for 6 to 7 minutes.

1. Preheat the grill.

2. In a small bowl, stir together the olive oil, lemon juice, and pepper. Brush over the tuna steaks.

3. Place the tuna on the hottest part of the grill. Cook for 10 minutes or to the desired level of doneness, using tongs to turn the tuna over halfway through cooking and taking care not to overcook.

4. Serve the grilled tuna with the Simple Salsa Verde (page 248).

Pork Satay with Spicy Peanut Sauce

Serves 6

Preparation time:
10 minutes
Marinating time:
30 minutes
Cooking time: 10 minutes

1½ pounds boneless pork
  loin
Spicy Peanut Sauce
  (page 252)

Using bamboo skewers to grill the pork? Be sure to soak them in water for 30 minutes to keep them from burning.

1. Cut the pork into 1" cubes.

2. Arrange the pork in a shallow glass dish. Stir in the peanut sauce.

3. Marinate the pork in the refrigerator for 30 minutes.

4. Heat the grill. Thread the pork onto bamboo skewers.

5. Grill the pork for about 10 minutes, until it is cooked through, turning occasionally.

Grilled Salmon

Serve this simple dish with Grilled Harvest Vegetables (page 217) or Instant Mashed Potato Salad (page 64) for a quick and easy meal.

Serves 4

Preparation time:
10 minutes
Cooking time: 15 minutes

1 cup peach yogurt
¼ cup olive oil
2 teaspoons dried dill
  leaves
½ teaspoon salt
4 salmon fillets, 8 ounces
  each

1. Preheat the grill.

2. In a small bowl, stir together the yogurt, olive oil, dill leaves, and salt.

3. Take a piece of aluminum foil and cut it into four rectangular pieces, each large enough to wrap around one salmon fillet.

4. Place the fillets in the foil squares and brush liberally with the yogurt mixture. Close up the foil packet.

5. Place the packets on the grill. Grill the salmon for 15 minutes or until it is cooked through.

Choosing Fish for the Grill

It's best to use a firm-fleshed, thickly cut fish that won't fall apart on the grill. Trout, swordfish, salmon, halibut, and red snapper are all good choices. Some delicate fishes like flounder may take on the taste of the charcoal and so aren't ideal candidates for grilling. You'll also want to avoid any fish that flakes easily, such as haddock or pollack.

Grilled Portobello Mushrooms

Serves 4

Preparation time:
5 minutes
Cooking time: 15 minutes

1 pound portobello
    mushrooms
½ stick unsalted butter
¼ cup olive oil
2 tablespoons balsamic
    vinegar
1 shallot, chopped
½ teaspoon salt
½ teaspoon dried parsley
½ teaspoon dried basil
    leaves

Flavorful portobello mushrooms are a great choice for grilling—cooking enhances their meaty flavor, and their high water content and thick texture means they won't dry out during cooking or fall apart on the grill.

1. Preheat the grill.

2. Wash the mushrooms and remove the stems.

3. In a small saucepan over low heat, melt the butter with the olive oil, balsamic vinegar, shallot, salt, parsley, and basil.

4. Place the mushroom caps on the grill with the gills facing upward. Brush the mushrooms with some of the melted butter mixture.

5. Grill the mushrooms for up to 10 minutes or until they are tender, turning halfway and brushing frequently with the melted butter mixture.

Grilled Harvest Vegetables

Soaking the vegetables before grilling helps prevent them from drying out. Serve the grilled vegetables with garlic aioli—a French garlic and oil sauce that is available at most supermarkets.

Serves 6

Preparation time:
30 minutes
Cooking time: 6 minutes

⅔ cup olive oil
3 red bell peppers, cut in
    half, seeds removed
2 sweet onions, peeled,
    cut into quarters
3 zucchini, thinly sliced
10 button mushrooms,
    cleaned, stems
    removed

1. Preheat the grill.

2. Soak all the vegetables in water for 30 minutes. Drain.

3. Use a pastry brush to brush the olive oil over the vegetables.

4. Lay the bell pepper halves, onions, and zucchini slices directly on the grill. Place the mushrooms in a grilling basket and lower onto the grill.

5. Grill the vegetables for 5 to 6 minutes or until they are cooked through, turning over halfway during cooking. (Cooking times for individual vegetables may vary slightly.)

Grill Baskets

Grill baskets are ideal for cooking smaller pieces of food such as shrimp or mushrooms that can fall through the grilling rack, or for fragile foods such as fish fillets. To ensure the food doesn't stick to the basket, spray it with a nonstick cooking spray, or brush with oil before adding the food. Depending on the design, the grill basket may have a long heat-proof handle to make it easier to manipulate the food. If yours does not, be sure to wear oven mitts.

Grilled Chicken Salad

Serves 4

Preparation time:
10 minutes
Cooking time: 15 minutes

⅓ cup olive oil
⅓ cup red wine vinegar
2 tablespoons soy sauce
1 teaspoon Dijon mustard
½ teaspoon salt, or to
taste
⅛ teaspoon black pepper,
or to taste
1 tablespoon minced
onion
1 pound boneless,
skinless chicken
breast halves
1 head lettuce
1 pint cherry tomatoes
1 English cucumber, thinly
sliced
½ cup crumbled feta
cheese
12 whole pitted olives,
chopped

A simple mixture of olive oil, red wine vinegar, soy sauce, and spices doubles as marinade and salad dressing in this easy recipe that is perfect for summer entertaining.

1. Preheat the grill. In a medium bowl, whisk together the olive oil, red wine vinegar, soy sauce, mustard, salt, pepper, and minced onion. Reserve ¼ cup to baste the chicken.

2. Place the chicken breasts on the grill and brush with the reserved marinade. Grill the chicken until it is cooked through, turning every 5 minutes and brushing with the marinade (total cooking time will be about 10–15 minutes).

3. While the chicken is grilling, combine the lettuce, tomatoes, and cucumber in a large salad bowl.

4. Let the chicken cool for a few minutes, and then shred, tearing it into small strips with your hands.

5. Mix the chicken into the salad. Whisk the remaining dressing one more time and then pour it into the salad and gently toss. Sprinkle the crumbled feta cheese and olives on top.

Chapter 15
Vegetable Sides

Microwave French Fries

Preparing French fries in the microwave is quicker and healthier than deep-frying them in hot oil. Be sure not to overcook the potatoes or they will deflate and become soft.

Serves 2

Preparation time:
5–7 minutes
Cooking time:
15–20 minutes

½ pound (2 medium) russet or red potatoes, peeled
¼ cup white vinegar
¼ teaspoon garlic salt
¼ teaspoon cayenne pepper

1. Scrub the potatoes under cold running water and use a paring knife to cut out any bruises or green spots. Cut into thin strips the size and shape of French fries.

2. Toss the cut potatoes in a bowl with the vinegar, stirring so that all the potato strips are coated.

3. Take approximately half the potato strips and arrange on a microwave-safe plate. Sprinkle the cut potatoes with the garlic salt.

4. Microwave the cut potatoes on high heat for 7 minutes, and then for 1 minute at a time until they are cooked through. (The potatoes will not brown like regular French fries, but will be fork-tender.)

5. Repeat with the remainder of the cut potatoes, sprinkling with the cayenne pepper instead of garlic salt.

Quick-Cooking with Potatoes

One way to speed up the preparation time when you're cooking potatoes is to leave on the peel. Potato peels add a crunchy texture, and carry fiber and vitamin B2 (riboflavin). Just be sure to scrub the potato skin under cold running water to remove any pesticide residue or other toxins.

Roasted Red Peppers

Roasting is a great way to bring out the sweet flavor of red bell peppers. To add extra color, try using a combination of red and yellow bell peppers. Green peppers can also be roasted; however, the flavor will not be as sweet.

Serves 4

Preparation time:
5 minutes
Cooking time: 15 minutes

4 red bell peppers
2 tablespoons olive oil

1. Preheat the broiler and line it with aluminum foil. Cut the stems off the red peppers; cut the peppers in half and remove the seeds.

2. Place the peppers on the broiling pan with the skin side facing up. Use a pastry brush to brush the peppers with the olive oil.

3. Broil the peppers for 15 minutes, or until most of the skin is blackened.

4. Use tongs to remove the peppers from the broiler and cover in aluminum foil or plastic wrap. Let the wrapped peppers stand for at least 10 minutes before removing the covering. Peel off the skins and cut into thin slices or squares as desired.

Versatile Peppers

Roasted red peppers add flavor to pasta dishes, heartier soups, and dips. You'll often find them used in combination with aromatic basil, pungent garlic, or cheese. Their sweet flavor pairs particularly well with goat cheese—for a quick snack, serve the roasted peppers and goat cheese on crusty bread.

Quick Green Beans Amandine

Serves 4

Cooking time:
7–10 minutes

2 cups canned French-
cut green beans
2 teaspoons butter or
margarine
2 teaspoons soy sauce
2 tablespoons slivered
almonds

Feel free to use your favorite brand of soy sauce in this recipe, and to substitute toasted sesame seeds or walnuts for the almonds if desired.

1. Heat the green beans to a boil in a small saucepan on medium heat.

2. Use a strainer to drain the juice from the beans.

3. Place the beans in a bowl or return them to the saucepan.

4. Immediately stir in the butter or margarine and the soy sauce.

5. Garnish with the slivered almonds. Serve immediately.

Roasted Fall Harvest Vegetables

Serves 4

Preparation time:
10 minutes
Cooking time:
35–40 minutes

1 butternut squash,
peeled, cut into 1"
cubes
2 shallots, peeled and cut
in half
4 carrots, peeled and cut
julienne
2 zucchini, cut into 1"
pieces
2 tablespoons olive oil
1½ teaspoons dried
oregano
1½ teaspoons dried basil
Salt and pepper, to taste

Roasting is a great way to bring out the natural sweetness of vegetables. You can combine leftovers with chicken broth to make roasted vegetable soup.

1. Preheat oven to 400°F.

2. In a large bowl, toss the prepared vegetables (the squash, shallots, carrots, and zucchini) with the olive oil, oregano, basil, salt, and pepper.

3. Spray a large baking sheet with cooking spray. Lay the butternut squash and carrots out on the baking sheet, cut-side down, and add the shallots. Roast for 20 minutes, stirring occasionally, then add the zucchini. Roast the vegetables for another 15 to 20 minutes, stirring a few times, until the vegetables are tender and browning at the edges.

Stir-Fried Broccoli in Oyster-Flavored Sauce

If your kitchen cupboard includes a selection of Asian sauces and seasonings, you can enhance the sauce by adding light and dark soy sauce and a few drops of toasted Asian sesame oil.

Serves 4

Preparation time:
5 minutes
Cooking time: 7 minutes

¼ cup canned or
   packaged chicken
   broth
2 tablespoons oyster
   sauce
1 teaspoon granulated
   sugar
2 tablespoons vegetable
   oil
2 slices ginger
½ onion, chopped
¼ teaspoon garlic salt,
   or to taste
1 pound broccoli florets
Salt and black pepper,
   to taste

1. Combine the chicken broth, oyster sauce, and sugar in a small bowl or measuring cup. Set aside.

2. Heat a large skillet over medium-high heat. Add the oil. When the oil is heated, add the ginger slices. Stir for a few seconds, then add the onion. Stir-fry the onion for about 2 minutes, until it begins to soften, and add in the garlic salt.

3. Add the florets, stir-frying for about 3 minutes until they are tender but crisp. Add 1 or 2 tablespoons water to the florets if they begin to dry out.

4. Stir the sauce and pour it over the broccoli. Bring to a boil and stir-fry for another minute to mix the sauce with the broccoli. Add salt and pepper as desired. Serve hot.

Oyster Sauce

Made from an extract of boiled oysters and seasonings, oyster sauce is available in the ethnic or international section of many supermarkets. Use it whenever you want to add a savory flavor to marinades and sauces. There are also several vegetarian brands available, made from either oyster or shiitake mushrooms.

Sesame Spinach

Serves 4

Preparation time:
5 minutes
Cooking time:
7–8 minutes

1 cup water
2 cups frozen spinach
2 teaspoons butter
2 teaspoons
   Worcestershire sauce
4 tablespoons toasted
   sesame seeds

Toasted sesame seeds add a fragrant, nutty flavor to this simple vegetable dish. Use margarine instead of butter if desired.

1. In a medium saucepan, bring the water to a boil. Add the frozen spinach and return to a boil.

2. Turn the heat down to medium, cover, and simmer until the spinach is heated through (about 5 minutes).

3. Drain the cooked spinach in a colander.

4. Place in a bowl and stir in the butter and Worcestershire sauce.

5. Garnish with the toasted sesame seeds.

How to Toast Sesame Seeds

Spread the seeds out in a frying pan and cook on low-medium heat, shaking the pan occasionally, until the seeds are fragrant and turn a light golden brown. If not using immediately, store the sesame seeds in a sealed container in the cupboard.

Thai-Style Creamed Corn

Homemade creamed corn takes only minutes to make and has much more flavor than store-bought. Thai basil adds a distinctive licorice flavor, but if it is unavailable you can substitute regular basil leaves.

1. In a small bowl, stir together the cornstarch and 1 tablespoon of the coconut milk.

2. In a small saucepan, heat the oil on medium-low heat. Stir in the garlic and shallot and sauté for 2 to 3 minutes until softened. Stir in the chopped jalapeño peppers. Add the corn and chicken broth and bring to a boil, stirring.

3. Stir in the brown sugar, salt, and pepper. Add the remaining coconut milk and bring to a boil. Turn the heat down and simmer for 5 minutes.

4. Stir the cornstarch slurry and add in the middle of the saucepan, stirring quickly to thicken. Stir in the chopped basil. Serve hot.

Serves 4

Preparation time:
5–10 minutes
Cooking time: 10 minutes

1 teaspoon cornstarch
¼ cup coconut milk, divided
1 tablespoon vegetable oil
1 teaspoon chopped garlic
1 shallot, chopped
1 teaspoon canned jalapeño peppers, chopped
2 cups frozen or canned corn
¼ cup chicken broth
1 tablespoon brown sugar
Salt and pepper, to taste
¼ cup chopped Thai basil leaves

Sautéed Cabbage with Apple

To turn this cabbage side dish into a lunch or light dinner, add leftover cooked ham, sausage, or ground beef.

Serves 4

Preparation time:
10 minutes
Cooking time: 12 minutes

2 tablespoons olive oil
2 apples, peeled, cored, and chopped
4 cups shredded green cabbage
¼ teaspoon paprika, or to taste
⅛ teaspoon garlic salt, or to taste
2 tablespoons red wine vinegar

1. Heat the olive oil in a skillet over medium heat. Add the apples and cabbage.

2. Turn the heat to low and cook for about 10 minutes, until the cabbage is wilted and the apple has softened.

3. Stir in the paprika, garlic salt, and red wine vinegar. Serve immediately.

Three Mushroom Stir-Fry

Stir-frying is a great way to bring out the flavor of fresh mushrooms. For extra color, try replacing the oyster mushroom with half of a red bell pepper, cut into chunks.

Serves 4

Preparation time:
5 minutes
Cooking time:
3–4 minutes

¼ pound fresh shiitake mushrooms
¼ pound fresh button mushrooms
1 oyster mushroom
1 tablespoon vegetable oil
1 shallot, chopped
1 tablespoon lemon juice
1 tablespoon red wine vinegar
Black pepper to taste, optional

1. Wipe the mushrooms clean with a damp cloth or brush with a mushroom brush. Thinly slice the shiitake and button mushrooms. Cut the oyster mushroom into thin pieces. (If you like, remove the leathery "gill" underneath the cap of the oyster mushroom.)

2. Add the oil to a heavy skillet preheated on medium-high heat. Add the shallot and the mushrooms. Stir-fry for a minute.

3. Stir in the lemon juice and red wine vinegar. Cook the vegetables for another minute, stirring continually to keep them from burning. Season with pepper if desired. Serve hot.

Stir-Fried Broccoli with Garlic

Stir-frying has the advantage of being both quick and healthy—the short cooking time means that vegetables retain more of their nutrients.

Serves 3

Preparation time:
5 minutes
Cooking time: 8 minutes

2 tablespoons olive oil
2 garlic cloves, peeled and finely chopped
½ teaspoon red pepper flakes, or to taste
½ pound broccoli florets
⅛ teaspoon salt, or to taste
2 tablespoons water
1 red bell pepper, seeded, cut into chunks
2 teaspoons lemon juice
2 teaspoons soy sauce

1. Heat the olive oil in a skillet on medium-high heat. Add the garlic cloves and red pepper flakes.

2. Add the broccoli. Stir briefly, sprinkling the salt over the broccoli while cooking, until the florets turn bright green.

3. Add the water and let the broccoli cook for 2 or 3 more minutes.

4. Add the red bell pepper. Stir in the lemon juice and soy sauce. Cook, stirring, for another minute. Serve immediately.

Preparing Vegetables Ahead of Time

One way to speed up meal-preparation time is to chop several days' worth of vegetables ahead of time. Store the vegetables for each meal in a sealed bag in the refrigerator until ready to use.

Simple Glazed Baby Carrots

Using tender baby carrots saves you from the work of having to peel and chop regular-size carrots.

Serves 4

Cooking time:
15–20 minutes

*1 tablespoon olive oil
1 pound baby carrots
1 cup orange juice
1 cup water
2 tablespoons butter
2 tablespoons brown
     sugar
Fresh parsley, for garnish,
     optional*

1. Heat the olive oil in a skillet over medium heat.

2. Add the carrots, orange juice, and water. Turn down the heat, cover, and simmer until the carrots are tender (about 12 minutes).

3. While the carrots are cooking, melt the butter and brown sugar in a saucepan, stirring to dissolve the sugar.

4. Add the brown sugar mixture to the carrots. Cook for another 5 minutes, or until the liquid is reduced and the carrots are nicely glazed. Garnish with the fresh parsley before serving.

Sautéed Asparagus

Blanching asparagus shortens the cooking time, making it easier to combine with other, quicker-cooking vegetables in sautéed or stir-fry dishes.

Serves 4

Preparation time:
10 minutes
Cooking time: 5 minutes

*1 pound asparagus, cut
     diagonally into 2"
     pieces
2 tablespoons olive oil
1 garlic clove, finely
     chopped
2 teaspoons finely
     chopped fresh
     gingerroot
1 red bell pepper,
     seeded, cut into thin
     strips
2 tablespoons soy sauce
¼ teaspoon red pepper
     flakes*

1. Fill a large saucepan with enough water to cover the asparagus and bring to a boil. Briefly blanch the asparagus, cooking in the boiling water for 1 minute. Remove the asparagus with a slotted spoon and rinse with cold water. Drain.

2. Heat the olive oil in a skillet on medium-high heat. Add the garlic, ginger, and asparagus.

3. Cook for 1 minute, then add the red bell pepper. Stir in the soy sauce and red pepper flakes. Cook until the asparagus is tender but still crisp. Serve hot.

Marinated Artichoke Hearts

Using frozen artichokes takes the work out of cleaning and boiling fresh artichokes. Serve them as a simple side dish or over cooked pasta.

Serves 2

Thawing time: 5 minutes
Preparation time:
5–10 minutes

8 frozen artichoke hearts,
 halved
¼ cup olive oil
¼ cup red wine vinegar
2 tablespoons lemon juice
¼ teaspoon garlic powder
Seasoned salt, to taste

1. Thaw the artichokes in the microwave according to the package directions.

2. In a small bowl, combine the olive oil, red wine vinegar, lemon juice, garlic powder, and seasoned salt.

3. Place the artichokes in a resealable bag. Pour in the dressing. Store in the refrigerator until ready to use.

Simple Steamed Mushrooms

While mushrooms are commonly grilled or sautéed, they can also be steamed. Serve this simple side dish with Lemon Beef (page 98) and a green salad for a complete meal.

Serves 2

Preparation time:
5 minutes
Cooking time: 5 minutes

4 large portobello
 mushrooms
1 cup chicken broth, or as
 needed
1 tablespoon balsamic
 vinegar
Black pepper, to taste

1. Wipe the mushrooms clean with a damp cloth. Separate the stems from the caps.

2. Bring the chicken broth to boil in a medium saucepan. (The pan should have about 1½" of liquid.) Place a metal steamer in the saucepan.

3. Place the mushroom pieces in the steamer.

4. Steam the mushrooms for 3 to 4 minutes. Use a pastry brush to brush on the balsamic vinegar. Season with the pepper.

5. Steam the mushrooms for 2 to 3 more minutes, until they are tender.

Speedy Stir-Fried Ratatouille

Serves 2

Preparation time:
10 minutes
Cooking time: 10 minutes

1 pound eggplant (one-
    half large eggplant),
    cut in ½" cubes
2 tablespoons vegetable
    or peanut oil
½ teaspoon salt, or to
    taste
1 zucchini, thinly sliced on
    the diagonal
1 onion, peeled and
    sliced
¼ teaspoon dried
    oregano, or to taste
1 red bell pepper, cut in
    ½" cubes
1 tablespoon chicken
    broth, or as needed
½ cup canned tomatoes
⅛ teaspoon black pepper,
    or to taste

This quick and easy dish makes a light lunch for two people or a side dish for four. Blanching the eggplant in the microwave takes only a couple of minutes, and helps prevent it from soaking up too much oil when it is stir-fried.

1. Place the eggplant in a microwave-safe dish and cover with water. Microwave the eggplant on high heat for 2 minutes, then continue microwaving for 30 seconds at a time as needed, until it is tender but still crisp.

2. Heat the oil and the salt in a heavy skillet on medium-high heat, tilting the skillet so that it covers the bottom of the pan and halfway up the sides.

3. Add the zucchini and the onion to the pan. Stir in the dried oregano. Cook the vegetables for 2 minutes, stirring constantly to keep them from burning.

4. Add the eggplant to the pan. Stir for a few seconds, then add the bell pepper. Cook, stirring for a few more seconds. (Total stir-frying time at this point should be about 3 minutes.) Stir in the chicken broth as needed, if the vegetables begin to dry out.

5. Turn the heat down to low-medium. Stir in the canned tomatoes. Simmer for 2 to 3 minutes, stirring occasionally to mix everything together. Stir in the pepper. Serve immediately.

Chinese Five-Spice Potatoes

Did you know: There are two basic types of potatoes—floury potatoes (such as fingerling potatoes) break down more easily, making them perfect for mashing and baking, while waxy potatoes (such as red potatoes) hold their shape better for roasting.

Serves 4

Preparation time:
10 minutes
Roasting time:
50 minutes

3 baking potatoes
2 tablespoons melted butter or margarine
2 teaspoons five-spice powder
½ teaspoon salt
Freshly ground black pepper, to taste

1. Preheat the oven to 375°F.

2. Wash the potatoes. Cut in half lengthwise, then crosswise into quarters. Cut each quarter in half.

3. Combine the melted butter or margarine, five-spice powder, salt, and pepper in a small bowl.

4. Lay the potatoes on a baking sheet. Use a pastry brush to brush the potatoes with the seasoned butter mixture. Bake the potatoes until golden brown and tender, about 50 minutes.

Fabulous Five-Spice Powder

An intriguing mix of sweet, sour, pungent, salty, and bitter, five-spice powder is an indispensable ingredient in Chinese cuisine. But that doesn't mean it needs to sit in the cupboard when you're not cooking Chinese food! Use this aromatic spice blend whenever you want to lend extra flavor to dry rubs and marinades for meat and poultry.

Garlic Mashed Potatoes

Serves 6

Preparation time:
5–10 minutes
Cooking time: 20 minutes

4 medium red potatoes
4 tablespoons butter or
    margarine
¼ cup milk
2 teaspoons garlic
    powder, or to taste
½ teaspoon salt, or to
    taste

Cooking the potatoes in the microwave speeds up the preparation time, since you don't have to wait for the water to boil. Serve these flavorful potatoes with Honey Mustard Pork Chops (page 119.)

1. Wash and peel the potatoes. Cut them roughly into bite-size chunks.

2. Place the potatoes in a deep microwave-safe dish and cover with water.

3. Microwave the potatoes at high heat for 10 minutes. Give the dish a quarter turn and continue microwaving for 1 or 2 minutes at a time until the potatoes are cooked through and can easily be pierced with a fork. (Total cooking time should be about 15 minutes.) Drain.

4. Place the potatoes in a large bowl. Add the butter or margarine and use a fork or a potato masher to whip the potatoes, while gradually adding the milk until the potatoes have reached the desired consistency (do not add more milk than is needed). Stir in the garlic powder and salt.

Chapter 16
Party Time

No-Cook Spring Rolls

Serves 8

Preparation time:
15 minutes

8 rice paper wrappers
2 cups packaged
   coleslaw mix
¼ cup hoisin sauce
1 teaspoon lime juice
1½ tablespoons water
⅛ teaspoon garlic
   powder, or to taste
¼ teaspoon red pepper
   flakes, or to taste
1 tablespoon chopped
   peanuts

These rolls are incredibly easy to make—the secret is rice paper wrappers, which only need to be briefly dipped in warm water before using. You'll find them in the refrigerated section of many local supermarkets.

1. Carefully dip each rice paper wrapper in a small bowl filled with warm water to moisten (about 20 seconds).

2. Lay the wrapper on a cutting board in front of you. Place about ¼ cup of the packaged coleslaw mix on the bottom half of the wrapper, being careful not to come too close to the edges.

3. Roll up the wrapper like a taco, tucking in the sides. Continue filling and rolling up the remainder of the rice paper wrappers.

4. In a small bowl, stir together the hoisin sauce, lime juice, water, garlic powder, and red pepper flakes. Garnish the dip with the chopped peanuts.

5. Serve the rolls cold with the hoisin dip.

No-Cook Substitutes for Rice Paper Wrappers

The beauty of rice paper wrappers is that once the wrapper is softened in water, it can be filled and served without any further cooking. While spring roll wrappers or even phyllo dough can be used as a substitute for rice paper wrappers, the rolls will then need to be fried after they are filled. If you're looking for a quick and easy no-cook substitute for rice paper wrappers, one option is to use a tortilla wrapper—try using one of the flavored wraps, such as spinach or roasted red pepper.

Italian-Inspired Bruschetta

Using canned diced tomatoes with seasonings means there is no need to chop and seed tomatoes in this take on the popular Italian appetizer.

1. Preheat the broiler on high heat. Spray a broiling rack with nonstick cooking spray.

2. Cut the garlic cloves in half. Rub both sides of each slice of bread with a garlic clove half.

3. In a medium bowl, stir together the diced tomatoes and olive oil. Season with salt and pepper to taste.

4. Spread the tomato mixture over each slice of bread. Sprinkle the Parmesan cheese on top.

5. Lay the bread slices out on the rack. Broil the toast on high heat for up to 2 minutes, until the cheese has melted and the bread is toasted.

Serves 8

Preparation time: 5 minutes
Cooking time: 2 minutes

2 cloves garlic
8 slices crusty French or Italian bread
¾ cup diced tomatoes with basil and garlic
1½ tablespoons extra-virgin olive oil
Salt and pepper, to taste
½ cup grated Parmesan cheese

Deviled Eggs

For a fancier presentation, use a pastry tube to fill the hollowed cooked egg white with the spicy egg yolk mixture.

1. Cut the eggs in half lengthwise. Use a spoon to carefully remove the yolks. Do not discard the cooked egg white.

2. Place the yolks in a small bowl. Use a fork to mash the yolks until they are fluffy. Stir in the mayonnaise, green onion, Worcestershire sauce, ketchup, curry powder, and pepper.

3. Carefully spoon a small amount of the mashed egg yolk mixture into each egg half. Chill until ready to serve.

Serves 6

Preparation time: 10 minutes

6 hard-boiled eggs, peeled
3 tablespoons mayonnaise
1 green onion, finely chopped
1 tablespoon Worcestershire sauce
1½ teaspoons ketchup
½ teaspoon curry powder
Black pepper, to taste

Microwave Tex-Mex Nachos

A processed cheese with a creamy texture, Velveeta's quick-melting properties make it an excellent choice for microwave recipes.

Serves 4

Preparation time:
5–8 minutes
Cooking time:
3–5 minutes

5 cups nacho chips
6 ounces Velveeta
   cheese, sliced
2 cups red kidney beans
1 tablespoon chili powder,
   or to taste
½ teaspoon ground cumin
3 tablespoons sour cream
½ cup sliced olives,
   optional

1. Lay out the nacho chips on a plate.

2. Place the Velveeta cheese in a 2-quart microwave-safe casserole dish. Microwave on high until the cheese is nearly melted, stopping and stirring every 30 seconds (total time will be about 1½ minutes).

3. Stir in the kidney beans, chili powder, ground cumin, and sour cream. Microwave on high heat for 1 minute, and then as needed until the cheese is melted and everything is heated through.

4. Spoon the cheese and bean mixture over the nacho chips. Garnish with the olives.

Simple Cheese and Fruit Platter

You can vary this basic arrangement by making use of fresh fruit in season.

Serves 8

Preparation time:
10 minutes

1 cup green seedless
   grapes
1 pint fresh blueberries
½ pint strawberries
2 cups sliced pineapple
½ pound cheddar cheese,
   cubed
½ pound Danish Havarti,
   sliced
2 packages water
   crackers

1. Rinse the grapes and blueberries in cold water. Drain and pat dry.

2 Rinse the strawberries, hull, and cut in half.

3. Arrange the fruit, cheese, and crackers on two large serving trays. Serve immediately.

Beef Ciabatta

Italian for "slipper," ciabatta is a fat, oval-shaped bread with a distinctive flavor that is reminiscent of sourdough bread.

Serves 6

Preparation time:
10 minutes
Cooking time:
10–12 minutes

1 loaf ciabatta bread
2 tablespoons vegetable
   oil
½ pound chorizo or
   andouille sausage,
   sliced
½ red onion, sliced
1 tomato, thinly sliced
½ cup sliced fresh
   mushrooms
½ red bell pepper, cut
   julienne-style
½ cup shredded
   mozzarella cheese

1. Cut the ciabatta loaf in half lengthwise.

2. Heat the vegetable oil in a heavy skillet over medium-high heat. Add the sausage and the onion. Sauté the onion for 4 to 5 minutes, until it is softened.

3. Add the tomato, pressing down so that it releases its juices. Add the mushrooms and bell pepper. Cook for about another 4 to 5 minutes, stirring, until the vegetables are tender but still crisp and heated through.

4. Spread the mixture on one half of the ciabatta loaf. Top with the mozzarella cheese. Add the other half and close up the sandwich. Cut into four equal slices.

Freezing Shredded Cheese

The easiest solution for what to do with leftover shredded cheese is to freeze it. You can freeze shredded cheese for up to two months. Thaw the cheese in the refrigerator and use as soon as possible.

Basic Guacamole

Salsa takes the work out of dicing tomatoes, while bottled jalapeño peppers replace fresh chili peppers in this simple guacamole recipe. If you wish, you can increase the heat by mixing in 1 teaspoon of chili powder.

Serves 4

Preparation time:
10 minutes

3 avocados
⅔ cup salsa
1 tablespoon bottled chopped jalapeño peppers
2 tablespoons finely chopped cilantro, or to taste
1 tablespoon lemon juice
1 (6-ounce) bag tortilla chips

1. Peel the avocados. With a knife, cut the avocados in half and remove the round pit in the middle. Place the pitted avocados in a medium bowl and mash with a fork or potato masher.

2. In a medium bowl, stir together the remaining ingredients except for the chips. Add the mashed avocado, stirring to mix it in. If the guacamole is too chunky, mash a bit more.

3. Serve the guacamole with tortilla chips.

Baked Pita Chips

These make a lighter alternative to taco or potato chips as a dip accompaniment. They go very nicely with an Italian salsa or with Roasted Red Pepper Dip (page 240).

Serves 6

Preparation time:
10 minutes
Cooking time:
10–15 minutes

3 pita wheels
2 tablespoons olive oil
1½ teaspoons lemon juice
½ teaspoon garlic salt, or to taste
½ teaspoon dried basil
½ teaspoon dried oregano
Black pepper, to taste

1. Preheat the oven to 350°F.

2. Cut each pita wheel into six even wedges.

3. In a small saucepan, heat the olive oil and lemon juice over low heat. Stir in the garlic salt, basil, oregano, and pepper.

4. Place the pita wedges on two baking sheets sprayed with nonstick cooking spray. Use a pastry brush to brush the olive oil and spice mixture on top.

5. Cook for 10 minutes, or until the pita wedges are crisp. Cool and serve.

Microwave Cheese Fondue

Be sure to stir the cheese frequently during the second half of cooking to keep it from curdling. For a nonalcoholic fondue, substitute 1 cup of apple juice for the white wine.

Serves 6

Preparation time:
5 minutes
Cooking time:
5–7 minutes

1 garlic clove, peeled and cut in half
4 cups shredded Swiss cheese
4 teaspoons cornstarch
¼ teaspoon nutmeg
⅛ teaspoon paprika, or to taste
1 cup dry white wine
2 teaspoons lemon juice
1 loaf French or garlic bread, sliced

1. Rub the garlic clove over the insides of a 2-quart casserole dish that is microwave-safe.

2. Combine the cheese, cornstarch, nutmeg, and paprika in the dish. Stir in the white wine and lemon juice.

3. Microwave the fondue on high heat for 3 minutes. Open the door and stir the fondue.

4. Continue microwaving the cheese fondue for 1 minute at a time, stirring each time, until the cheese is completely melted (total cooking time is about 5 minutes).

5. Serve the fondue in the casserole dish, with the bread for dipping.

Fondue Facts

The secret to making fondue is to use hard, aged cheeses such as Swiss Emmental and Gruyère—the high fat content means they melt easily. The high acid content in dry white wine also helps melt the cheese.

Easy Garlic Toast

Balsamic vinegar gives a sharp kick to the garlic butter spread. Bread cooks quickly in the broiler—start checking the garlic toast after one minute to make sure it doesn't burn.

Serves 12

Preparation time:
10 minutes
Cooking time:
1–2 minutes

12 (1") slices crusty
   French bread (one-
   half loaf)
¾ cup butter, softened
¾ teaspoon garlic powder
⅛ teaspoon salt, or to
   taste
⅛ teaspoon black pepper,
   or to taste
½ teaspoon dried basil
   leaves
1 teaspoon lemon juice
1 teaspoon balsamic
   vinegar

1. Preheat the broiler on high heat. Spray a broiling rack with nonstick cooking spray.

2. In a small bowl, beat together the softened butter, garlic powder, salt, pepper, basil, lemon juice, and balsamic vinegar.

3. Spread the garlic butter over one side of the bread slices (about 1½ tablespoons per bread slice). Store any leftover garlic butter in a sealed container in the refrigerator to use on bread or toast as desired.

4. Lay the bread slices out on the rack.

5. Broil the toast on high heat for up to 2 minutes, until the butter has melted and the bread is toasted.

Roasted Red Pepper Dip

Serve this flavorful red-pepper dip with Baked Pita Chips (page 238) and an assortment of cut vegetables such as carrots, cauliflower, and broccoli.

Serves 4

Preparation time:
10 minutes

Roasted Red Peppers
   (page 221)
½ cup Italian basil pesto
   sauce
½ cup low-fat plain yogurt
1 tablespoon olive oil

1. Cut the roasted peppers into small squares if needed.

2. In a large bowl, stir together the pesto sauce and low-fat yogurt. Stir in the roasted peppers and olive oil.

3. Use immediately, or store in a sealed container within the refrigerator until ready to use.

Greek Hummus Dip

Can't find chickpeas at the local supermarket? Look for them under their other name, garbanzo beans.

1. Process all the ingredients in a blender or food processor until smooth.

2. Place the dip in a sealed container in the refrigerator for 1 hour, to give the flavors a chance to blend.

Make-Ahead Hummus

Hummus is one of the few party dips that freezes well. Store the hummus in a resealable plastic bag or a small container before freezing. Thaw the hummus in the refrigerator. If the dip is a bit dry, stir in one or two teaspoons of olive oil before serving.

Crab and Cream Cheese Dip

Rich mascarpone cheese—the key ingredient in Italian tiramisu—adds a touch of decadence to this tasty dip. You can substitute canned crabmeat for fresh lump crabmeat in this recipe—be sure to drain the meat before using.

1. Combine the ingredients in a medium bowl.

2. Cover and chill for 1 hour to give the ingredients a chance to blend.

Yields 1½ cups

Preparation time:
15 minutes

1½ cups canned chickpeas, rinsed and drained
2 tablespoons reserved juice from the chickpeas
3 tablespoons lemon juice
2 tablespoons creamy peanut butter
¼ teaspoon garlic powder
¼ teaspoon paprika, or to taste
¼ teaspoon ground cumin
⅛ teaspoon salt, or to taste
Black pepper, to taste

Yields 2 cups

Preparation time:
10 minutes

½ pound cream cheese, softened
¼ cup mascarpone, softened
8 ounces fresh lump crabmeat
1 tablespoon lemon juice
2 teaspoons Worcestershire sauce
1½ green onions, finely chopped
½ teaspoon garlic powder, or to taste
¼ teaspoon paprika, or to taste

Chili con Queso Dip

Yields 1¾ cups

Preparation time:
5 minutes
Cooking time:
7–10 minutes

½ cup Monterey jack
  cheese
½ cup cream cheese
½ cup canned diced
  tomatoes
½ teaspoon onion powder
2 tablespoons jarred red
  chili peppers

Traditionally, this spicy Tex-Mex dip is meant to be served with square queso chips, but tortilla chips or Baked Pita Chips (page 238) work just as well.

1. Combine all the ingredients in a medium microwave-safe bowl, stirring to mix everything together.

2. Microwave on high heat for 3 minutes. Stir and microwave for 1 minute at a time until the cheese is melted. Stir again before serving.

Skillet con Queso

Don't have a microwave? This tasty dip can also be prepared on the stovetop. Replace the onion powder with ¼ cup chopped onion and sauté with the chili peppers in one tablespoon of olive oil, until the onion is softened. Add the tomatoes, heat to boiling, and let simmer for 2 minutes. Top with the cheeses and cook over low heat until the cheese is melted. You can also load up the dish with one diced green bell pepper.

Chapter 17
Make-Ahead Marinades and Sauces

Simple Stir-Fry Sauce

Yields ½ cup

Preparation time:
5 minutes

1 tablespoon soy sauce
1 tablespoon red wine
    vinegar
1 tablespoon brown sugar
2 tablespoons hoisin
    sauce
¼ cup water
1 teaspoon Asian sesame
    oil
Black pepper, to taste

This sauce is a great way to finish off a simple meat and vege-table stir-fry. You can prepare the sauce ahead of time and store it in a sealed container in the refrigerator until ready to use.

1. In a medium bowl, combine all the ingredients.

2. If not using the sauce immediately, refrigerate in a sealed container and use within 3 to 4 days.

Easy White Sauce for Vegetables

Serves 4

Cooking time:
10 minutes

4 tablespoons unsalted
    butter
3 tablespoons flour
1 cup milk
½ teaspoon ground
    nutmeg, or to taste
Salt and black pepper, to
    taste

One of the simplest sauces to make, white sauce is an excellent way to liven up fish, vegetables, or cooked pasta. Use this white sauce recipe with about 2½ cups of cooked vegetables.

1. In a small saucepan, melt the butter on low heat. Add the flour and blend it into the melted butter, stirring continually until it thickens and forms a roux.

2. Slowly add the milk and continue stirring with a whisk until the mixture has thickened. Stir in the nutmeg, salt, and pepper. Serve immediately.

Beautiful Béchamel Sauce

Believed to have been created by a chef working in the court of French King Louis XIV, the official name of white sauce is béchamel sauce, after Louis de Bechameil, a chief steward in the King's Court. In addition to standing on its own, white sauce forms the base of many other famous French sauces. Rich Mornay sauce is made by adding eggs, cream, and shredded cheese to the basic sauce, while velouté sauce is made with stock instead of milk.

White Sauce for Seafood

This simple sauce goes nicely with poached whitefish, such as sole. You can dress it up by combining the milk with a good stock or white wine, and adding fresh chopped parsley or chives at the end of cooking.

1. In a small saucepan, melt the butter on low heat. Add the flour and blend it into the melted butter, stirring continually until it thickens and forms a roux (3 to 5 minutes). Stir in the dill weed.

2. Increase the heat to medium. Slowly add the milk and the cream, stirring with a whisk until the mixture has thickened.

3. Stir in the nutmeg and pepper.

4. Stir in the lemon juice. Serve immediately.

Serves 4

Cooking time: 10 minutes

4 tablespoons unsalted butter
3 tablespoons flour
½ teaspoon dried dill weed
¾ cup milk
¼ cup heavy cream or whipping cream
½ teaspoon ground nutmeg, or to taste
⅛ teaspoon black or white pepper, or to taste
1 teaspoon lemon juice

Teriyaki Sauce

This recipe replaces the mirin found in classic Japanese teriyaki sauce with white grape juice and lemon juice. If you like, you can increase the amount of brown sugar to 4 teaspoons.

In a small saucepan, combine all the ingredients and bring to a boil, stirring to dissolve the brown sugar. Serve the sauce immediately.

Yields ⅔ cup

Preparation time: 2 minutes
Cooking time: 5 minutes

1 green onion, finely chopped
⅓ cup Japanese soy sauce
¼ cup white grape juice
1 teaspoon lemon juice
2 teaspoons bottled chopped fresh ginger
3 teaspoons brown sugar

Marinade for Beef or Pork

Yields about 1¼ cup

Preparation time:
5 minutes

½ cup soy sauce (such as
    Kikkoman)
4 tablespoons red wine
    vinegar
4 tablespoons vegetable
    oil
2 tablespoons brown
    sugar
2 tablespoons liquid
    honey
3 garlic cloves, crushed
½ teaspoon crushed red
    pepper

This marinade would go nicely with up to two pounds of beef steak that is going to be grilled or broiled. The recipe is very adaptable, and can easily be doubled if you're planning to barbecue for a crowd.

1. In a medium bowl, whisk together the soy sauce, red wine vinegar, and vegetable oil. Whisk in the remaining ingredients.

2. Pour the marinade over the meat. Cover and marinate in the refrigerator for at least 4 hours. Discard the excess marinade before cooking, or boil for 5 minutes if planning to use as a basting sauce for the meat.

What Makes a Marinade?

A good marinade tenderizes and enhances the flavor of meat, poultry, and seafood. All marinades contain an acid—such as flat beer, lemon juice, vinegar, or soy sauce—that flavors and tenderizes food by breaking down its proteins. A combination of herbs and spices is usually added for extra flavor. Finally, vegetable oil may be added to disperse the flavor more quickly, and help prevent the food from drying out.

Orange-Cilantro Marinade

This marinade pairs nicely with a firm-fleshed fish such as whitefish, or with shrimp. Serve the fish with Healthy Brown Rice (page 151) and a plain salad for a complete meal.

Yields ⅔ cup

Preparation time:
10 minutes

¼ cup orange juice
¼ cup extra-virgin olive oil
2 teaspoons lime juice
Zest of 1 orange
3 tablespoons freshly
    chopped cilantro
3 teaspoons minced
    garlic
½ teaspoon salt
¼ teaspoon freshly
    ground black pepper
1 teaspoon Tabasco
    sauce

1. In a small bowl, whisk together the orange juice and olive oil.

2. Whisk in the remaining ingredients.

3. Store in a sealed container in the refrigerator. Use the marinade within three days.

Marinating Times

Deciding how long to marinate food can be a little tricky. Food that has been left too long in a marinade can develop a "mushy" texture. A general rule is to marinate meat and poultry for at least one hour. On the other hand, delicate fish should not be marinated for more than 30 minutes. However, total marinating time will depend on the amount of acid in the marinade—the more acid a marinade contains, the less marinating time is required.

Simple Salsa Verde

Yields 1 cup

Preparation time:
10 minutes

Although most people think of salsa as a dip for tortilla chips, the word salsa is simply the Spanish word for sauce. You can use this flavorful dip with chips, grilled meat, or seafood, or even pair it with ¾ pound of cooked pasta.

6 canned tomatillos,
　sliced
½ sweet onion, peeled
　and chopped
2 tablespoons jarred
　chopped jalapeño
　peppers
½ bunch chopped fresh
　cilantro leaves (about
　3 tablespoons)
1 tablespoon lime juice
1 tablespoon reserved
　tomatillo juice, or to
　taste
¼ teaspoon garlic powder
　or 2 cloves garlic,
　minced
½ teaspoon salt
1 teaspoon chili powder,
　or to taste
⅛ teaspoon freshly
　ground black pepper,
　or to taste

1. Briefly process the tomatillos, sweet onion, chopped jalapeños, and cilantro in a food processor.

2. Add lime juice, reserved tomatillo juice, garlic powder or minced garlic, salt, chili powder, and pepper. Process until the salsa has a chunky consistency. Store in a sealed container in the refrigerator until ready to use.

Types of Salsa

While many people are familiar with the classic Mexican salsa that combines tomatoes and herbs with hot chili peppers and tart lime juice, there are many variations. In Mexican salsa verde, green tomatillos take the place of tomatoes (verde is Spanish for "green"). A spicy fruit salsa that is often served as a salad, pico de gallo means "beak of the rooster," and refers to the spicy chili peppers used in the seasoning. And salsa ranchera or ranch sauce is a peppery sauce meant to be served with heuvos rancheros, the Mexican version of fried eggs.

Teriyaki Marinade

*Use this simple marinade to make Teriyaki Chicken (page 209).
It would also go very nicely with beef.*

Yields ⅔ cup

Preparation time:
5 minutes

2 teaspoons grated fresh
    gingerroot
¼ cup soy sauce
2 tablespoons brown
    sugar
¼ cup pineapple juice
1 shallot, peeled and
    chopped
¼ cup pineapple tidbits

1. Combine all the ingredients in a large bowl. Pour into a large resealable plastic bag.

2. Add the chicken or beef that is to be marinated. Reseal the bag and marinate in the refrigerator for about 1 hour, turning occasionally so that all the food is coated in the marinade.

Quick and Easy Teriyaki Marinade for Stir-Fries

With a little adjusting, this simple marinade can be used to make a quick and easy stir-fry. Place ¾ to 1 pound sliced beef in a bowl, and add 2 tablespoons pineapple juice, 2 tablespoons soy sauce, 1 teaspoon fresh gingerroot, and 1 teaspoon brown sugar. Marinate the beef for 20 minutes. Before you begin stir-frying, remove the beef with a slotted spoon, discarding any excess marinade.

Spicy Barbecue Sauce

This thick tomato-based sauce goes very nicely with grilled pork.

Yields 1 ⅓ cups

Preparation time:
5 minutes
Cooking time: 15 minutes

1 tablespoon olive oil
¼ cup chopped onion
2 cloves garlic, crushed
1 cup tomato paste
2 tablespoons
    Worcestershire sauce
2 tablespoons white or
    cider vinegar
1 tablespoon brown sugar
1 tablespoon Dijon mustard
⅛ teaspoon cayenne
    pepper, or to taste

1. Heat the oil in a medium saucepan over medium heat.

2. Add the onion and garlic. Cook, stirring, until the onion begins to soften.

3. Stir in the tomato paste, Worcestershire sauce, vinegar, sugar, mustard, and cayenne pepper.

4. Turn the heat down and simmer for 10 minutes, stirring occasionally.

Alfredo Sauce

This classic butter and cream sauce was invented by an Italian restaurateur in the 1920s. Whether or not to add flour as a thickener is a matter of personal preference—you can leave it out if desired.

Yields 1¼ cups

Preparation time:
5 minutes
Cooking time: 10 minutes

4 tablespoons unsalted
    butter
3 tablespoons flour
1 cup heavy cream or
    whipping cream
⅓ cup grated Parmesan
    cheese
¼ teaspoon ground
    nutmeg, or to taste
¼ teaspoon red pepper
    flakes, optional
Black pepper, to taste
2 tablespoons chopped
    fresh basil

1. In a small saucepan, melt the butter on low heat. Add the flour and blend it into the melted butter, stirring continually until it thickens and forms a roux (3 to 5 minutes).

2. Increase the heat to medium. Slowly add the cream, stirring with a whisk until the mixture has thickened.

3. Add the Parmesan cheese and continue stirring with a whisk until the mixture has thickened.

4. Remove from the heat. Stir in the nutmeg, red pepper flakes, pepper, and basil.

5. Keep warm until the pasta is ready.

No-Cook Pasta Sauce

*This is a quick and easy version of Italian tonnato sauce,
without the anchovies. Serve the sauce with 8 ounces
of cooked pasta. Sprinkle the cooked pasta with
¼ cup of Parmesan cheese if desired.*

Serves 4

Preparation time:
5 minutes

2 tablespoons capers
1 (6-ounce) can tuna in
    oil, undrained
1 cup low-fat mayonnaise
2 tablespoons lemon juice
¼ teaspoon garlic
    powder, or to taste
½ teaspoon salt
Black pepper, to taste

1. Rinse the capers to remove excess salt.

2. Process the tuna and mayonnaise in a blender or food processor.

3. Add the other ingredients and continue processing until smooth.

4. Store the sauce in a sealed container in the refrigerator until ready to serve.

Storing Sauce

Leftover sauce can be stored in a sealed container in the refrigerator for up to three days. Reheat the sauce before serving, thinning with a small amount of water if necessary. For longer storage, freeze the sauce in ice cube trays for up to three months.

Spicy Peanut Sauce

This easy dipping sauce takes only five minutes to make, and goes nicely with spring rolls or other Asian dumplings. If you don't have fish sauce, you can substitute 2 tablespoons of soy sauce.

Yields 1 cup

Preparation time:
5 minutes
Cooking time: 5 minutes

½ cup coconut milk
½ cup peanut butter
2 tablespoons lime juice
1 tablespoon soy sauce
1 tablespoon fish sauce
1 garlic clove, minced
½ teaspoon red pepper
    flakes, or to taste

1. In a small saucepan, heat the coconut milk.

2. Stir in the peanut butter, lime juice, soy sauce, fish sauce, garlic, and red pepper flakes.

3. Heat, stirring occasionally, until the peanut butter is melted and the ingredients combined.

4. Store in a sealed container in the refrigerator until ready to use.

Quick and Easy Brown Sauce

This flavorful sauce pairs nicely with beef and green vegetables. In Chinese cuisine, brown sauce (made with oyster sauce and soy sauce and minus the butter) is often featured in beef and broccoli stir-fries.

Serves 2

Preparation time:
5 minutes
Cooking time: 5 minutes

1½ tablespoons butter
1 tablespoon flour
½ cup beef broth
1 tablespoon
    Worcestershire sauce
½ teaspoon honey
    mustard
½ teaspoon granulated
    sugar
⅛ teaspoon red pepper
    flakes, optional

1. In a small saucepan, melt the butter on low heat. Add the flour and blend it into the melted butter, stirring continually until it thickens and forms a roux.

2. Add the beef broth. Stir in the Worcestershire sauce, mustard, sugar, and red pepper flakes if using. Bring to a boil, stirring continually.

3. Use the sauce immediately or store in a sealed container in the refrigerator until ready to use.

Chapter 18
Beverages

Easy No-Boil Apple-Flavored Iced Tea

This recipe is so simple, you don't even need to brew the tea! For extra flavor, add 1 cup orange or cranberry juice to the chilled tea before serving.

Serves 4

Preparation time:
5 minutes
Chill: Overnight

2 bags Earl Grey black
   tea
2 cups apple juice
2 cups water
2 tablespoons honey
Ice cubes, as desired

1. Combine the tea bags, apple juice, and water in a large glass pitcher. Leave in the refrigerator overnight.

2. Stir in the honey. Serve the iced tea over ice cubes.

Sun-Brewed Tea

As its name implies, sun tea is tea that is brewed outdoors in the sun. Fans of sun tea claim that it has a more delicate flavor than tea prepared with boiling water. However, health professionals warn that heating water without bringing it to a full boil means that harmful bacteria in the water or on the teabags may not be destroyed.

Homemade Café Mocha

Café mocha is the perfect pick-me-up on a cold winter's day. You can jazz up this drink for guests by replacing the low-fat milk with whole milk, and garnishing with chocolate syrup, whipped cream, and grated chocolate.

Serves 1

Heating time: 5 minutes

1 cup low-fat milk
2 teaspoons instant coffee
2 tablespoons sweetened
   hot chocolate
¼ teaspoon ground
   cinnamon

Bring the ingredients to boil in a medium saucepan, stirring frequently to dissolve the chocolate. Serve warm.

Gingery Tea

This simple drink is believed to aid digestion. Make the tea stronger or weaker by increasing or reducing the amount of ginger as desired.

Serves 2

Preparation time:
5 minutes
Steeping time:
15 minutes

1 cup water
1 tablespoon freshly grated gingerroot
2 teaspoons honey, or to taste
Lemon slices, for garnish

1. Bring the water to a boil.

2. Place the ginger in a cup and pour ¾ cup of the water over.

3. Let the tea steep for 15 minutes (longer if you want a stronger tea).

4. Stir in the honey. Garnish with lemon slices.

Selecting Fresh Ginger

Look for ginger that has a fresh unwrinkled skin, firm body, and a nice tan color. Store the ginger in a cool, dark place until ready to use.

Masala Chai

This spiced milk drink from India is traditionally made with strong black tea.

Serves 3

Preparation time:
5 minutes
Cooking time: 10 minutes

2 cardamom pods
3 whole cloves
1½ cups water
1½ cups light cream
1 tablespoon granulated sugar
¼ teaspoon ground ginger
1 cinnamon stick, broken into pieces
2 bags Earl Grey black tea

1. Crush the cardamom and cloves with a mortar and pestle, or by rolling over them with a rolling pin.

2. In a medium saucepan, bring the water and cream to a boil. Add the sugar, stirring to dissolve.

3. Add the crushed spices, ginger, and cinnamon. Bring back to a boil.

4. Add the teabags, then remove the pan from the heat and let stand for 5 minutes. Strain and serve.

Indian Spiced Chai

This is a quick and easy version of Masala chai, made with ground spices and tea bags instead of tea leaves.

Serves 1

Cooking time:
8–10 minutes

1 cup water
2 black tea bags
1 cup light cream
1½ teaspoons granulated
  sugar
¼ teaspoon ground
  cardamom
⅛ teaspoon ground
  ginger
¼ teaspoon ground
  cinnamon

1. Bring the water to a boil. Add the tea and let steep for 3 minutes.

2. While the tea is steeping, in a small saucepan, bring the cream, sugar, ground cardamom, ground ginger, and ground cinnamon to a boil, stirring to dissolve the sugar.

3. Add the brewed tea to the milk and spices.

4. Simmer for a minute and serve.

Thirst-Quenching Chai

This popular Asian beverage is made with brewed black tea, milk, and spices. There are numerous recipes for chai; the most popular, Masala chai, is a spicy beverage containing many of the same spices found in Indian curries.

Easy Iced Coffee

Of course, nothing beats the taste of brewed coffee, but this easy drink made with instant coffee is great when you want a cold drink in a hurry.

Serves 2

Preparation:
5 minutes

2½ teaspoons instant
    coffee
1½ cups water
½ cup heavy cream or
    whipping cream
4 teaspoons liquid honey
¼ teaspoon ground
    cinnamon
4 ice cubes

Combine all the ingredients in a blender. Process for about 15 to 30 seconds, until smooth.

Flavorful Ice Cubes

The next time you're making Classic Lemonade (page 259), Easy Iced Coffee, or other flavorful drinks, prepare more than you need and freeze the extra in ice cube trays. Use the ice cubes to add extra flavor to fruit or alcoholic drinks.

Mexican-Inspired Hot Chocolate

This is a quick and easy version of champurrado, a hot spiced drink made with Mexican chocolate.

Serves 1

Preparation time:
5 minutes
Cooking time:
5–10 minutes

1 cup warm water
3 tablespoons
    unsweetened cocoa
3 tablespoons brown
    sugar, or to taste
⅛ teaspoon ground
    aniseed
⅛ teaspoon cayenne
    pepper
1 cup milk
½ teaspoon vanilla extract

1. In a small saucepan, bring the water and unsweetened cocoa to a boil over low heat.

2. Stir in the brown sugar, ground aniseed, and cayenne pepper.

3. In a separate small saucepan, bring the milk to a boil. Add the milk to the chocolate mixture and heat to boiling.

4. Stir in the vanilla extract. Serve hot.

Two-Step Asian Bubble Tea

*This is the Southeast Asian version of a comforting warm milk
and tea drink, made with chewy tapioca pearls.*

Serves 4

Chill: Overnight
Cooking time: 30 minutes

*2 Earl Gray black tea
    bags
12 cups water, divided
1 cup tapioca pearls
4 cups milk
Ice cubes, as desired*

1. The night before, prepare the iced tea, following the instructions in Easy No-Boil Apple-Flavored Iced Tea (page 254), but replacing the 2 cups of apple juice and 2 cups of water with 4 cups water.

2. In a large saucepan, bring 8 cups of water to a boil. Cook the tapioca pearls in the boiling water according to the package directions. Cool and rinse under cold water.

3. Combine the iced tea, milk, and ice cubes in a cocktail shaker. Shake thoroughly to mix together.

4. Divide the cooked tapioca pearls between four glasses, laying out one-quarter of the pearls at the bottom of each glass. Pour 1 cup of the tea/milk mixture into each glass. Do not stir. Serve with a thick straw.

Bubble Tea Accompaniments

Bubble tea just tastes better when it's served in a see-through plastic cup, with a thick straw for sipping. Feel free to top the bubble tea with a sugary syrup, using brown or white sugar (or both!) and whatever ratio of sugar to water that you prefer.

Classic Lemonade

The secret to good lemonade lies in using boiling water, so that the sugar fully dissolves. While freshly squeezed lemons will give a more intense flavor, you can use bottled lemon juice if desired.

1. In a medium saucepan, bring the water and sugar to a boil, stirring to dissolve the sugar.

2. Stir in the lemon juice.

3. Chill until ready to serve.

Extra Special Lemonade

There are many variations on classic lemonade. To make pink lemonade, replace half of the lemon juice with cranberry juice. Raspberry lemonade is made by adding fresh or thawed frozen raspberries to the lemon juice, sugar, and water mixture. And for a quick and easy version of a Gin Fizz, spike this Classic Lemonade with ¼ cup gin.

Red and Blue Berry Smoothie

Chilling the banana firms it up, adding more texture to the smoothie. If available, use a frozen mixed-berry blend.

1. Peel the banana and chill for 15 minutes. Chop into a few pieces.

2. Put the banana, berries, milk, and cinnamon into a blender. Process until liquefied.

3. Add the ice cubes and process again.

4. Pour the smoothie into a large drinking glass and sprinkle the granola on top.

Serves 4

Preparation time:
10 minutes
Chill time: 20 minutes

2 cups water
1 cup sugar
½ cup lemon juice

Serves 1

Chill time: 15 minutes
Assemble time:
5 minutes

1 banana
½ cup frozen raspberries
½ cup frozen blueberries
1 cup milk
⅛ teaspoon ground
   cinnamon, or to taste
4 ice cubes
1 tablespoon granola,
   optional

Green Tea Smoothie

Serves 2

Chill time: 15 minutes
Preparation time:
5 minutes

1 medium banana
1 cup water
1 green tea bag
4 crushed ice cubes
½ cup low-fat peach
    yogurt
½ cup orange juice
1 tablespoon granulated
    sugar

Peach yogurt provides a handy substitute for fresh fruit in this quick and easy smoothie that includes healthy green tea. On days when you have more time, you can replace the peach yogurt with one chopped fresh peach, pitted and sliced, and ½ cup of milk.

1.   Peel the banana and chill for 15 minutes. Chop into a few pieces.

2.   Bring the cup of water to a boil. Add the tea bag and let steep for 3 minutes.

3.   Remove the tea bag and add the ice cubes to chill.

4.   Pour the tea into the blender. Add the yogurt, orange juice, and sugar.

5.   Process until smooth.

Smoothie or Milkshake?

While you can't make a milkshake without milk and ice cream, in a smoothie the dairy products are optional. The main ingredients that make up a smoothie are fruit, fruit juice, and ice. While the fruit provides flavor, ice cubes or crushed ice give the smoothie a thick texture that is similar to a milkshake.

Chocolate Espresso

This rich drink is perfect for days when you want to treat yourself to something special. You can adjust the ratio of hot chocolate to coffee as desired.

Bring all the ingredients to a boil in a medium saucepan, stirring. Serve hot.

Dark Chocolate

There is evidence that chocolate may be good for you! Dark chocolate contains compounds called flavonoids that may help prevent cancer and heart disease. And the saturated fat in chocolate is stearic acid, a fatty acid that does not raise blood cholesterol levels. Chocolate contains a monounsaturated fat, oleic acid, which actually helps lower blood cholesterol levels.

Serves 1

⅓ cup instant coffee crystals
3 tablespoons sweetened hot chocolate
½ cup water
¼ cup milk
¼ cup light cream
¼ teaspoon ground nutmeg
¼ teaspoon ground cinnamon

Chapter 19
Desserts

Chocolate Chow Mein Clusters

Serves 4

Preparation time:
5 minutes
Cooking time:
5–10 minutes

2 cups dry crispy chow
    mein noodles
2 cups coconut chocolate
    macaroon candy
⅓ cup light cream

Kids love this sweet treat, but for a more adult version, you can add 2 or 3 teaspoons of liqueur. Grand Marnier, amaretto, or kirsch brandy are all good choices. If chocolate macaroon candy is unavailable, feel free to use chocolate rosebuds.

1. Place the chow mein noodles in a large bowl.

2. To melt the coconut chocolate macaroon candy on the stovetop, place the macaroons and cream in a bowl over a saucepan half-filled with water, making sure the water doesn't touch the bottom of the bowl. Bring the water to a near boil over medium-low heat, stirring the chocolate macaroon candy constantly so that the chocolate doesn't burn.

3. To melt the chocolate in a microwave, place the chocolate macaroon candy and cream in a microwave-safe bowl. Melt on high heat for 1 minute, stir, and continue microwaving for 30 seconds at a time until the chocolate is melted.

4. Stir the chocolate into the noodles. Chill for 10 to 15 minutes.

Chocolate Melting Tips

Unfortunately for cooks with a sweet tooth, chocolate scorches easily when heated. When melting chocolate in the microwave, always be sure to stir the chocolate between cooking periods. For stovetop melting, make sure the bottom of the bowl containing the chocolate does not come in contact with the heated water.

Skillet Bars

The secret to this recipe is to use quick-cooking oats, which are thinner than regular cooking oatmeal and have been steamed.

1. Place the quick-cooking oats in a large mixing bowl. Set aside.

2. In a skillet, melt the butter on medium-low heat. Add the sugars and cook until they are dissolved and bubbling.

3. Stir in the dried fruit, stirring to mix it in with the dissolved sugar. Push to one side of the skillet.

4. Turn the heat up to medium and add the evaporated milk in the other half of the skillet. When the milk is just starting to boil, stir to mix it in with the dried fruit and sugar mixture.

5. Pour the mixture into the bowl with the quick-cooking oats and mix thoroughly. Press onto a greased 8" × 8" or 9" × 9" baking pan. Chill.

Serves 6

Preparation time:
5 minutes
Cooking time:
10–15 minutes

3 cups quick-cooking
   oats
3 tablespoons butter
¾ cup brown sugar
¾ cup granulated sugar
1½ cups dried fruit and
   nut mix
¾ cup unsweetened
   evaporated milk

Fast Chocolate Fondue

Serves 4

Preparation time:
5–10 minutes
Cooking time:
2–4 minutes

1 pint fresh strawberries
2 (3.5-ounce) Toblerone
*   bars*
⅓ cup half-and-half
*   cream*
½ teaspoon almond
*   extract*
25 vanilla wafers

A microwave is perfect for melting chocolate—no more standing over a stove and constantly stirring and adjusting the temperature to make sure the chocolate doesn't burn!

1. Wash the strawberries, drain, and remove the hulls on top.

2. Break the chocolate bars into several pieces.

3. Place the chocolate and cream in a microwave-safe bowl. Microwave at high heat for 1 minute, stir, and then microwave for another minute. Stir in the almond extract.

4. Continue microwaving for 15 seconds at a time, stirring each time, until the chocolate is melted. (Be sure not to burn the chocolate.)

5. Serve the fondue with the strawberries and vanilla wafers for dipping.

Decadent Chocolate Fondue

Chocolate fondue is the perfect choice when you need to make a delicious dessert in a hurry. Many dessert pots are microwave-safe, meaning you can cook and serve the fondue in the same dish. Instead of strawberries, you can use other firm fresh fruit in season, or canned fruit such as pineapple.

Easy Blueberry Ice Cream Parfait

Parfaits are the perfect quick dessert—elegant, easy to make, and full of flavor. To transform this into a low-calorie dessert, simply use sugar-free strawberry preserves and replace the ice cream with your favorite flavor of yogurt.

1. Line the bottom of each parfait glass with ¼ cup of blueberries.

2. Spoon ¼ cup of the ice cream on top of the blueberries.

3. Spoon ¼ cup of the strawberry preserves on top of the ice cream.

4. Garnish with the mint leaves.

Serves 6

Preparation time:
10 minutes

1½ cups fresh or frozen (thawed) blueberries
1½ cups chocolate chip ice cream
1½ cups strawberry preserves
Mint leaves, for garnish

Microwave S'mores

The classic campfire treat, invented in the early twentieth century, s'mores are easy to make at home in a microwave oven.

Serves 6

Preparation time:
5 minutes
Cooking time:
3–5 minutes

12 whole graham
    crackers (2-part
    square)
1 cup semisweet
    chocolate chips
½ cup mini marshmallows

1. Lay 6 graham crackers in a microwave-safe shallow baking dish.

2. In a small bowl, stir together the chocolate chips and marshmallows.

3. Arrange the chocolate and marshmallows over the graham crackers.

4. Microwave on high heat for 1½ minutes, and then for 15 or 30 seconds at a time until the chocolate and marshmallows are melted.

5. Remove and top each s'more with a graham cracker to make a sandwich.

Stovetop S'mores

Don't have a microwave? Don't worry, you don't need to start up a campfire in the backyard—s'mores can also be made on the stovetop. Just melt the marshmallows and chocolate over low heat, according to the instructions for melting chocolate in Chocolate Chow Mein Clusters (page 264). Spread a portion of the chocolate over half the graham crackers and lay the remaining crackers on top, pressing down to make a sandwich.

Steamed Pears

Brushing the peeled pears with lemon juice helps prevent them from browning. Be sure to use a firm pear (such as Bartlett) that is not overripe.

Serves 4

Preparation time:
7–10 minutes
Cooking time:
5–10 minutes

4 Bartlett pears
4 tablespoons liquid
   honey
3 tablespoons golden
   raisins
¼ teaspoon ground
   cinnamon
2 tablespoons lemon juice

1. Peel and core the pears.

2. In a small bowl, stir together the honey, raisins, and ground cinnamon.

3. Stand the pears in a deep-sided, microwave-safe casserole dish. Brush the pears with the lemon juice. Carefully spoon the honey mixture into the core of each pear.

4. Cover the dish with microwave-safe plastic wrap.

5. Microwave the pears on high heat for 5 minutes. Give the dish a quarter turn and then microwave for 1 minute at a time until the pears are cooked through (they should be tender and easy to pierce with a fork).

How Does a Microwave Work?

Microwaves are electromagnetic waves that operate within the same frequency as radio waves. When the microwaves hit the food, they cause water molecules in the food to jiggle and vibrate. This molecular movement creates the heat that cooks the food. The need for water molecules to create heat means that it's best to stick with foods with a high liquid content.

Microwave Fudge

Serves 6

Preparation time:
5 minutes
Cooking time:
4–5 minutes

1½ cups semisweet
    chocolate chips
½ cup margarine
1½ cups sweetened
    condensed milk
2 teaspoons vanilla
    extract
2 cups chopped pecans

Sweetened condensed milk gives a rich, caramel-like flavor to this easy fudge recipe. The recipe calls for margarine, but you can, of course, use butter if desired.

1. Grease an 8" × 8" baking pan.

2. Combine the chocolate chips, margarine, condensed milk, and vanilla extract in a microwave-safe dish.

3. Microwave on high heat for 2 minutes. Stir and microwave for 1 minute. Stir and microwave for another minute. Continue microwaving for short periods as needed, stirring each time, until the chocolate is thoroughly melted. (Take care not to burn the chocolate.)

4. Pour the mixture into the baking pan. Stir in the pecans.

5. Cover and refrigerate or freeze until set.

Five-Minute Chocolate "Mousse"

Serve this simple dessert in tall parfait glasses, topped with chocolate sprinkles or maraschino cherries.

Serves 6

Preparation time:
5 minutes
Chill time: 1 hour

2 teaspoons instant coffee
    granules
2½ cups whipping cream
2 cups semisweet
    chocolate chips
4 tablespoons granulated
    sugar
1 teaspoon vanilla extract

1. In a medium heavy saucepan, heat the coffee granules and whipping cream until hot but not boiling (this will help melt the chocolate chips). Stir frequently to dissolve the coffee granules.

2. Place the chocolate chips and sugar in a blender. Add the vanilla extract and the heated cream.

3. Process for a minute, or until smooth and the chocolate chips are melted.

4. Pour into serving dishes, cover, and chill for about 1 hour.

Basic Peanut Butter Cookies

Serves 10

Preparation time:
10 minutes
Cooking time: 12 minutes

1 cup chunky peanut
    butter
1 cup margarine, room
    temperature
½ cup granulated sugar
½ cup brown sugar
1 teaspoon vanilla extract
1 large egg
¾ cup chocolate chips
1 teaspoon baking soda
½ teaspoon salt
1½ cups all-purpose flour

While rolling the cookies, keep the remainder of the cookie dough covered in plastic wrap so that it doesn't dry out. Feel free to replace the chocolate chips with raisins if desired.

1. Preheat the oven to 375° F. Grease 2 9" × 13" baking sheet.

2. In a large mixing bowl, stir together the peanut butter, margarine, sugars, vanilla extract, and the egg, mixing well. Stir in the chocolate chips.

3. In a separate medium mixing bowl, stir the baking soda and salt with the flour. Gradually stir the flour into the creamed peanut butter mixture with a wooden spoon.

4. Roll the dough into balls about 1–1½" in diameter. Place on the baking sheets, approximately 2" apart. (You will have more cookies than can fit on the 2 sheets and will need to use one of them again.) Press down in the middle of each cookie with a wet fork.

5. Bake for 12 minutes, or until the cookies are browned around the edges and a toothpick placed in the middle comes out clean. Cool and store in a sealed container.

Freezing Cookies

Fresh-baked cookies can be frozen and enjoyed later. To freeze, place the cookies in individual resealable plastic bags, or between layers of wax paper in a sealed container. For best results, do not freeze the cookies for longer than three months.

Low-Cal Raspberry Parfait

This light, healthy dessert is perfect for weeknights.
You can replace the raspberries with blueberries
or other seasonal fruit as desired.

Serves 8

Preparation time:
7–10 minutes

2 cups plain fat-free
    yogurt
1 teaspoon vanilla extract
2 cups fresh or frozen
    thawed raspberries
2 cups Instant Granola
    (page 19) or store-
    bought granola

1. In a medium mixing bowl, stir together the yogurt and vanilla extract.

2. Line the bottom of a parfait or dessert glass with ¼ cup of raspberries.

3. Spoon ¼ cup of the yogurt mixture on top of the raspberries.

4. Sprinkle ¼ cup of the granola on top of the yogurt.

5. Continue with the remainder of the parfaits.

No-Bake Cookies

Serves 6

Preparation time:
5 minutes
Cooking time:
15–20 minutes

2½ cups Rice Krispies
   cereal
1½ cups dried fruit and
   nut mixture
2 tablespoons butter
1 cup granulated sugar
½ cup sweetened
   condensed milk
1 teaspoon vanilla extract

Light, crunchy Rice Krispies cereal is perfect for making these easy no-bake cookies. You can replace ½ cup of the dried fruit and nuts with ½ cup of dried cranberries if desired.

1. Combine the Rice Krispies cereal and the fruit and nut mixture in a large mixing bowl. Set aside.

2. In a skillet, melt the butter and sugar on medium-low heat. Cook, stirring constantly, until the sugar is dissolved and bubbling (5 to 6 minutes).

3. Add the sweetened condensed milk and bring to a boil, stirring constantly, until it is just bubbling and is thickened (5 to 6 minutes).

4. Pour into the bowl with the Rice Krispies and dried fruit and nut mixture. Stir in the vanilla extract. Chill in the coldest part of the refrigerator for 5 minutes.

5. Roll into small balls and place on two greased 9" × 13" baking sheets. Cool until ready to serve.

Evaporated or Condensed Milk?

Both evaporated and condensed milk have approximately 60 percent of the water removed through an evaporation process. However, in the case of condensed milk, the evaporated milk is sweetened with sugar. This makes it perfect for desserts and cookies such as the ones in this recipe.

Pan-Fried Pineapple Rings with Brown Sugar

This simple dessert features the classic combination of tart pineapple and brown sugar. Use sweetened or unsweetened coconut flakes as desired.

Serves 4

Preparation time:
5 minutes
Cooking time:
6–7 minutes

¼ cup brown sugar
¼ cup reserved, canned pineapple juice
1 teaspoon vanilla extract
2 tablespoons coconut flakes
2 teaspoons margarine
1 (20-ounce) can pineapple rings, drained

1. In a medium saucepan, heat the brown sugar, pineapple juice, and vanilla extract over medium to medium-low heat, stirring to dissolve the sugar. Turn the heat down to low and keep warm.

2. Place the coconut flakes in a frying pan over medium heat. Cook for a minute, stirring or shaking the pan.

3. Melt the margarine in the pan. Add the pineapple and cook, continuing to shake the pan. Continue cooking until the coconut is browned and the pineapple is heated through (total cooking time for the coconut is 2 to 3 minutes). Remove the pan from the heat.

4. Pour the brown sugar and pineapple mixture on top. Serve immediately.

Easy Rice Pudding

Serves 4

Preparation time:
5 minutes
Cooking time: 10 minutes

1 cup instant rice
1 cup boiling water
6 tablespoons orange
    juice
1½ cups plain yogurt
2 tablespoons granulated
    sugar
1½ teaspoons ground
    cinnamon
¾ cup golden raisins

The cinnamon and sugar blend in this recipe also goes nicely on toast. Simply spread the cinnamon and sugar on two slices of buttered toast and enjoy!

1. Prepare the instant rice in the boiling water (see Basic Cooked Instant Rice, page 146, for instructions). Set aside.

2. Stir the orange juice into the yogurt.

3. Stir in the sugar and ground cinnamon and raisins.

4. Stir in the cooked rice.

Raisin Softening Tip

Place the raisins in a microwave-safe bowl and drizzle with water (2 teaspoons per ½ cup of raisins). Cover with plastic wrap and microwave on high heat for 30 seconds, and then for 15 seconds at a time until the raisins are softened and fragrant. The total cooking time for ½ cup of raisins should be about 45 seconds.

Make-Ahead Freezer Cookie Dough

The higher than usual proportion of butter to flour in this make-ahead recipe helps keep the dough from drying out.

Yields about 48 cookies

Preparation time:
20 minutes
Chill time: at least 2 hours

2 sticks unsalted butter,
   softened
1 cup granulated sugar
1 tablespoon lemon juice
2 cups all-purpose flour
¼ teaspoon salt
½ cup dried cranberries
½ cup dried fruit and
   nut mix

1. In a large mixing bowl, cream together the butter and sugar. Blend in the lemon juice.

2. Using an electric mixer set at low speed, gradually add the flour and salt until you have a soft dough.

3. Gradually add the cranberries and dried fruit and nut mixture.

4. Roll the dough into two separate logs. Wrap each log firmly in plastic wrap and chill until ready to bake.

Marshmallow Gelatin Dessert

For best results, make sure the cranberry juice is cold. To speed up the setting time, use a metal mold (gelatin sets more quickly in a metal container).

Serves 4

Preparation time:
5 minutes
Cooking time: 5 minutes
Chill time: about 1 hour

1 envelope unflavored gelatin
4 tablespoons sugar
1 cup boiling water
½ cup cranberry juice
½ cup reserved pineapple juice
1 cup drained pineapple tidbits
1 cup mini marshmallows

1. In a medium mixing bowl, stir together the gelatin and sugar. Add the boiling water, stirring until the gelatin is fully dissolved.

2. Stir in the cranberry juice and reserved pineapple juice.

3. Pour into a bowl or serving mold. Chill until mixture has thickened but not completely set.

4. Stir in the pineapple and marshmallows.

5. Continue chilling until fully set.

Pineapple Facts

Did you know: Fresh pineapple is never used in gelatin desserts because it contains an enzyme, bromelain, that prevents gelatin from setting. However, canned pineapple is safe to use, since the enzyme is destroyed during the canning process.

Cranberry Chews

Dried cranberries and lemon juice add a tart flavor to these chewy cookies. This recipe yields about 40 cookies.

Serves 8

Preparation time: 15 minutes
Cooking time: 10 minutes

1½ cups all-purpose flour
½ teaspoon baking soda
¾ teaspoon ground
  cinnamon
½ teaspoon salt
1½ sticks unsalted butter,
  softened
¾ cup granulated sugar
1 large egg
1 tablespoon lemon juice
¾ cup dried cranberries

1. Preheat the oven to 350°F. Grease two 9" × 13" baking sheets.

2. In a bowl, stir together the flour, baking soda, ground cinnamon, and salt.

3. In a separate large mixing bowl, use an electric mixer to mix together the butter and sugar. Gradually beat in the egg and lemon juice. Blend in the flour mixture. Stir in the dried cranberries.

4. Drop a heaping teaspoon of dough onto the baking sheet. Space the cookies on the cookie sheets about 2" apart. Press down gently with a fork.

5. Bake the cookies for 10 minutes, or until the edges are golden brown and crisp. Remove and let cool.

Rice Krispies Squares

Serves 8

Preparation time:
5 minutes
Cooking time: 5 minutes

½ stick unsalted butter
4 cups regular-size
    marshmallows
1 teaspoon vanilla extract
6 cups Kellogg's Rice
    Krispies cereal
1 cup salted cashews

Vanilla extract and cashews add extra flavor to this easy-to-make treat. You can replace the cashews with peanuts or pecans if desired.

1. Place the butter in a microwave-safe bowl. Microwave on high heat for 45 seconds, and then for 15 seconds at a time or as needed until the butter is melted.

2. Stir in the marshmallows and the vanilla extract. Microwave on high heat for 45 seconds. Continue microwaving and stirring until the marshmallows are melted.

3. Stir in the Rice Krispies and the cashews.

4. Spread out the mixture in a greased 9" × 13" pan.

5. Serve immediately or chill until ready to serve.

Rice Krispies—Perfect for Desserts

Invented by employees at Kellogg's in the late 1930s, the original Rice Krispies dessert consisted of Rice Krispies cereal, marshmallows, and melted butter. Today, recipes abound for more elaborate versions with peanut butter, chocolate, coconut, or even ice cream.

Easy Chocolate Chip "Ice Cream"

Chocolate chip and peppermint make a classic combination.

1. In a heavy saucepan, bring the water and sugar to a boil, stirring to dissolve the sugar.

2. Place the milk in a large bowl. Stir in the peppermint extract.

3. Stir in the sugar and water mixture. Stir in the egg.

4. Place in the freezer.

5. When the milk is partially frozen, stir in the chocolate chips. Continue freezing. Let thaw briefly before serving.

Serves 6

Preparation time:
5 minutes
Cooking time:
5–10 minutes

⅓ cup water
⅔ cup sugar
2 cups milk
1½ teaspoons peppermint
  extract
1 egg, beaten
1⅓ cups semisweet
  chocolate chips

Chapter 20

Quick Baked Breads, Cakes, and Pies

Coffee Cake

Serves 6

Preparation time:
10 minutes
Cooking time:
30–35 minutes

2 cups flour
1½ teaspoons baking
    powder
1 teaspoon baking soda
½ teaspoon salt
1 teaspoon ground
    cinnamon
½ teaspoon ground
    nutmeg
¼ teaspoon ground
    ginger
½ banana
½ cup vegetable oil
1 teaspoon vanilla extract
1½ cups French vanilla
    yogurt

*There's no beating and mixing required in this quick and easy
cake recipe. For an added touch, top the cake with a mixture of
¾ cup vanilla yogurt, 3 tablespoons granulated sugar, and
1½ tablespoons pineapple juice. Brush over the cake
during the last 10 minutes of baking.*

1.   Preheat the oven to 350°F. Grease an 8" × 8" cake pan.

2.   In a medium mixing bowl, combine the flour, baking powder, baking
     soda, salt, cinnamon, nutmeg, and ginger. In a large mixing bowl, mash
     the banana with a potato masher. Whisk in the vegetable oil and vanilla
     extract.

3.   Add the dry ingredients and the vanilla yogurt alternately to the wet
     ingredients. Stir until well combined.

4.   Pour the batter into the prepared cake pan.

5.   Bake at 350°F for 30 to 35 minutes, or until a toothpick inserted in the
     middle comes out clean.

Do You Need to Sift?

*Sifting dry ingredients in a baking recipe serves several purposes, from
lightening flour to thoroughly blending all the dry ingredients and
removing any clumps. Now that most commercially produced flour is
pre-sifted, many recipes skip this step. If a recipe does call for sifted flour,
be sure to sift before measuring so as not to affect the recipe propor-
tions. If a recipe doesn't call for sifting, be sure to thoroughly combine
the dry ingredients with a fork.*

Quick Banana Bread

As the name implies, quick breads are quicker and easier to make than yeast-based bread. You can add ½ cup of cranberries to the bread batter just before baking.

1. Preheat the oven to 350°F. Grease a 9" × 5" bread pan.

2. In a large mixing bowl, mash the bananas. Whisk in the milk, reserved pineapple juice, egg, and vanilla extract.

3. In a separate mixing bowl, combine the flour, baking powder, baking soda, sugar, salt, and ground cinnamon.

4. Gradually stir the dry ingredients into the wet ingredients. Stir in the crushed pineapple.

5. Pour the batter into the prepared bread pan, spreading it out evenly. Bake at 350°F for 60 minutes, or until a toothpick placed in the middle of the bread comes out clean.

Quick Breads

If you've ever whipped up a batch of muffins, you have experienced cooking quick breads. Instead of yeast, quick breads rely on baking powder and baking soda for lift. Quick breads are less labor-intensive (no need for rolling and punching out bread dough), and take less time to make than standard yeast-based bread doughs.

Serves 8

Preparation time:
15 minutes
Baking time: 60 minutes, or as needed

1½ cups mashed bananas (3 large bananas)
¼ cup milk
¼ cup reserved pineapple juice
1 large egg
1 teaspoon vanilla extract
2 cups all-purpose flour
1 teaspoon baking powder
½ teaspoon baking soda
1 cup granulated sugar
½ teaspoon salt
½ teaspoon ground cinnamon
1 cup drained crushed pineapple

Quick Zucchini Bread

This recipe is a great way to introduce children to zucchini. You will need two zucchini for this recipe—be sure to drain any excess liquid from the grated zucchini before stirring it into the batter.

Serves 8

Preparation time:
15 minutes
Baking time: 60 minutes

1½ cups mashed bananas
   (3 large bananas)
⅓ cup milk
½ cup vanilla-flavored
   yogurt
1 large egg
1 teaspoon vanilla extract
2 cups all-purpose flour
2 teaspoons baking
   powder
½ teaspoon baking soda
1 cup granulated sugar
½ teaspoon salt
½ teaspoon ground
   cinnamon
2 cups grated zucchini

1. Preheat the oven to 350°F. Grease a 9" × 5" bread pan.

2. In a large mixing bowl, mash the bananas. Whisk in the milk, yogurt, egg, and vanilla extract.

3. In a separate mixing bowl, combine the flour, baking powder, baking soda, sugar, salt, and cinnamon.

4. Gradually stir the dry ingredients into the wet ingredients. Stir in the grated zucchini.

5. Pour the batter into the prepared pan, spreading it out evenly. Bake at 350°F for 60 minutes, or until a toothpick stuck in the middle of the bread comes out clean.

Adjusting for Altitude

Reduced air pressure means that baking at an altitude above 3,000 feet can wreak havoc with recipes—cakes fall and quick breads lack flavor. If baking at a high altitude is affecting how your quick breads turn out, one solution is to reduce the amount of baking powder. Experts recommended using ¼ less teaspoon for every teaspoon called for in the recipe.

Easy Chocolate Cake

Souring the milk with lemon juice adds extra flavor to this simple cake that doesn't require any mixing or beating.

1. Preheat the oven to 350°F. Grease an 8" × 8" baking pan.

2. In a small bowl, sour the milk by stirring in the lemon juice.

3. In a large bowl, combine the flour, salt, baking soda, and sugar. Stir in the chocolate.

4. Stir in the vegetable oil, soured milk, vanilla extract, and vinegar. Do not beat but make sure the mixture is well blended.

5. Pour the batter into the prepared cake pan. Bake the cake for 30 to 35 minutes, until cooked through (begin checking the cake after 30 minutes). Cool. Carefully remove the cake from the pan.

Serves 8

Preparation time:
10–15 minutes
Cooking time:
30–35 minutes

1 cup milk
1 tablespoon lemon juice
1½ cups all-purpose flour
½ teaspoon salt
1 teaspoon baking soda
1 cup granulated sugar
1 package sweetened
    hot chocolate (3
    tablespoons)
⅓ cup vegetable oil
1 teaspoon vanilla extract
1 tablespoon white
    vinegar

Sour Cream Cake

Serves 8

Preparation time:
15 minutes
Cooking time:
40–45 minutes

1 banana, mashed
2 tablespoons vegetable
    oil
¼ cup pineapple juice
1 teaspoon vanilla extract
1 cup all-purpose flour
1 teaspoon baking soda
½ teaspoon salt
½ cup granulated sugar
¾ cup sour cream
¾ cup crushed pineapple

This cake tastes even better the next day. Feel free to increase the amount of sugar to ¾ cup if desired.

1. Preheat the oven to 350°F. Grease an 8" × 8" cake pan.

2. In a large mixing bowl, mash the banana with a potato masher. Whisk in the vegetable oil, pineapple juice, and vanilla extract. In a medium mixing bowl, combine the flour, baking soda, salt, and sugar.

3. Stir about half the dry ingredients into the wet ingredients. Stir in ½ cup sour cream, then the remaining half of the dry ingredients. Stir in the remaining ¼ cup sour cream and the crushed pineapple.

4. Pour the batter into the prepared cake pan.

5. Bake at 350°F for 40 minutes, or until a toothpick inserted in the middle comes out clean.

How to Measure Flour

While many types of recipes are fairly forgiving, accurate measurements are critical in baking. When measuring flour, always spoon the flour loosely into a measuring cup, and then pull the edge of a knife across the top to level it off. Never pack the flour into the cup, or use a measuring cup with a pouring lip that can't be leveled off at the top.

Easy Cake Mix Cherry Cobbler

Blending the cake mix and butter gives this cobbler a nice crisp topping. However, you can also cut the butter into several small pieces and lay them on top of the cake mix before baking.

1. Preheat oven to 350°F. Grease two 8" × 8" cake pans.

2. In a large mixing bowl, stir together the pineapple and cherry pie filling. Pour the cake mix into a large mixing bowl. Cut the butter into the cake mix with a knife, and then use your fingers to combine the cake mix and butter until it has a crumb-like texture.

3. Spread half of the pineapple and cherry pie mixture into each pan. Sprinkle half the cake mix on top of the fruit mixture in each pan.

4. Bake the cakes for 60 minutes, or until the topping is crisp and browned.

5. While the cakes are baking, in a large bowl stir the lime juice into the Cool Whip topping, blending thoroughly. Spread over the baked cakes.

Delicious Dump Cake

Another name for Easy Cake Mix Cherry Cobbler is Dump Cake. One of the easiest cakes to make, dump cake gets its name from the fact that the ingredients are dumped into the pan, with no beating or mixing. Feel free to vary the basic recipe by experimenting with different cake mix flavors, and replacing the cherry pie with apple pie filling or canned fruit.

Serves 8

Preparation time:
10 minutes
Cooking time: 60 minutes

1 (19-ounce) can crushed
   pineapple with juice
1 (20-ounce) can cherry
   pie filling
1 package yellow cake
   mix
1½ sticks butter, softened
⅓ cup frozen lime juice,
   thawed
1½ cups Cool Whip Lite
   whipped topping,
   thawed

Cherry and Apple Crumble

Serves 6

Preparation time:
15 minutes
Cooking time:
30–40 minutes

1 cup all-purpose flour
1 teaspoon ground
    cinnamon
½ stick butter, softened
¼ cup brown sugar
1 cup cherry pie filling
1 cup apple pie filling

Using pie filling instead of fresh fruit takes most of the work out of this popular dessert. If you don't want to combine the two flavors, you can substitute one (20-ounce) can of cherry, apple, or your own favorite fruit pie filling.

1. Preheat the oven to 350°F. Grease a 9" × 9" pan.

2. Place the flour in a medium mixing bowl. Stir in the ground cinnamon. Cut the butter into the bowl, then use your fingers to combine the flour and butter until it has a crumb-like texture. Stir in the brown sugar, again using your fingers to mix it in.

3. Put the two pie fillings into the bottom of the pan, stirring to combine.

4. Sprinkle the crumb mixture over the pie filling.

5. Bake the crumble at 350°F for 30 minutes, or until the top is browned and crisp and the filling is bubbling. Place on a wire rack to cool for about 20 minutes before serving.

Crisp or Crumble?

Both of these desserts consist of fruit that is topped with a crumb coating and baked. However, while flour is the main ingredient in a crumble topping, crisp toppings usually include oats.

Cream Cheese Apple Pie

Sweetened condensed milk adds a decadent touch to this simple frozen dessert. Sift the sugar if needed to prevent any clumps from forming in the dessert.

Serves 6

Preparation time:
10 minutes

1 (8-ounce) package
    cream cheese
½ teaspoon vanilla extract
½ teaspoon ground
    cinnamon
⅓ cup sweetened
    condensed milk
1 pre-made 9" graham
    cracker pie crust
1 cup applesauce

1. In a large mixing bowl, combine the cream cheese, vanilla extract, and ground cinnamon.

2. Stir in the sweetened condensed milk. Do not beat, but stir until the cream cheese has a smooth texture and all the ingredients are well combined.

3. Spoon the mixture into the pie crust.

4. Freeze until it has set.

5. Spoon the applesauce on top and serve.

Five-Ingredient Frozen Lemon Pie

Sweetened condensed milk lends texture and flavor, while Cool Whip adds a sweet decadence to this easy recipe that kids will love. Be sure to use a quality lemon juice from concentrate, such as ReaLemon.

Serves 6

Preparation time:
5–8 minutes

1 cup Cool Whip Lite
    whipped topping,
    thawed
½ cup sweetened
    condensed milk
½ cup lemon juice
1½ tablespoons
    sweetened coconut
    flakes
1 pre-made 9" graham
    cracker pie crust

1. In a medium mixing bowl, combine the Cool Whip topping, sweetened condensed milk, lemon juice, and coconut flakes.

2. Spoon the mixture into the pie crust.

3. Cover and freeze until set. Let thaw for 5 minutes before serving.

Fun with Cool Whip

Cool Whip is a nondairy imitation whipped cream that is used to make frozen pies and as a dessert topping. The beauty of Cool Whip is that there's no whipping involved—it's ready to use straight from the container. However, if you're one of those people who think that it tastes a little bland, you can stir in some fruit juice for extra flavor.

Frozen Lime Pie

Flavorful French vanilla yogurt takes the place of sweetened condensed milk in this recipe, reducing the total calorie count. Minute Maid frozen limeade works well in this recipe.

Serves 8

Preparation time:
5–8 minutes

½ cup frozen lime juice, thawed
½ teaspoon salt
1 cup French vanilla-flavored yogurt
1 cup Cool Whip Lite whipped topping, thawed
2 pre-made 6" graham cracker pie crusts

1. In a medium mixing bowl, stir the lime juice and salt into the yogurt.

2. Add the Cool Whip topping. Stir until thoroughly blended.

3. Spoon the mixture into the pie crusts, using a knife to spread out evenly.

4. Cover and freeze until set. Let thaw for 5 minutes before cutting and serving.

Serves 6

Preparation time:
5–10 minutes

¾ cup mango-flavored
    yogurt
¾ cup Cool Whip Lite
    whipped topping,
    thawed
2 tablespoons sweetened
    condensed milk
1 pre-made 9" graham
    cracker pie crust
½ cup pecans

Yogurt Pecan Pie

Pecans and mango-flavored yogurt give this simple dessert a tropical flavor. To enhance the effect, you can stir 1 to 2 tablespoons of sweetened coconut flakes into the whipped topping mixture before spreading it over the pie crust.

1. In a medium mixing bowl, combine the yogurt, Cool Whip, and sweetened condensed milk, blending thoroughly.

2. Spread the mixture into the pie crust, using a knife to spread it out evenly.

3. Cover and freeze until set.

4. Let thaw for 5 minutes before serving. Garnish with the pecans.

Make Your Own Graham Cracker Crust

Pie crusts made with graham crackers are perfect for frozen desserts such as this one. If pre-made graham cracker pie crusts aren't available at your local supermarket, it's easy to make your own. Melt ½ stick of unsalted butter and stir in 1½ cups crushed honey graham wafers. Press into a 9" × 9" pie pan. Store in the refrigerator until ready to use.

Cinnamon Crumb Cake

A simple crumb coating made with flour, butter, and brown sugar is a great way to finish off a coffee cake. To quickly soften butter, place it on a microwave-safe plate and microwave for 10 to 15 seconds, 5 seconds at a time, as needed.

Serves 6

Preparation time:
5–10 minutes
Cooking time:
30–35 minutes

1 cup flour
½ stick butter, softened
¼ cup brown sugar, packed
1 Coffee Cake (page 284)

1. Preheat the oven to 350°F. Grease an 8" × 8" cake pan.

2. Place 1 cup flour in a medium mixing bowl. Cut the butter into the bowl, then use your fingers to combine the flour and butter until it has a crumb-like texture. Add the brown sugar, again using your fingers to mix it in.

3. Follow the directions for Coffee Cake (page 284).

4. When you are ready to bake the cake, sprinkle the crumb coating over the top of the cake before placing it in the oven.

5. Bake the cake at 350°F for 30 to 35 minutes, or until a toothpick inserted in the middle comes out clean.

Appendix A
Menu Suggestions

From the Garden and the Sea

Quick Tuna with Marinara Sauce (page 136)
Creamy Risotto Side Dish (page 150)
Quick Zucchini Bread (page 286)

Backyard Barbecue

Grilled Salmon (page 215)
Spicy Mexican Potato Salad (page 74)
French or Italian Bread
Easy Iced Coffee (page 257)

Classic Italian

Pan-Fried Garlic Chicken Thighs with Sun-Dried Tomatoes (page 90)
Savory Rice with Portobello Mushrooms (page 158)
Roasted Red Peppers (page 221)

Chinese Takeaway

Easy Egg Drop Soup (page 58)
Beef and Broccoli Stir-Fry (page 94)
Three Mushroom Stir-Fry (page 226)
Cooked Rice

Asian Flavors

Pork Satay with Spicy Peanut Sauce (page 214)
Steamed Coconut Rice (page 153)
Thai-Style Creamed Corn (page 225)

Warming Winter Meal

Rosemary Lamb Chops (page 113)
Simple Glazed Baby Carrots (page 228)
Sautéed Asparagus (page 228)
Cooked Noodles

Fall Harvest

Turkey Meat Loaf (page 89)
Roasted Fall Harvest Vegetables (page 222)
Easy Garlic Toast (page 240)

Midweek Break

Glazed Ham (page 198)
Garlic Mashed Potatoes (page 232)
Quick Green Beans Amandine (page 222)
Low-Cal Raspberry Parfait (page 273) or Easy Blueberry Ice Cream Parfait (page 267)

Appendix B
Glossary of Basic Cooking Terms

al dente:
An Italian term literally meaning "to the tooth," al dente is used to describe the state to which pasta should be cooked. Pasta that is cooked al dente has no taste of flour remaining, but there is still a slight resistance and chewiness when it is bitten into. Like Italian pasta, Chinese egg noodles should be cooked al dente.

baste:
To spoon liquid over a food while it is cooking. Meat, seafood, or poultry may be basted with a marinade during broiling or grilling, while meat or poultry is frequently basted with drippings from the bottom of a pan during roasting.

blanch:
To partially cook food by plunging it briefly into boiling water. Blanching is used to loosen the skin on fruit or nuts, or to partially cook food before finishing cooking by another method (such as stir-frying). Normally, blanched food is immediately plunged into ice water to stop the cooking process. Depending on the purpose, blanching times will vary from a few seconds to minutes.

blend:
To thoroughly mix two or more ingredients together until they are smooth and indistinguishable from one another. Liquid or wet ingredients are blended together, as in a shake, salad dressing, or sauce.

boil:
To cook food by immersing it in water that has been heated to the point where bubbles are regularly breaking on the surface. Although boiling is an excellent quick-cooking method, it is less healthy than steaming, as some of the nutrients may be lost in the cooking water.

braise:
To cook meat in a small amount of liquid in a tightly covered pan. Normally, the meat is browned before braising. Popular braising liquids include wine and broth.

broil:
To cook food by radiant heat (the transfer of heat from a heated surface). In the case of broiling, the heated surface is located above the food.

brown:
Browning food consists of heating it in a small amount of oil to seal in the juices. Browning food is not stirred, but is turned over halfway through cooking. Normally, the food is not browned for more than five minutes on each side.

caramelize:
Caramelization comprises heating sugar until it liquefies into a caramel-colored syrup. Carmelizing vegetables refers to heating vegetables (such as pearl onions) until they release their natural sugars.

chop:
To cut food into small pieces. While the chopped pieces of food don't need to be uniform, they should be roughly the same size to cook evenly.

dash or pinch:

A inexact measurement, equal to approximately 1/16 teaspoon.

deep-fry:

To cook food by immersing it in hot oil. Once the food is deep-fried, it is removed with a slotted spoon or a mesh container and drained. While deep-frying is very quick, it can take several minutes for the oil to heat to the correct temperature. An electric deep-fat fryer heats the oil more quickly.

deglaze:

To heat liquid in a pan or roasting pan that has been used to cook meat or poultry. A rubber spatula is used to scrape up leftover browned bits from the cooked meat. The browned bits gradually mix with the liquid, adding extra flavor. Deglazing does not take much time, and is a great way to add extra flavor to the dish.

dice:

To cut food into half-inch cubes.

dredge:

To coat food with a dry ingredient, such as flour or bread crumbs, before it is fried. Dredging the food before frying gives a crunchy coating and seals in flavor.

grill:

Like broiling, grilling consists of cooking food through the transfer of heat from a heated surface. Unlike broiling, however, the heated surface is located below the food.

marinate:

To soak food such as meat or poultry in a liquid before cooking. Marinating tenderizes food and adds flavor. Since marinades used to flavor raw food can carry bacteria, it is best not to add leftover marinade to food while it is cooking. Instead, prepare more marinade than you need and set aside a portion to add to the food.

mince:

To cut food into very small pieces. Minced food is cut more finely than either chopped or diced food. Garlic and ginger are frequently minced before being added to stir-fries.

sauté:

To quickly cook food over high heat in a small amount of butter or oil.

simmer:

To cook food in water that has been brought almost to a boil. When water is simmering, the bubbles are rising slowly, and often breaking before reaching the surface. In cooking, liquid is often brought to a boil and then simmered at a lower heat.

steam:

To cook food by placing it over water that has been brought to a boil. The steam produced by the boiling water cooks the food.

stir-fry:

To quickly cook food over high heat by stirring it continually in a small amount of oil. Unlike sautéing, food is cut into smaller, uniform pieces before it is stir-fried.

Appendix C
Food Doneness Chart

How can you tell when food is done? One way is to check the appearance: ground beef will have no trace of pink and fish will flake easily with a fork. However, the safest way to ensure that food is cooked all the way through is to test the internal temperature. Insert a meat thermometer into the thickest part of the meat, without touching any bone. Here are the internal doneness temperatures for various types of food:

Food	Temperature
Ground Beef	165°F
Whole Chicken	160°F
Chicken Thighs	160°F
Chicken Breasts	170°F
Pork	165°F
Steak, Medium Rare	145°F
Steak, Medium	160°F
Steak, Well Done	170°F

Index

THE EVERYTHING SERIES!

BUSINESS & PERSONAL FINANCE

Everything® Accounting Book
Everything® Budgeting Book, 2nd Ed.
Everything® Business Planning Book
Everything® Coaching and Mentoring Book, 2nd Ed.
Everything® Fundraising Book
Everything® Get Out of Debt Book
Everything® Grant Writing Book, 2nd Ed.
Everything® Guide to Buying Foreclosures
Everything® Guide to Fundraising, $15.95
Everything® Guide to Mortgages
Everything® Guide to Personal Finance for Single Mothers
Everything® Home-Based Business Book, 2nd Ed.
Everything® Homebuying Book, 3rd Ed., $15.95
Everything® Homeselling Book, 2nd Ed.
Everything® Human Resource Management Book
Everything® Improve Your Credit Book
Everything® Investing Book, 2nd Ed.
Everything® Landlording Book
Everything® Leadership Book, 2nd Ed.
Everything® Managing People Book, 2nd Ed.
Everything® Negotiating Book
Everything® Online Auctions Book
Everything® Online Business Book
Everything® Personal Finance in Your 20s & 30s Book, 2nd Ed.
Everything® Personal Finance in Your 40s & 50s Book, $15.95
Everything® Project Management Book, 2nd Ed.
Everything® Real Estate Investing Book
Everything® Retirement Planning Book
Everything® Robert's Rules Book, $7.95
Everything® Selling Book
Everything® Start Your Own Business Book, 2nd Ed.
Everything® Wills & Estate Planning Book

COOKING

Everything® Barbecue Cookbook
Everything® Bartender's Book, 2nd Ed., $9.95
Everything® Calorie Counting Cookbook
Everything® Cheese Book
Everything® Chinese Cookbook
Everything® Classic Recipes Book
Everything® Cocktail Parties & Drinks Book
Everything® College Cookbook
Everything® Cooking for Baby and Toddler Book
Everything® Diabetes Cookbook
Everything® Easy Gourmet Cookbook
Everything® Fondue Cookbook
Everything® Food Allergy Cookbook, $15.95
Everything® Fondue Party Book
Everything® Gluten-Free Cookbook
Everything® Glycemic Index Cookbook
Everything® Grilling Cookbook
Everything® Healthy Cooking for Parties Book, $15.95
Everything® Holiday Cookbook
Everything® Indian Cookbook
Everything® Lactose-Free Cookbook
Everything® Low-Cholesterol Cookbook

Everything® Low-Fat High-Flavor Cookbook, 2nd Ed., $15.95
Everything® Low-Salt Cookbook
Everything® Meals for a Month Cookbook
Everything® Meals on a Budget Cookbook
Everything® Mediterranean Cookbook
Everything® Mexican Cookbook
Everything® No Trans Fat Cookbook
Everything® One-Pot Cookbook, 2nd Ed., $15.95
Everything® Organic Cooking for Baby & Toddler Book, $15.95
Everything® Pizza Cookbook
Everything® Quick Meals Cookbook, 2nd Ed., $15.95
Everything® Slow Cooker Cookbook
Everything® Slow Cooking for a Crowd Cookbook
Everything® Soup Cookbook
Everything® Stir-Fry Cookbook
Everything® Sugar-Free Cookbook
Everything® Tapas and Small Plates Cookbook
Everything® Tex-Mex Cookbook
Everything® Thai Cookbook
Everything® Vegetarian Cookbook
Everything® Whole-Grain, High-Fiber Cookbook
Everything® Wild Game Cookbook
Everything® Wine Book, 2nd Ed.

GAMES

Everything® 15-Minute Sudoku Book, $9.95
Everything® 30-Minute Sudoku Book, $9.95
Everything® Bible Crosswords Book, $9.95
Everything® Blackjack Strategy Book
Everything® Brain Strain Book, $9.95
Everything® Bridge Book
Everything® Card Games Book
Everything® Card Tricks Book, $9.95
Everything® Casino Gambling Book, 2nd Ed.
Everything® Chess Basics Book
Everything® Christmas Crosswords Book, $9.95
Everything® Craps Strategy Book
Everything® Crossword and Puzzle Book
Everything® Crosswords and Puzzles for Quote Lovers Book, $9.95
Everything® Crossword Challenge Book
Everything® Crosswords for the Beach Book, $9.95
Everything® Cryptic Crosswords Book, $9.95
Everything® Cryptograms Book, $9.95
Everything® Easy Crosswords Book
Everything® Easy Kakuro Book, $9.95
Everything® Easy Large-Print Crosswords Book
Everything® Games Book, 2nd Ed.
Everything® Giant Book of Crosswords
Everything® Giant Sudoku Book, $9.95
Everything® Giant Word Search Book
Everything® Kakuro Challenge Book, $9.95
Everything® Large-Print Crossword Challenge Book
Everything® Large-Print Crosswords Book
Everything® Large-Print Travel Crosswords Book
Everything® Lateral Thinking Puzzles Book, $9.95
Everything® Literary Crosswords Book, $9.95
Everything® Mazes Book
Everything® Memory Booster Puzzles Book, $9.95

Everything® Movie Crosswords Book, $9.95
Everything® Music Crosswords Book, $9.95
Everything® Online Poker Book
Everything® Pencil Puzzles Book, $9.95
Everything® Poker Strategy Book
Everything® Pool & Billiards Book
Everything® Puzzles for Commuters Book, $9.95
Everything® Puzzles for Dog Lovers Book, $9.95
Everything® Sports Crosswords Book, $9.95
Everything® Test Your IQ Book, $9.95
Everything® Texas Hold 'Em Book, $9.95
Everything® Travel Crosswords Book, $9.95
Everything® Travel Mazes Book, $9.95
Everything® Travel Word Search Book, $9.95
Everything® TV Crosswords Book, $9.95
Everything® Word Games Challenge Book
Everything® Word Scramble Book
Everything® Word Search Book

HEALTH

Everything® Alzheimer's Book
Everything® Diabetes Book
Everything® First Aid Book, $9.95
Everything® Green Living Book
Everything® Health Guide to Addiction and Recovery
Everything® Health Guide to Adult Bipolar Disorder
Everything® Health Guide to Arthritis
Everything® Health Guide to Controlling Anxiety
Everything® Health Guide to Depression
Everything® Health Guide to Diabetes, 2nd Ed.
Everything® Health Guide to Fibromyalgia
Everything® Health Guide to Menopause, 2nd Ed.
Everything® Health Guide to Migraines
Everything® Health Guide to Multiple Sclerosis
Everything® Health Guide to OCD
Everything® Health Guide to PMS
Everything® Health Guide to Postpartum Care
Everything® Health Guide to Thyroid Disease
Everything® Hypnosis Book
Everything® Low Cholesterol Book
Everything® Menopause Book
Everything® Nutrition Book
Everything® Reflexology Book
Everything® Stress Management Book
Everything® Superfoods Book, $15.95

HISTORY

Everything® American Government Book
Everything® American History Book, 2nd Ed.
Everything® American Revolution Book, $15.95
Everything® Civil War Book
Everything® Freemasons Book
Everything® Irish History & Heritage Book
Everything® World War II Book, 2nd Ed.

HOBBIES

Everything® Candlemaking Book
Everything® Cartooning Book
Everything® Coin Collecting Book
Everything® Digital Photography Book, 2nd Ed.

Everything® Drawing Book
Everything® Family Tree Book, 2nd Ed.
Everything® Guide to Online Genealogy, $15.95
Everything® Knitting Book
Everything® Knots Book
Everything® Photography Book
Everything® Quilting Book
Everything® Sewing Book
Everything® Soapmaking Book, 2nd Ed.
Everything® Woodworking Book

HOME IMPROVEMENT

Everything® Feng Shui Book
Everything® Feng Shui Decluttering Book, $9.95
Everything® Fix-It Book
Everything® Green Living Book
Everything® Home Decorating Book
Everything® Home Storage Solutions Book
Everything® Homebuilding Book
Everything® Organize Your Home Book, 2nd Ed.

KIDS' BOOKS

All titles are $7.95
Everything® Fairy Tales Book, $14.95
Everything® Kids' Animal Puzzle & Activity Book
Everything® Kids' Astronomy Book
Everything® Kids' Baseball Book, 5th Ed.
Everything® Kids' Bible Trivia Book
Everything® Kids' Bugs Book
Everything® Kids' Cars and Trucks Puzzle and Activity Book
Everything® Kids' Christmas Puzzle & Activity Book
Everything® Kids' Connect the Dots
    Puzzle and Activity Book
Everything® Kids' Cookbook, 2nd Ed.
Everything® Kids' Crazy Puzzles Book
Everything® Kids' Dinosaurs Book
Everything® Kids' Dragons Puzzle and Activity Book
Everything® Kids' Environment Book $7.95
Everything® Kids' Fairies Puzzle and Activity Book
Everything® Kids' First Spanish Puzzle and Activity Book
Everything® Kids' Football Book
Everything® Kids' Geography Book
Everything® Kids' Gross Cookbook
Everything® Kids' Gross Hidden Pictures Book
Everything® Kids' Gross Jokes Book
Everything® Kids' Gross Mazes Book
Everything® Kids' Gross Puzzle & Activity Book
Everything® Kids' Halloween Puzzle & Activity Book
Everything® Kids' Hanukkah Puzzle and Activity Book
Everything® Kids' Hidden Pictures Book
Everything® Kids' Horses Book
Everything® Kids' Joke Book
Everything® Kids' Knock Knock Book
Everything® Kids' Learning French Book
Everything® Kids' Learning Spanish Book
Everything® Kids' Magical Science Experiments Book
Everything® Kids' Math Puzzles Book
Everything® Kids' Mazes Book
Everything® Kids' Money Book, 2nd Ed.
**Everything® Kids' Mummies, Pharaoh's, and Pyramids
    Puzzle and Activity Book**
Everything® Kids' Nature Book
Everything® Kids' Pirates Puzzle and Activity Book
Everything® Kids' Presidents Book
Everything® Kids' Princess Puzzle and Activity Book
Everything® Kids' Puzzle Book

Everything® Kids' Racecars Puzzle and Activity Book
Everything® Kids' Riddles & Brain Teasers Book
Everything® Kids' Science Experiments Book
Everything® Kids' Sharks Book
Everything® Kids' Soccer Book
Everything® Kids' Spelling Book
Everything® Kids' Spies Puzzle and Activity Book
Everything® Kids' States Book
Everything® Kids' Travel Activity Book
Everything® Kids' Word Search Puzzle and Activity Book

LANGUAGE

Everything® Conversational Japanese Book with CD, $19.95
Everything® French Grammar Book
Everything® French Phrase Book, $9.95
Everything® French Verb Book, $9.95
Everything® German Phrase Book, $9.95
Everything® German Practice Book with CD, $19.95
Everything® Inglés Book
Everything® Intermediate Spanish Book with CD, $19.95
Everything® Italian Phrase Book, $9.95
Everything® Italian Practice Book with CD, $19.95
Everything® Learning Brazilian Portuguese Book with CD, $19.95
Everything® Learning French Book with CD, 2nd Ed., $19.95
Everything® Learning German Book
Everything® Learning Italian Book
Everything® Learning Latin Book
Everything® Learning Russian Book with CD, $19.95
Everything® Learning Spanish Book
Everything® Learning Spanish Book with CD, 2nd Ed., $19.95
Everything® Russian Practice Book with CD, $19.95
Everything® Sign Language Book, $15.95
Everything® Spanish Grammar Book
Everything® Spanish Phrase Book, $9.95
Everything® Spanish Practice Book with CD, $19.95
Everything® Spanish Verb Book, $9.95
Everything® Speaking Mandarin Chinese Book with CD, $19.95

MUSIC

Everything® Bass Guitar Book with CD, $19.95
Everything® Drums Book with CD, $19.95
Everything® Guitar Book with CD, 2nd Ed., $19.95
Everything® Guitar Chords Book with CD, $19.95
Everything® Guitar Scales Book with CD, $19.95
Everything® Harmonica Book with CD, $15.95
Everything® Home Recording Book
Everything® Music Theory Book with CD, $19.95
Everything® Reading Music Book with CD, $19.95
Everything® Rock & Blues Guitar Book with CD, $19.95
Everything® Rock & Blues Piano Book with CD, $19.95
Everything® Rock Drums Book with CD, $19.95
Everything® Singing Book with CD, $19.95
Everything® Songwriting Book

NEW AGE

Everything® Astrology Book, 2nd Ed.
Everything® Birthday Personology Book
Everything® Celtic Wisdom Book, $15.95
Everything® Dreams Book, 2nd Ed.
Everything® Law of Attraction Book, $15.95
Everything® Love Signs Book, $9.95
Everything® Love Spells Book, $9.95
Everything® Palmistry Book
Everything® Psychic Book
Everything® Reiki Book

Everything® Sex Signs Book, $9.95
Everything® Spells & Charms Book, 2nd Ed.
Everything® Tarot Book, 2nd Ed.
Everything® Toltec Wisdom Book
Everything® Wicca & Witchcraft Book, 2nd Ed.

PARENTING

Everything® Baby Names Book, 2nd Ed.
Everything® Baby Shower Book, 2nd Ed.
Everything® Baby Sign Language Book with DVD
Everything® Baby's First Year Book
Everything® Birthing Book
Everything® Breastfeeding Book
Everything® Father-to-Be Book
Everything® Father's First Year Book
Everything® Get Ready for Baby Book, 2nd Ed.
Everything® Get Your Baby to Sleep Book, $9.95
Everything® Getting Pregnant Book
Everything® Guide to Pregnancy Over 35
Everything® Guide to Raising a One-Year-Old
Everything® Guide to Raising a Two-Year-Old
Everything® Guide to Raising Adolescent Boys
Everything® Guide to Raising Adolescent Girls
Everything® Mother's First Year Book
Everything® Parent's Guide to Childhood Illnesses
Everything® Parent's Guide to Children and Divorce
Everything® Parent's Guide to Children with ADD/ADHD
Everything® Parent's Guide to Children with Asperger's
    Syndrome
Everything® Parent's Guide to Children with Anxiety
Everything® Parent's Guide to Children with Asthma
Everything® Parent's Guide to Children with Autism
Everything® Parent's Guide to Children with Bipolar Disorder
Everything® Parent's Guide to Children with Depression
Everything® Parent's Guide to Children with Dyslexia
Everything® Parent's Guide to Children with Juvenile Diabetes
Everything® Parent's Guide to Children with OCD
Everything® Parent's Guide to Positive Discipline
Everything® Parent's Guide to Raising Boys
Everything® Parent's Guide to Raising Girls
Everything® Parent's Guide to Raising Siblings
**Everything® Parent's Guide to Raising Your
    Adopted Child**
Everything® Parent's Guide to Sensory Integration Disorder
Everything® Parent's Guide to Tantrums
Everything® Parent's Guide to the Strong-Willed Child
Everything® Parenting a Teenager Book
Everything® Potty Training Book, $9.95
Everything® Pregnancy Book, 3rd Ed.
Everything® Pregnancy Fitness Book
Everything® Pregnancy Nutrition Book
Everything® Pregnancy Organizer, 2nd Ed., $16.95
Everything® Toddler Activities Book
Everything® Toddler Book
Everything® Tween Book
Everything® Twins, Triplets, and More Book

PETS

Everything® Aquarium Book
Everything® Boxer Book
Everything® Cat Book, 2nd Ed.
Everything® Chihuahua Book
Everything® Cooking for Dogs Book
Everything® Dachshund Book
Everything® Dog Book, 2nd Ed.
Everything® Dog Grooming Book

Everything® Dog Obedience Book
Everything® Dog Owner's Organizer, $16.95
Everything® Dog Training and Tricks Book
Everything® German Shepherd Book
Everything® Golden Retriever Book
Everything® Horse Book, 2nd Ed., $15.95
Everything® Horse Care Book
Everything® Horseback Riding Book
Everything® Labrador Retriever Book
Everything® Poodle Book
Everything® Pug Book
Everything® Puppy Book
Everything® Small Dogs Book
Everything® Tropical Fish Book
Everything® Yorkshire Terrier Book

REFERENCE

Everything® American Presidents Book
Everything® Blogging Book
Everything® Build Your Vocabulary Book, $9.95
Everything® Car Care Book
Everything® Classical Mythology Book
Everything® Da Vinci Book
Everything® Einstein Book
Everything® Enneagram Book
Everything® Etiquette Book, 2nd Ed.
Everything® Family Christmas Book, $15.95
Everything® Guide to C. S. Lewis & Narnia
Everything® Guide to Divorce, 2nd Ed., $15.95
Everything® Guide to Edgar Allan Poe
Everything® Guide to Understanding Philosophy
Everything® Inventions and Patents Book
Everything® Jacqueline Kennedy Onassis Book
Everything® John F. Kennedy Book
Everything® Mafia Book
Everything® Martin Luther King Jr. Book
Everything® Pirates Book
Everything® Private Investigation Book
Everything® Psychology Book
Everything® Public Speaking Book, $9.95
Everything® Shakespeare Book, 2nd Ed.

RELIGION

Everything® Angels Book
Everything® Bible Book
Everything® Bible Study Book with CD, $19.95
Everything® Buddhism Book
Everything® Catholicism Book
Everything® Christianity Book
Everything® Gnostic Gospels Book
Everything® Hinduism Book, $15.95
Everything® History of the Bible Book
Everything® Jesus Book
Everything® Jewish History & Heritage Book
Everything® Judaism Book
Everything® Kabbalah Book
Everything® Koran Book
Everything® Mary Book
Everything® Mary Magdalene Book
Everything® Prayer Book

Everything® Saints Book, 2nd Ed.
Everything® Torah Book
Everything® Understanding Islam Book
Everything® Women of the Bible Book
Everything® World's Religions Book

SCHOOL & CAREERS

Everything® Career Tests Book
Everything® College Major Test Book
Everything® College Survival Book, 2nd Ed.
Everything® Cover Letter Book, 2nd Ed.
Everything® Filmmaking Book
Everything® Get-a-Job Book, 2nd Ed.
Everything® Guide to Being a Paralegal
Everything® Guide to Being a Personal Trainer
Everything® Guide to Being a Real Estate Agent
Everything® Guide to Being a Sales Rep
Everything® Guide to Being an Event Planner
Everything® Guide to Careers in Health Care
Everything® Guide to Careers in Law Enforcement
Everything® Guide to Government Jobs
Everything® Guide to Starting and Running a Catering
    Business
Everything® Guide to Starting and Running a Restaurant
**Everything® Guide to Starting and Running
    a Retail Store**
Everything® Job Interview Book, 2nd Ed.
Everything® New Nurse Book
Everything® New Teacher Book
Everything® Paying for College Book
Everything® Practice Interview Book
Everything® Resume Book, 3rd Ed.
Everything® Study Book

SELF-HELP

Everything® Body Language Book
Everything® Dating Book, 2nd Ed.
Everything® Great Sex Book
**Everything® Guide to Caring for Aging Parents,
    $15.95**
Everything® Self-Esteem Book
Everything® Self-Hypnosis Book, $9.95
Everything® Tantric Sex Book

SPORTS & FITNESS

Everything® Easy Fitness Book
Everything® Fishing Book
Everything® Guide to Weight Training, $15.95
Everything® Krav Maga for Fitness Book
Everything® Running Book, 2nd Ed.
Everything® Triathlon Training Book, $15.95

TRAVEL

Everything® Family Guide to Coastal Florida
Everything® Family Guide to Cruise Vacations
Everything® Family Guide to Hawaii
Everything® Family Guide to Las Vegas, 2nd Ed.
Everything® Family Guide to Mexico
Everything® Family Guide to New England, 2nd Ed.

Everything® Family Guide to New York City, 3rd Ed.
**Everything® Family Guide to Northern California
    and Lake Tahoe**
Everything® Family Guide to RV Travel & Campgrounds
Everything® Family Guide to the Caribbean
Everything® Family Guide to the Disneyland® Resort, California
    Adventure®, Universal Studios®, and the Anaheim
    Area, 2nd Ed.
Everything® Family Guide to the Walt Disney World Resort®,
    Universal Studios®, and Greater Orlando, 5th Ed.
Everything® Family Guide to Timeshares
Everything® Family Guide to Washington D.C., 2nd Ed.

WEDDINGS

Everything® Bachelorette Party Book, $9.95
Everything® Bridesmaid Book, $9.95
Everything® Destination Wedding Book
Everything® Father of the Bride Book, $9.95
Everything® Green Wedding Book, $15.95
Everything® Groom Book, $9.95
Everything® Jewish Wedding Book, 2nd Ed., $15.95
Everything® Mother of the Bride Book, $9.95
Everything® Outdoor Wedding Book
Everything® Wedding Book, 3rd Ed.
Everything® Wedding Checklist, $9.95
Everything® Wedding Etiquette Book, $9.95
Everything® Wedding Organizer, 2nd Ed., $16.95
Everything® Wedding Shower Book, $9.95
Everything® Wedding Vows Book, 3rd Ed., $9.95
Everything® Wedding Workout Book
Everything® Weddings on a Budget Book, 2nd Ed., $9.95

WRITING

Everything® Creative Writing Book
Everything® Get Published Book, 2nd Ed.
Everything® Grammar and Style Book, 2nd Ed.
Everything® Guide to Magazine Writing
Everything® Guide to Writing a Book Proposal
Everything® Guide to Writing a Novel
Everything® Guide to Writing Children's Books
Everything® Guide to Writing Copy
Everything® Guide to Writing Graphic Novels
Everything® Guide to Writing Research Papers
Everything® Guide to Writing a Romance Novel, $15.95
Everything® Improve Your Writing Book, 2nd Ed.
Everything® Writing Poetry Book